Turning the Century:
A Bits and Bytes Reader
for Developing Writers

Phoebe Reeves
YouthBuild San Antonio

Prentice Hall, Upper Saddle River, New Jersey 07458

Library of Congress Cataloging-in-Publication Data

Reeves, Phoebe.
    Turning the century : a bits and bytes reader for developing
writers / Phoebe Reeves.
        p.   cm.
    Includes index.
    ISBN 0-13-081305-2
    1. College readers.   2. Internet (Computer network)—Problems,
exercises, etc.   3. English language—Rhetoric—Problems, exercises,
etc.   4. English language—Grammar—Problems, exercises, etc.
5. Report writing—Problems, exercises, etc.   I. Title.
PE1417.R435   2000
808′.0427—dc21   99-12253
                                                                          CIP

Editor-in-Chief: *Leah Jewell*
Senior Acquisitions Editor: *Maggie Barbieri*
Editorial Assistant: *Joan Polk*
Production Liaison: *Fran Russello*
Project Manager: *Marianne Hutchinson* (Pine Tree Composition)
Prepress and Manufacturing Buyer: *Mary Ann Gloriande*
Cover Director: *Jayne Conte*
Cover Designer: Bruce *Kenselaar*

This book was set in 10/12 Bookman Light by Pine Tree Composition
and was printed and bound by Courier Companies, Inc.
The cover was printed by Phoenix Color Corp.

For permission to use copyrighted material, grateful acknowledgment is made to the
copyright holders on pages 359 to 361, which are hereby made part of this copyright
page.

Printed in the United States of America

10 9 8 7 6 5 4 3 2 1

ISBN 0-13-081305-2

Prentice-Hall International (UK) Limited, *London*
Prentice-Hall of Australia Pty. Limited, *Sydney*
Prentice-Hall Canada Inc., *Toronto*
Prentice-Hall Hispanoamericana, S.A., *Mexico*
Prentice-Hall of India Private Limited, *New Delhi*
Prentice-Hall of Japan, Inc., *Tokyo*
Pearson Education Asia Pte. Ltd., *Singapore*
Editora Prentice-Hall do Brasil, Ltda., *Rio de Janeiro*

Contents

Note: Internet web sites are subject to change without notice. Occasionally a site will leave a forwarding address to its new location as a link for the user (you). If a site listed here in *Turning the Century* has changed and left no forwarding address, then it should be used simply as a sample site. Based on that sample site, you and your teacher can select and use an active related site in place of the original site listed here. All readings listed as Internet sources can be accessed by using key word searches or by typing their Internet addresses into any of the major search engines.

Preface

"Why should I learn to read, think, and write critically?" you ask. "What's it going to do for me?"

Everything. It will open up the whole world to you. Reading, thinking, and writing critically will educate you both academically and professionally and will put you in charge of what you want to do with your life. Why? Because these skills give you strength—school strength, career strength, life strength.

"So how do I do it? How do I read, think, and write well?" you ask.

You start by reading and thinking, all the time, every opportunity you get. Reading and thinking teach you to write because they give you something valuable to say. Reading and thinking inevitably lead you to research because once you discover you have something valuable to say, you want to make sure you know what you're talking about—after all, reading, thinking, and writing both invite and force you to participate in the public world.

Writing allows you to articulate your life in a way that nothing else does. Writing gives you a loud, passionate voice even when you think no one could possibly be listening, that no one could possibly care. Writing records history, tells the stories of our lives long after our bodies have left the earth. Writing makes thoughts matter; writing makes your ideas count.

If you can read well and write well, those two skills will teach you to think well and learn well. You see how any one of these three skills leads back to the other two. Of course, writing is difficult. In certain ways writing is the most challenging of the three skills. But I urge you to accept and meet the challenge writing poses to you. Take that challenge because writing enables you to take the world apart so that you can see what makes it tick. You've got to know how and when you're being manipulated by information and how and when to manipulate information if you're going to stay ahead in both academics and the professional world—if you're going to have any control over your life and the direction it takes.

As we fast approach the turn of the century, you are entering a crucial life class, and right now, the world around you is making for a particularly interesting teacher. Much of that has to do with the onslaught of information virtually everyone has access to now, thanks to the sometime angel, sometime demon, the Internet. The Internet has made us a real global village by removing the barrier of geography through the dissemination of information—*all* information. Reading—and the source of reading, publishing—has been yanked out of the hands of a select gathering of publishers and thrust into a new realm, one to which everyone has access and to which everyone can contribute: the Internet. You can travel the world in moments, see the sun shining in real time on Melville Island in Australia even if rain is beating at the window of your office in East Pittston, Maine. You can find out in moments something (whether right or wrong) about any topic, subject, person, place, or thing, so you have unlimited information at your fingertips. Trash and treasures all heaped in the same box—and you can take what you want! How will you determine which is which? You'll need to ask a lot of questions and get a lot of answers. You'll need to research. A lot. You'll also need to exchange information with other people, people who are experts in their fields, and people who aren't. A lot. You'll need to talk *and* listen (most often you'll do better to do the latter *a lot* before you start talking). And, last but not least, you'll need to write—you guessed it—a lot.

The title of this reader *Turning the Century: A Bits and Bytes Reader for Developing Writers* will show you how to read on computers, write and read on computers, read and write cutting-edge material, look at how words can be packaged, presented, and understood as we reach the millennium. From a rattlesnake queen beauty contest to magic protection bottles, to Spanish cats and personal history identification chips, the readings in *Turning the Century: A Bits and Bytes Reader for Developing Writers* have been selected from books and web sites on the Internet for their colorful language, imagination, and creativity. This combination means you should be prepared to look at the composition of material you read and write stylistically and imagistically, as more than just words that you read from left to right in lines across a page.

Here's an analogy to help you think about why it's important for you to open up your reading and writing perspective: when you first learn to drive, one of the key rules to learn is that the world outside your car is constantly changing, even though you have the road and its solid or broken yellow lines to follow to keep you and your car going "straight." If you never look beyond the hood of your car and the yellow lines on the road just in front of your car, you run the risk of getting into a serious accident. It is the same with reading and writing: you've got the opportunity to "see" language now, not just read it. And, while that may not seem like a life-or-death difference to you right now, when that critical piece of information races across the "road" in front of you and you're still just reading the next word instead of the whole essay, story, and/or web site, you may end up crashing academically and professionally.

That's why you want to take advantage of the fact that the Internet pastes language into unusual collages, visual, written, and both visual *and* written. Discovering possibilities and connections in these patterns will enrich the "book" that you may even finally have taken for granted. No longer!

The readings in *Turning the Century* have been chosen to stimulate you to read, think, and write actively and creatively. But you need to have something to say back to the world because you will get so much more from it than if you just sit there looking around you, bored. *You don't have time to be bored!*

In *Art Objects: Essays on Ecstasy and Effrontery*, British author Jeanette Winterson makes this point very well. She writes of her experience with a painting that changes her "life-look" on art: "I was dog-dumb. The usual response of 'this painting has nothing to say to me' had become 'I have nothing to say to this painting.' And I desperately wanted to speak." *Turning the Century* wants to provide you with more than one opportunity to achieve a kind of life-opening experience similar to Winterson's. And, if you really take the challenge to read, think, and write seriously, the "art" (writing, thoughts, ideas) that stuns you speechless could come from the person sitting next to you in class. It could even come from you.

Phoebe Reeves

Acknowledgments

I wrote *Turning the Century: A Bits and Bytes Reader for Developing Writers* because I want all young people, dropouts and graduates, from those of you who are just facing the beginning of an education to those of you who have prematurely left the system, that reading and writing is *the* ticket to your life's journey.

Thank you to all the reviewers: Christian R. Weisser, University of South Florida; Deborah Weaver Parker, Albuquerque TVI Community College; Bonnie Ronson, Hillsborough Community College; Patrick McGann, Pikes Peak Community College; Suzanne G. Weisar, San Jacinto College South; Keith Coplin, Colby Community College; Harvey Rubinstein, Hudson County Community College; Mary Helen Halloran, University of Wisconsin, Milwaukee; Janet Cutshall, Sussex County Community College; Leslie Dennen, University of San Francisco through Prentice Hall who provided valuable editorial commentary and lively pedagogical debates to me over the process of writing and rewriting this textbook, and Joan Polk who always came through for me at Prentice Hall.

Thank you to Mary Jo Southern who gave me the idea for *Turning the Century.* Thank you and deep gratitude to Fred Courtright who has always located and retrieved my oddball reading selections, wherever they may be from around the world and/or deep in the machine of the Internet, and who helped me see through the publication of my first novel *The Revenant.* Thank you and drinks on The Riverwalk to Maggie Barbieri who has been both my editor and my friend throughout.

Thank you and love to my parents Bruce and Polly who first showed me how to write and how to be a teacher *and* a pupil.

And lastly, all my love and gratitude to my husband Juris who teaches me that every day presents a new classroom and another graduation.

Turning the Century: A Bits and Bytes Reader for Developing Writers is dedicated to all the people who want to get somewhere in this world.

Introduction

HOW TO USE THIS BOOK

Turning the Century is divided into four parts:

1. *What's in the Mind of God?*
2. *Fashion Victims, Fashion Plates, or Fashion Scholars?*
3. *Media Rare, Mediocre, or Well-Done?*
4. *Technology: Genius, Nightmare, or Possibility?*

Within each part, you'll find a collection of approximately eleven brief readings, nonfiction and fiction, text- and Internet-based. These readings will challenge you to look at spirituality, fashion, media, and technology—fairly standard subjects for a number of introductory college courses—in very different ways from those in which you or your classmates have been used to looking at them.

A brief introduction will precede each reading (giving you some background and/or commentary and/or questions about the reading), followed by the reading itself, and followed by a Words to Know section (where you will define each of the listed words). Then you will find a Questions section (which will help you to create questions which directly or indirectly relate to the reading), followed by a Writing Activities section (which will ask you to use your questions to create a variety of writing projects). Finally, you will find a Grammar and Style Questions section.

The difficulty of the readings and their accompanying writing activities vary. For your class's convenience, some writing activities have been designed to work in conjunction with others. However, both the readings and the writing activities have also been selected and designed to be used in any order. You and your instructor can mix and match them in any combination you choose.

The primary goals of working with *Turning the Century* are twofold:

1. For you to build your writing from a series of sentences, to a series of paragraphs, to a series of papers;
2. For you to develop a global sensibility about your own reading, thinking, and writing as well as the reading, thinking, and writing of others, now that you're all citizens of a global village. (After all, if the stock market crashes in Asia, you may lose your job in Kansas.)

The content of your writing will evolve from reaction-writing to idea-writing, and you will compose your own subjects, topics, and writing projects based on the readings. At the same time, you will learn how to evaluate both your printed source material and the Internet material. How do you determine what is "quality" reading and writing and what is "junk"? Does its value depend on the number of words? On its political correctness? On whether the words are printed on paper or appear on a screen? On if a giant publisher has published those words versus a local homeless shelter publishing them? On if the words are shaped like a home page instead of an essay? On if the composition of words comes from the United States rather than some other country?

Keep the following in mind as you use *Turning the Century* for your reading and writing projects:

1. The introductions to the readings provide you with a doorway to the readings, to give you a starting point from which to react, to respond to them. They are not the last word or even the first word on "getting everything you're supposed to get out of the readings." The introductions may include background on the reading and its writing style, or its author, or an editorial commentary from the author of this reader, or questions for you to answer as you read and write, or all of these elements. Use them to build, not replace, your own ideas and thoughts.

2. The readings are unconventional choices. I can almost guarantee you won't find 95 percent of them in any other reader. Remain open-minded to the very different sorts of topics the readings will in-

troduce as well as how they put a new spin on topics about which you might have thought you knew everything. An important "how-to" evaluation for Internet sources, written and assembled by UCLA College Librarian Esther Grassian, follows this section of the Introduction. It provides straightforward, analytical questions you can ask about any Internet source to determine its worth, both in terms of your gaining information from it and in terms of using it as a source in your own writing.

3. In the **Words to Know** section, rather than treat the list of words you must define as a series of dictionary-copying exercises, use these words in talking with people when you get the opportunity. Use them in your writing and in your speech because *word usage* (not words alone) builds your vocabulary. Besides, people get tired of hearing the same words over and over. Don't forget the average person uses a vocabulary of perhaps a thousand words. A thousand words—that's all! If you take into account that about two hundred of those thousand are strictly for survival communication, that leaves only about eight hundred "nonessential" words. And, how many words do you think there are in the world?

It is important to realize that the word lists mentioned above may be difficult. Use the following resources to help you define them:

1. Dictionary and/or thesaurus: Use a dictionary and/or a thesaurus to determine the meaning.
2. Context: See if you can determine the meaning from the context of the entire sentence—that is, given the rest of the sentence and how the word is used in that sentence, what does the word appear to mean?
3. Group Discussion: Discuss with other people what they think the words mean and why. Many times, you will find you and your classmates will be able to exchange expertise and information in this way.
4. Fabricated vocabulary: Sometimes the authors of these readings will have made up certain words for particular reasons. The dictionary won't be of much use to you in these cases, so you will have to research possible meanings using other sources, including context.

4. Following the readings in the **Questions** section you will be asked to formulate your own questions, ranging from simple to complex, about what you have read. The two types of questions you will form are called the Text/You/Other Question and the Three-Layered Question. Within the category of Text/You/Other Question building, you can develop seven types of individual questions: single-level (three simple kinds), bi-level (mixing two of the simple kinds), and text/you/other (mixing all three of the simple kinds).

Single-Level Questions

1. *Text Question:* A Text Question is based solely on information found in a particular reading. This question can only be composed and answered by someone who had read the specific reading that it concerns.

2. *You Question:* A You Question is based on your experiences, values, and ideas. At the same time, it is also connected to some larger theme or subject based in the reading. While a You Question would be connected to themes or subjects in the reading, unlike a Text Question, someone else would not have had to have read the reading in order to answer your You Question.

3. *Other Question:* An Other Question is based on your knowledge of history, other peoples and cultures, knowledge of other literature, science, and any other relevant outside world subjects. While an Other Question would also be connected to themes or subjects in the reading, someone else would not have had to have read the reading in order to answer your Other Question.

Bi-Level Questions

These questions combine two of the three questions listed above. Read carefully through the definitions of each type of question again before combining them so that you know which questions are dependent on the reading for at least part of their answer versus those which are inspired by, but not dependent on, the reading for their answer.

4. *Text/You Question*
5. *Text/Other Question*
6. *You/Other Question*

Tri-Level Questions

These are the most complex form of questions, as they combine all three single-level types. All tri-level questions will be dependent on the text for at least part of their answers. Again, be sure to review the definitions for each type of single-level question so you understand what you're putting together for your Tri-level questions.

7. *Text/You/Other Question*

Three-Layered Questions

The Three-Layered Question takes the form of a three-sentence paragraph, composed of three parts:

1. A specific quotation from the reading (this quotation should be as concise as possible, and it should be a quotation that really catches your attention, one which really appeals to you). This is the first sentence of the three;

2. followed by a one sentence comment directly speaking to the quotation or closely relating to the quotation. This comment can point out something significant in or regarding the quotation, or perhaps set the quotation within a particular context, (i.e. historical, gender, political, literary, scientific, philosophical, artistic, religious, ethnic). This is the second sentence of the three;

3. and ends with the actual question. This question will be explored in writing. The question should logically follow the train of thought introduced by the quote and the comment. (Again, this question, like the Text/You/Other question or any in-depth question works best if its phrasing follows the what, who, where, when, how, or why format—*not* the "yes" or "no" answer format.)

Why do you need to learn how to compose these two types of questions for your writing? Although their structure may appear complicated at first, the format of these two particular types of questions is specifically designed to make you use all your critical thinking skills in your reading and writing. Therefore, it is important that you work with their structure, even if it feels awkward at first. Very soon, creating questions in this manner will become second nature to you.

5. The **Writing Activities** section will provide you with a list of writing activities based on the reading you've just finished—and, in some cases, previous readings. You may use these writing activities as a springboard to writing your papers and/or you may modify—even change them—to suit your particular writing project goals.

6. This final section, called the **Grammar and Style** section, will ask you to answer a brief list of relevant grammar and style questions as they apply to the current reading and occasionally other readings in *Turning the Century* chosen by you and your classmates. You will occasionally need to tailor the questions to fit your selected readings, so this activity will require you to revise as well as answer the standard questions given to you in the questions section on an individual basis. If the grammar and style question involves your examining or analyzing more than one reading, you will need to make some comparative or contrasting statements as well. You will also be expected to have a grammar and style handbook and to look up specific grammar and style rules on a regular basis. You will then select particular rules to use in your written answers to the grammar and style questions. This kind of grammar and style "research" will help you to learn the rules, not as the *purpose* of writing, but as part of the *structure* of writing (i.e. *one* of the key elements that holds writing together, and that depends on rules, not in and of themselves, but rules within a particular situation, context). The reason the grammar aspect of reading and writing is being shown to you in this manner is because you need to learn how grammar functions as an essential part of making the map of your writing. Think of grammar as a set of road signs as well as a set of visual mood cues that give writing motion and feeling, both for the writer and for the reader.

Grammar is based on universally accepted methods of presenting information, whether orally or in writing (you may find that often it can be easier to hear and speak than to write). Every style of writing has its own grammar rules. Sometimes in great literature, (and by this, I am not limiting the term to fiction, or to Shakespeare and other classic writers of his ilk), the authors will invent their own grammar rules so that readers are brought into these authors' worlds and the grammar of those worlds.

The contributions grammar makes to writing are clarity and consistency. As you go through this course, look at the selected readings in this text and identify how the various authors make their intentions clear and consistent grammatically. This helps you develop your own sense of effective grammar. You should also have a grammar handbook with you as you answer these questions to refresh your memory on punctuation and other grammatical rules you may need to review.

NOTE: The focus of this section is on you taking responsibility not just for trying to memorize grammar and style rules, but for actually learning grammar and style rules as they directly impact on how readers read and understand your writing. You have a reason for writing what you write as do all writers. Grammar and style aid you in making sure that your reason gets across to your reader, that your reader can understand your writing.

A certain number of the following questions will follow each reading. You may find you need to revise and modify certain of these questions to accompany each of the reading and writing projects you will do with this reader. You will be answering two to three questions per reading. Write your answers in full, using specific details and examples.

1. Compare and contrast author _____'s reading _____ with author _____'s reading _____. How do they use grammar to get their points across? How does their use of grammar to get their points across differ? What are the common features of both? Use specific grammar rules and details in your answer.

2. Look at the uses of narrative punctuation from a journalist reading and a story-telling reading. How are they (commas, quotation marks) used to create context? Use specific reading examples as well as specific grammar rules and details in your answer.

3. Examine the use of punctuation in three different readings. How is punctuation used to emphasize the authors' tone?

4. Select a text reading and a reading from the Internet. Analyze these examples. What is the difference in grammatical style and why? Use specific reading examples as well as specific grammar rules and details in your answer.

5. Using a standard grammar reference (i.e., Strunk and White's *Elements of Style*), find three exceptions (from any of the readings in this reader) to the rules such a standard reference has created, and discuss why the authors broke those rules.

6. Look at "exotic" punctuation (e.g., dashes, parentheses, exclamation points) within any of this text's readings, discuss what effect the authors' use of these kinds of punctuation have on the reader. What does this use of grammar tell you about the written word as opposed to the spoken word?

7. Part of good grammatical usage is the concise and active expression of thoughts and ideas. Looking through the readings, find concise, active, grammatical expressions, put them into your own words, and see how you can make them still more concise.

8. Take wordy, general grammatical expressions from your own writing that you've done based on these readings and revise to make them concise, active grammatical expressions.

9. One of the most difficult tasks for any new writer is to express time and timelines consistently and to match actions to those times and timelines. Take a paragraph from one of the readings that has a strong sense of either past, present, or future tense, and rewrite it using a different verb tense (i.e., if it was written in the present tense, rewrite it in the past tense, and so forth). What is the effect of such a change? Were you consistent in your new selection of verb tense in your revision? And, if you had difficulty with consistency, without referring back to the text, restore the original tense and see how closely the paragraph matches how the author originally wrote it.

10. One of the best ways to learn grammar, in addition to learning the names and rules of grammatical elements, is to read other people's writing and determine how and why they write well. Take a grammatically imperfect piece of your own work, read two or three readings from this reader, and rewrite your piece afterwards. Is it grammatically better? Why or why not? What was the impact of seeing how other people put together words?

The work that you do using this book will help you to create writing that will reflect YOU—an interesting *and* interested reader, thinker, and writer. The kind of reading, thinking, and writing you will learn to do in the exercises in this book will serve you throughout your academic and professional careers—and your life.

THINKING CRITICALLY ABOUT WORLD WIDE WEB RESOURCES*

The World Wide Web has a lot to offer, but not all sources are equally valuable or reliable. Here are some points to consider.

Content and Evaluation

- Who is the audience?
- What is the purpose of the Web page and what does it contain?
- How complete and accurate are the information and the links provided?
- What is the relative value of the Web site in comparison to the range of information resources available on this topic? (Note: Be sure to check with a librarian.)
  - What other resources (print and nonprint) are available in this area?
  - What are the date(s) of coverage of the site and site-specific documents?
  - How comprehensive is this site?
    - What are the link selection criteria if any?
    - Are the links relevant and appropriate for the site?
    - Is the site inward-focused, pointing outward, or both?
    - Is there an appropriate balance between inward-pointing links ("inlinks") and outward-pointing links ("outlinks")?
    - Are the links comprehensive or do they just provide a sampler?
    - What do the links offer that is not easily available in other sources?
    - Are the links evaluated in any way?
    - Is there an appropriate range of Internet resources (e.g., links to gophers)?
    - Is multimedia appropriately incorporated?
- How valuable is the information provided in the Web page (intrinsic value)?

*Prepared June 1995 by Esther Grassian, Electronic Services Coordinator, UCLA College Library. Copyright © 1997. All Rights Reserved. Permission is granted for unlimited noncommercial use of this guide. To contact the author, send mail to estherg@library.ucla.edu.

Source and Date
- Who is the author or producer?
- What is the authority or expertise of the individual or group that created this site?
  - How knowledgeable is the individual or group on the subject matter of the site?
  - Is the site sponsored or co-sponsored by an individual or group that has created other Web sites?
- Is any sort of bias evident?
- When was the Web item produced?
- When was the Web item mounted?
- When was the Web item last revised?
- How up to date are the links?
- How reliable are the links; are there blind links, or references to sites which have moved?
- Is contact information for the author or producer included in the document?

Structure
- Does the document follow good graphic principles?
- Do the graphics and art serve a function or are they decorative?
- Do the icons clearly represent what is intended?
- Does the text follow basic rules of grammar, spelling and literary composition?
- Is there an element of creativity, and does it add to or detract from the document itself?
- Can the text stand alone for use in line-mode (text only) Web browsers as well as multimedia browsers, or is there an option for line-mode browsers?
- Is attention paid to the needs of the disabled (e.g., large print and graphics options; audio)?
- Are links provided to Web "subject trees" or directories—lists of subject-arranged Web sources?

Other
- Is appropriate interactivity available?
- When it is necessary; to send confidential information out over the Internet, is encryption (i.e., a secure coding system) available? How secure is it?
- Are there links to search engines or is a search engine attached to (embedded in) the Web site?

PRACTICE READING
AND WRITING SELECTION

Pet Shop Fish: Touched by Deity?— Muslims Say Marks on Fish's Fins Spell Out Allah in Arabic

This Associated Press article, which appeared in the San Francisco Examiner *June 29, 1997, at first read may seem outrageous, bizarre, ridiculous—you are certain to come up with any number of emotional reactions to it. But why? Do research, either in the library or on the Internet and find out how many "signs from God" have appeared and where over the last five years, the last ten years, the last century. How many could you find? What does constitute a true sign from God? How do you know?*

Introduction This piece is written as journalism, in the style of a newspaper article. The effect is to convey to you an event taking place here in the United States, but also to play with your emotions and religious beliefs in a sensationalist or exaggerated manner.

Can a fish be a sign from Allah?

A group of Muslims in this San Joaquin County community certainly is convinced. The albino tiger oscar fish reportedly has markings on its right fluorescent orange flank that spell out the word "Allah" in Arabic.

And now the fish, which lived most of its four years on a discount pet store shelf, suddenly is a local celebrity.

Hyatullah Ahmadi, 27, bought the fish last week for $36. Since then, as many as 50 Muslims a day have flocked to his home to gawk at the fish.

A Muslim doctor said he's willing to pay up to $1,000 for the unusual pet that's being dubbed the "Allah fish." But Ahmadi has no plans of selling the fish and says he plans to keep it forever as a symbol of God's power.

"It's very, very distinctly written," said Taj Khan, president of Lodi Muslim Mosque, who has seen the fish several times.

A comparison of the fish's tail-markings and the letters "alif," double "laum" and "ha" that spell out the Arabic word for God, indicates a strong resemblance.

"It's a sign of Allah," said Ahmadi, a student of the Holy Book of Islam, the Koran. "If he wants to write his name on any kind of animal or thing, he can do it."

The fish has never had so much attention.

From an obscure existence on a pet store shelf with few prospective customers, the albino fish has leapt up in status. He has received a flood of guests since moving into a brand new salt water aquarium at the Ahmadi home. The Allah fish also shares its quarters with a second Oscar, purchased as a companion.

Interest in the pearly white fish with the unusual markings increased sharply about six weeks ago, said Bryan Dimas, who works at Discount Pet store.

"A lot of Arabian guys started coming in and staring at our fish for a long time," Dimas said. "They didn't ask questions. They just asked if we knew what it said."

"They drew a picture of how you would write (Allah in Arabic), but I didn't think it looked anything like it," he said.

Khan said other objects, including fruit and vegetables, have had similar markings. What it all means remains unclear, he said.

"In England, there was a tomato that said Allah three weeks ago," he said. "I don't know how you interpret this. It probably means different things to different people."

WORDS TO KNOW

NOTE: When you write the definitions of the following words, make it a point to use at least three of them in conversation over the next day and three of them in your next writing assignment. Many times you'll find it difficult or impossible to use them in everyday speech or writing. What then is the point of defining them? Of learning them? At the very least, in all the following cases where you have unusual vocabulary terms to define, attempt to use them. How does attempting to use vocabulary that feels awkward or different change your view of your common speech and writing patterns? Learning how to use new vo-

cabulary means just that—using the words. Write specifically how, where, when, and why you used the words and discuss with your class.

Lodi—
Allah—
Islam—
Koran—
albino—

QUESTIONS

Create a simple Text Question, a simple You Question, and a simple Other Question. For examples, look just above the introduction paragraph to this reading. (And, in this case, please see the same questions that have been provided for you following this reading and writing selection.)

WRITING ACTIVITIES

1. Write a one-sentence reaction to this reading. Share your reaction with your classmates. How do they respond? What do you wish you had added to your reaction writing? Why?
2. Write a one-paragraph reaction to this reading. Share your reaction with your classmates. How do they respond? What do you wish you had added to your reaction writing? Why?

GRAMMAR AND STYLE

1. What specific form or forms of punctuation in this reading makes it identifiable as a newspaper article and why?
2. How would you describe the tone (tone means the "voice" or "mood" of the writing) of this article and why? Is that tone typical of a newspaper article? Why or why not?

PRACTICE QUESTIONING SESSION AND SAMPLE QUESTIONS BASED ON "PET SHOP FISH"

Ask yourself the following to help you to generate ideas for composing each question:

1. Text Question—what are you asking about the text?
2. You Question—what does the text make you think about in your own life?
3. Other Question—what does the text make you think about in the world?

SIMPLE QUESTIONS

1. Text Question—What kind of fish is it that bears the marks that spell out Allah?
2. You Question—Where have you seen "marks of God"?
3. Other Question—What marks or signs of God have received public attention in the last five years?

BI-LEVEL QUESTIONS

1. Text/You Question—What specifics/details in "Petshop Fish" struck you as particularly interesting and why?
2. Text/World Question—Where in the world has reported the largest number of "God signs" such as the Pet shop fish?
3. You/World Question—What famous "God signs" or religious signs, either in the United States or elsewhere in the world, have you actually seen/visited?

TEXT/YOU/OTHER QUESTION

Using the Pet shop fish as well as other specific miracles from around the world, what do you think constitutes a true sign from God (or the Gods) and why?

Ask yourself the following to help you to generate ideas for composing your Three-Layered Question:

1. What quote from the reading most interested you?
2. What comment (a sentence, two sentences maximum) would you make about the quote?
3. What question would you ask based on your quote and comment(s)?

THREE-LAYERED QUESTION

"In England, there was a tomato that said Allah three weeks ago," says Taj Khan. As we reach the millennium, people are seeing and can expect to see many more such "signs." Which signs seem the most meaningful, the most ridiculous and why?

Now that you have seen a sample of each type of question, read the following definition segment for each of the different kinds and levels of questions. This way, you will be prepared to create your own questions and in doing so, your own writing projects to accompany the readings.

WHAT'S IN THE MIND OF GOD?

"Door Gods" and "Dragon"

C. A. S. Williams

All the inhabitants of Oriental countries and especially those of the Flowery Land, are gifted with a vivid imagination—a quality of important constructive value. This high development of the imaginative powers is very largely due to the reaction created by the complicated symbolism of the ancient folklore. . . . From the earliest ages the Chinese have had a firm credence in the prevalence of occult influences, and a general trust in amulets and charms and other similar preservatives against the spirits of evil, although nowadays the Government is making efforts to dissuade people from these superstitious beliefs.

—C. A. S. Williams, *Chinese Symbolism and Art Motifs*

Introduction C. A. S. Williams's piece is written using a combination of historical factual data, research, and legends ("Door Gods"). He also occasionally uses categories to organize his information ("Dragon"). The effect allows Williams to present you with information to introduce you to Chinese cultural symbolism and art motifs and how they have patterned Chinese culture.

DOOR GODS
（門神）

According to the legend, the Emperor T'ai Tsung of the T'ang dynasty （唐太宗） was once disturbed at night by the throwing of bricks and tiles outside his bedroom and the hooting of demons and spirits. His Majesty and all the inmates of the palace were much alarmed and the Ministers of State were informed. General Ch'in Shu-pao （秦叔寶） stepped forward, and addressing the Emperor said: "Your servant has during his whole life killed men as he would split open a gourd and piled up carcasses as he would heap up ants; why should he be afraid of ghosts? Let your servant, in company with Yü Ch'ih Ching-tê (尉遲敬德), arm ourselves, and keep watch standing." The Emperor granted his request, and during the night he experienced no further alarm, at which he was much pleased, but remarked: "These two men, watching all night had no sleep." He therefore commanded a painter to draw two pictures of men clad in full armour, holding in their hands a gemmed battle-axe, and having a whip, chain, bow and arrows girt on their loins, with their hair standing on end according to their usual manner. These were suspended on the right and left doors of the palace, and the evil spirits were said to be subdued. Subsequent ages imitated this precedent, and have ever since made the champions Ch'in and Yü the tutelary deities of the doorways, the former being depicted with a white face and the latter with a black face.

It is also recorded that Shên Shu (神荼) and Yü Lü (鬱壘), two brothers of remote antiquity, lived on Mount Tu So (度朔) under a peach-tree, and were said to have power over all the disembodied spirits (鬼). They bound the wicked ones with reeds (葦) and fed the tigers with them. On New Year's Eve their coloured portraits or gaudy pictures of tigers are pasted on the doors of houses as a talisman against evil spirits.

When these painted effigies are not depicted in full, the characters 文 承 and 武 尉 are written instead upon squares of red paper, which are pasted upon the doors.

DRAGON
（龍）

"The Eastern dragon is not the gruesome monster of mediæval imagination, but the genius of strength and goodness. He is the spirit of change, therefore of life itself. . . . Hidden in the caverns of inaccessible mountains, or coiled in the unfathomed depth of the sea, he awaits the time when he slowly rouses himself into activity. He unfolds himself in the storm clouds; he washes his mane in the blackness of the seething whirlpools. His claws are in the fork of the lightning, his scales begin to glisten in the bark of rain-swept pine trees. His voice is heard in the hurricane, which, scattering the withered leaves of the forest, quickens a new spring."[1]

The Shuo Wên dictionary (說文)—A.D. 200—states that of the 369 species of scaly reptiles, such as fishes, snakes, and lizards, the dragon is the chief; it wields the power of transformation, and the gift of rendering itself visible or invisible at pleasure. In the spring it ascends to the skies, and in autumn it buries itself in the watery depths. It covers itself with mud in the autumnal equinox, and emerges in the spring; thus announcing by its awakening the return of nature's energies, it became naturally the symbol of the productive force of moisture, that is of spring, when by means of genial rains and storms all nature renewed itself. It may be noted that the crocodile was worshipped by the ancient Egyptians, and the theory has been advanced that the Chinese dragon is merely a modified form of the alligator found occasionally to the present day in the Yangtze River, for the emergence of the latter from hibernation synchronises with the coming of spring, when the dragon is believed to be exerting its beneficient influence; it is, however, difficult to trace an analogy between this fabulous animal and any other natural species, for the body of the dragon seems to be distinctly serpentine, its head is made up of parts of those of various other animals, the teeth are those of a mammalian carnivore, while the legs and claws are those of a bird. Moreover, as it is a beneficent creature, it cannot be compared with the ferocious dragon of heraldry and mediæval mythology. "The dragon seems to perpetuate the tradition of primæval flying saurians of geologic times, now known only through their fossilized remains. The Lamas and Chinese Buddhists have assimilated them with the mythical serpents (Naga) of Indian myth."[2] Fossil remains of the Stegodon, Mastodon, Elephant, etc., are occasionally unearthed in various parts of North China. The bones are called Dragon's Bones (龍骨), and the fossil ivory is termed Dragon's Teeth (龍齒); they are powdered, levigated, and used medicinally in the treatment of various ailments such as chorea, spermatorrhæa ague, and hemorrhages.

"There are three chief species of dragons; the *lung* (龍), which is the most powerful and inhabits the sky; the *li* (螭), which is hornless and lives in the ocean; and the *chiao* (蛟), which is scaly and resides in marshes and dens in the mountains. The *lung* is however the only authentic species, and is thus described. 'It has nine resemblances, or forms, viz.: the head of a camel, the horns of a deer, eyes of a rabbit, ears of a cow, neck of a snake, belly of a frog, scales of a carp, claws of a hawk, and palm of a tiger. There is a ridge of scales along its back, eighty-one in number; the scales on its throat lie towards the head, and those on the head are disposed like the ridges in a chain of mountains. On each side of its mouth are whiskers, and a beard hangs under its chin, where also is placed a bright pearl; it cannot hear, which is the reason why deaf persons are called *lung* (聾). Its breath proceeds from the mouth like a cloud; being sometimes changed into water, at other times into fire; its voice is like the jingling of copper pans. There are several varieties;

some are horned and others hornless, some are scaleless, and one kind has no wings. It is the common opinion that the dragon, being a divine animal, dies of its own accord. It eats swallows' flesh, for which reason, when people pray to the dragon for rain they throw swallows into the water.' The *chiao*, which inhabits the marshes and dens, differs but little from the dragon of the sky. It is described as having a small head and neck, without horns, a breast of a crimson colour, back striped green, and sides yellow; has four legs, but is otherwise like a snake, and about thirteen feet long."[3]

"Another Chinese authority informs us that the dragon becomes at will reduced to the size of a silkworm, or swollen till it fills the space of Heaven and Earth. It desires to mount—and it rises till it challenges the clouds; to sink—and it descends until hidden below the fountains of the deep. The Chinese most thoroughly believe in the existence of this mysterious and marvellous creature; it appears in their ancient history; the legends of Buddhism abound with it; Taoist tales contain circumstantial accounts of its doings; the whole country-side is filled with stories of its hidden abodes, its terrific appearances; it holds a prominent part in the pseudo-science of geomancy; its portrait appears in houses and temples, and serves even more than the grotesque lion as an ornament in architecture, art designs, and fabrics. It has, however, been less used for ornamental purposes since the overthrow of the Monarchy."[4]

A primitive form of dragon is known as *k'uei* (夔). It is a beneficent creature, said to exert a restraining influence against the sin of greed, and it generally occurs in conventional form on ancient Chinese bronzes. Other varieties are the Celestial Dragon (天龍), which protects and supports the mansions of the gods; the Spiritual Dragon (神龍), which produces wind and rain to benefit mankind; the Dragon of Hidden Treasures (伏藏龍), which mounts guard over the wealth concealed from mortal eye; the Winged Dragon (應龍); the Horned Dragon (虬龍); the Coiling Dragon (蟠龍), which inhabits the waters; and the Yellow Dragon (黃龍), which emerged from the River Lo (洛河) to present the elements of writing to the legendary Emperor Fu Hsi. "Modern superstition has further originated the idea of four Dragon Kings (龍王)—identified with the *Nagas* or Serpent Spirits of the Hindoos—each bearing rule over one of the four seas which form the border of the habitable earth; and the subterranean palaces which form their respective abodes are named as follows: in the east sea, 清華宮; in the south sea, 丹陵宮; in the west sea, 素靈宮; in the north sea, 元冥宮."[5]

There are said to be nine distinct offshoots of the dragon, and they are respectively distinguished by special characteristics. These creatures, according to the *Ch'ien Chü'eh Lei Shu* (潛確類書), by Ch'ên Jen-hsi (陳仁錫), are as follows:

1. *P'u-lao* (蒲牢), carved on the tops of bells and gongs, in token of its habit of crying out loudly when attacked by its arch-enemy the whale;

2. *Ch'iu-niu* (囚牛), carved on the screws of fiddles, owing to its taste for music;

3. *P'i-hui* (贔屭), carved on the top of stone tablets, since it was fond of literature; it is also said to represent a male and female tortoise bowed down by grief, and is largely used as a pedestal for tomb-stones, one head looking each way. It is a river god, and is believed to be endowed with supernatural strength;

4. *Pa-hsia* (霸下), carved at the bottom of stone monuments, as it was able to support heavy weights;

5. *Chao-fêng* (朝風), carved on the caves of temples, owing to its liking for danger;

6. *Chih-wên* (蚩吻), carved on the beams of bridges, because of its fondness for water. It is also placed on the roofs of buildings to keep off fires. It likes to gaze and look out, and is sometimes symbolised by the figure of a fish with uplifted tail;

7. *Suani-ni* (狻猊), carved on Buddha's throne, on account of its propensity for resting. It has also been identified with the *Shih-tzŭ* (獅子) or symbolic lion;

8. *Yai-tzŭ* (睚眦), carved on sword-hilts, and where the blade joins the handle, in memory of its lust for slaughter;

9. *Pi-kan* (狴犴), carved on prison gates, as it was addicted to litigation and quarrelling, and loved to use its energy and strength, being very fierce. It is a scaly beast with one horn.

On the shores of the North Lake at Peking there stands what is known as the "Nine Dragon Spirit Screen." This screen is of brick faced with a marvellous design of glazed coloured tiles set together in the form of nine coiling and writhing dragons. They are so beautifully fashioned that they actually seem to be alive and ready to fight in protection of the Emperor against all evil spirits and marauders in the sacred precincts. As there are nine main species of dragon, so this protective screen symbolises all the dragons in existence. It was originally erected before the Temple of Ten Thousand Buddhas—long since destroyed by fire. Another fine screen of a similar nature is also to be seen in the Forbidden City near the Hsi Ch'ing Mên (Gate of the Bestowal of Rewards).

Slightly different collections of dragon spawn are given in the

Shêng An Wai Chi (升庵外集), and other publications, which also mention the *Chiao-t'u* (椒圖), carved on doorhandles because it likes to close things; the *T'ao-t'ieh* (饕餮), carved on covers and sides of food-vessels as a warning against its gluttonous nature; and the *Cha-yü* (𤟤貐), which has the head of a dragon, tail of a horse, and claws of a tiger; this monster is 4 *chang* (40 feet) long, and loves to eat men; it appears in the world if the ruling sovereign shows a lack of virtue; amongst other relatives of the dragon may be mentioned the *Lang-pei* (狼狽), said to be amphibious and supposed to have short hind legs unsuitable for locomotion, so that one animal rides upon another of the species, the latter making use of its long fore legs. This combination is a symbol of two persons joined together for evil purposes.

"The dragon is said to be the emblem of vigilance and safeguard. The ancients and the moderns have both spoken of this fabulous being. Consecrated by the religion of the earliest people, and particularly the Chinese nation; having become the object of their mythology, the minister of the will of their gods, the guardian of their treasures."[6] By the ancients a water-spout was thought to be a living dragon, and swelling waves—"enchanted." The monster is said to possess the power of raising great waves to injure men and boats.

The round red object which seems to be the constant appurtenance of the dragon is variously described as the sun, the moon, the symbol of thunder rolling, the egg emblem of the dual influences of nature, the pearl of potentiality—the loss of which betokens deficient power—or the "night-shining pearl" (夜明珠), which Professor Giles defines as a carbuncle or ruby. The Chinese imperial coat of arms from the Han to the Ch'ing dynasty consisted of a pair of dragons fighting for a pearl. "A Minister of State—Chi Liang, Marquis of Sui—walking abroad on a certain occasion, found a wounded snake, to which he gave medicine and saved its life. Afterwards, when he was again abroad in the evening, he saw the snake holding a brilliant pearl in its mouth, and as he approached it, the snake is said to have addressed him thus: 'I am the son of His Majesty the Dragon, and while recreating myself was wounded; to you, Sir, I am indebted for the preservation of my life, and have brought this pearl to recompense you for your kindness.' The Minister accepted the pearl and presented it to his Sovereign, who placed it in his hall, where by its influence the night became as day."[7]

The dragon is the fifth of the symbolic creatures corresponding to the Twelve Terrestrial Branches (*q.v.*). "According to the *I Ching*, the symbol *chên* (震), corresponding to the third of the four primary developments of the creative influence, is synonymous with *lung*, the dragon; and, in conformity with this dictum, the powers and functions of nature governed by the forces thus indicated, such as the East, Spring, etc., are ranked under the symbol 青 龍, the Azure Dragon, which also designates the eastern quadrant of the uranosphere."[8]

Since the reign of Kao Tsu (高 祖) of the Han dynasty, 206 B.C., the five-clawed dragon was the emblem of imperial power; the Emperor's throne, his robes, and articles of household use, etc., all bore the device of this scaly monster. It was also assigned to the use of the Emperor's sons, and princes of the first and second rank. Princes of the third and fourth rank were allowed the use of the four-clawed dragon, while princes of the fifth rank, and certain officials, were only entitled to employ a serpent-like creature with five claws as their emblem. The following description of court ceremonial, as practiced early in the seventeenth century, will serve as an illustration of the vanished splendour of the past: "When the Emperor of China takes his seat on the dragon throne, flags, chowries, and satin umbrellas are arranged on his right and left hand, and a band of music plays in a large building to the southward. On his right are the military officers, and on his left the civil officers; and they all, at a given signal, bow their heads nine times. The Emperor comes out of his palace in the following manner: He is seated in a sedan chair covered with yellow satin, with three rows of fringe, twelve chowries and twelve flags, upwards of twenty spears having the points sheathed, ten led horses with saddles and bridles complete, and upwards of twenty horses with the brothers and sons of the Emperor dressed in yellow satin jackets, and armed with bows and swords. Immediately in front of the Emperor is carried an umbrella of yellow satin with three rows of fringe, and having the figure of a dragon worked upon it in gold thread, and upwards of a hundred men in charge of the women (eunuchs) surround the Emperor's chair. The band of music which plays when the Emperor comes out or enters the palace, consists of a pipe with six stops, two trumpets, a lyre, and an alligator harp."[9]

The Dragon Boat Festival, known variously as 端 陽 節, 中 元 節, 解 糭 節, or 龍 舟 節, is held on the 5th day of the 5th moon, and presents a very animated scene. Long, narrow boats, holding sixty or more rowers, race up and down the river in pairs with much clamour, as if searching for someone who has been drowned. The festival is popularly believed to have been instituted in memory of a statesman named Ch'ü Yüan (屈原), a native of Ying (郢), who

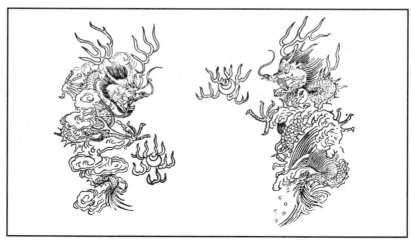

DRAGON OF THE CLOUDS   DRAGON OF THE SEA

drowned himself in the River *Mi-lo* (汨 羅) in 295 B.C., after having been falsely accused by one of the petty princes of the State, and as a protest against the corrupt condition of the government. The people, who loved the unfortunate courtier for his virtue and fidelity, sent out boats in search of the body, but to no purpose. They then prepared a peculiar kind of rice-cake called *tsung* (糉), made of glutinous rice and wrapped in leaves, and, setting out across the river in boats with flags and gongs, each strove to be first on the spot of the tragedy, and to sacrifice to the spirit of the loyal statesman. This mode of commemorating the event has been carried down to posterity as an annual holiday. A dragon boat generally measures 125 feet in length, 2½ feet in depth, and 5½ feet in width, and costs about $500. The bow of the boat is ornamented or carved with a dragon's head, and the stern with a dragon's tail, and carries men beating gongs and drums, and waving flags to inspire the rowers to renewed exertions. Accidents frequently occur during these races and the local authorities in some districts have accordingly restricted or forbidden the practice. It is quite probable that the festival had an earlier origin, and was possibly inaugurated with the object of propitiating the beneficent dragon in the hope that he would send down sufficient rain for the crops.

AUTHORITIES

1. Okakura: *The Awakening of Japan*, pp. 77–78.
2. Waddell: *Lamaism*, p. 395.
3. *The Chinese Repository*, Notices of Natural History, Vol. VII, 1839, p. 252.
4. Dyer Ball: *Things Chinese*, 5th Ed.: Dragon.
5. Mayers: *Chinese Reader's Manual*, Pt. I, No. 451.
6. *Encyclopaedia Londinensis:* Heraldry, Vol. IX, p. 421.
7. *The Chinese Repository*, Vol. IV, 1835, p. 238.
8. Mayers: *Chinese Reader's Manual*, Pt. 1, No. 451.
9. *The Chinese Repository*, Vol. IX, Nov., 1840, Art. 11, p. 453.

WORDS TO KNOW

NOTE: When you write the definitions of the following words, make it a point to use at least three of them in conversation over the next day and three of them in your next writing assignment. Many times you'll find it difficult or impossible to use them in everyday speech or writing. What then is the point of defining them? Of learning them? At the very least, in all the following cases where you have unusual vocabulary terms to define, attempt to use them. How does attempting to use vocabulary that feels awkward or different change your view of your common speech and writing patterns? Learning how to use new vocabulary means just that—using the words. Write specifically how, where, when, and why you used the words and discuss with your class.

Tang Dynasty—
T'ai Tsung—
Ch'in Shu-pao—
carcasses—
Yü Ch'ih Ching-tê—
gemmed—
girt—
subsequent—
tutelary—
disembodied—
gaudy—
talisman—

effigies—
depicted—
ascends—
mediaeval—
inaccessible—
equinox—
Yangtze River—
synchronises—
beneficient—
heraldry—
saurians—
levigated—
chorea—
spermatorrhaea—
hemorrhages—
circumstantial—
abodes—
geomancy—
betokens—
carbuncle—
uranosphere—
clamour—

QUESTIONS

Create a simple Text Question, a simple You Question, and a simple Other Question. Do the questions interest you? Share them with your classmates. Do they interest your classmates? Why or why not? Note their comments as well as your own and revise the questions.

WRITING ACTIVITIES

1. Write a one-sentence answer to one of your questions. Share your answer with your classmates. How do they respond? What do you wish you had added to your answer to make it more interesting? More compelling?

2. Write a one-paragraph answer to one of your questions. Share your answer with your classmates. How do they respond? What do you wish

you had added to your answer to make it more interesting? More compelling?

3. Try the above activities on another question. What do you find happening to your writing this second time around, and why?

GRAMMAR AND STYLE QUESTIONS

1. An important element of good usage is the concise and active expression of thoughts and ideas. Look through "Door Gods" and "Dragon" and find concise, active, phrases. Rewrite these phrases in your own words, and see how you can make them still more concise.

2. Take wordy, general expressions from your own writing that you've done based on these two readings and revise them to make them concise, active expressions that are correct grammatically. What did you change grammatically and why? What did you change stylistically, and why? (Grammar means your punctuation, and style means the manner in which you write what you write, i.e. do you use short or long sentences? Do you use humor? These are just a few examples of style and what it means.)

The Story of False Face

Mad Bear

In the 70's, interest in American Indian culture and tradition began to grow, and we began to get many dozens of letters from non-Indian people—young people, mostly, students and "seekers"—who were aspiring to meet teachers of their own—shamans, medicinepeople, wise ones who could help them in their spiritual development. Non-Indians wanted to meet Indians. In those days there was a natural hunger and longing among those of our contemporary modern society—among those many Indians still called "the newcomers"—for personal identity. That decade was known as the "me generation," and there was some question among some traditional elders—the would-be teachers—as to just what was being sought and why. Over time, interest in the tradition led to understanding of how tradition works. Traditional Indians are custodians of the land, medicinepeople are healers and helpers, and the ancient wisdom, as it is sustained and shared, accrues to the village, the land, the wildlife, and Earth Herself.

In the 90's, the interest and concern grows yet greater, and the cause ever clearer. We now long for a healthier planet. We now long to practice stewardship rather than dominion. We long to learn the natural humility and ecological harmony that is intrinsic to the Native tradition, to experience our interconnectedness with Earth and with all of life—and thus to better preserve a genuine quality of life for all our relations in coming generations. So now, when we come to them, The Wisdom Keepers come to us.

—Doug Boyd, "Wisdomkeepers Speak: The Earth Speaks"

Introduction Doug Boyd's piece is written using narration, relaying a series of events that have happened (in this case to him), and storytelling. He's placed a story within a story (Mad Bear is telling him the story of False Face during a visit they have together, and Boyd, in turn, is telling both of these stories to you as reader). The effects help emphasize the importance of story as the through-line, not only of how we live, but how we learn.

The Story of False Face was among the first of many tales and legends I heard from Mad Bear. The False Face that hung on the dark, paneled wall of his den was the first one I ever saw. It looked like a mask to me—an impossibly disordered and grotesque face whose nose, cheeks, chin, and protruding lips had been pushed horribly off center. I learned it was a living deity. His hair grew.

He was a wooden carving, a hollow face hung high on a peg near the ceiling. The coarse, dried "hair" that draped down past the chin on either side of the face appeared to be glued to the top of the head. But it grew. Over the years of our acquaintance, I often stayed at Mad Bear's Tuscarora cabin; and whenever there was a sufficient gap of time between my visits, I was sure that those dry, yellow thatches hung perceptibly closer to the floor. It was never mentioned by Mad Bear nor by me.

Over time I began to feel grateful that I had never inquired or remarked about that sacred object, or worse yet, pointed at it or even waved a hand in its direction before I knew what it was. Whenever an occasional visitor performed such an infraction, I could see Mad Bear's discomfort.

On my first visit to Mad Bear's place, we ate and drank coffee and started plans for our upcoming adventures, as I listened to his cheerful voice and easy laughter, I believe my eyes remained long fixed upon that False Face. I watched it hanging there, still and breathless and looking very much alive.

Mad Bear noticed. He stopped talking and watched me for moment. Then he turned in his chair to face the Being on the wall and spoke something in his own language. "This is False Face," he said to me, still facing the wall. "He is in my keeping. I feed him and watch over him. He goes with me to ceremonies, and I take him to the traditional rites that are for him and his people. I belong to the False Face Society. To me this is a big responsibility and a big, big honor."

He paused and turned to look at me. I had no questions. They weren't necessary. He would tell me what he wished, and nothing more.

"I will tell you his story—who he is and how he came to look like that. But he is gone on now, evolved beyond this. These Beings have graduated and gone to a higher world—and they are high, high, high, beyond us. Yet we keep the False Face in this form and we pay our honor and respect to it. It reminds us of a lesson far ahead of us—a hard lesson that we have yet to learn.

"I call him False Face even though that wasn't his name at his time. That was never the name of him or his people but that is how we refer to it. False Face had studied and learned all the basic things in the universe. Then he had prepared and developed himself in all the medicine ways. It took centuries of hard work, but eventually he developed all the spiritual powers known on this earth. He knew all the ways of the Creator.

"One day False Face stood out in a large field looking at the skies and at the mountains in the distance. And he thought to himself: Knowing as I do all the ways of the Creator, all things in this world are possible for me. I now understand how all things are done. Why, if it should be my will, those mountains should have to move.

"And then he heard the voice of the Creator whom he knew as the Great Lord of the Universe. The voice said, 'Yes, I am the Lord and the mountains are there by my will.'

"False Face paused for a moment. Many times he had heard the voice of the Creator; but now he was thinking only of himself. Speaking aloud, he announced in a powerful voice: 'I have come to know the ways of the Lord and I can duplicate them all! I can move these mountains if I wish!'

"And the Creator repeated: 'Yes, I am the Lord and I can move mountains.'

"'Not you!' shouted False Face. 'I am referring to myself. I am talking about me. Have I developed all this for nothing? Can I do nothing myself? I have learned all the rules of power and creation! Do you still think I am useless without you?'

"'You are never without me,' the Great Spirit answered in a gentle voice, 'for I am always with you.'

"'But I know all your secrets now,' False Face protested. 'I know how you do all these things.'

"'It is because you have come to me,' said the Great Spirit.

"In spite of all that he had learned, in spite of all his training and wisdom, False Face experienced a rush of great pride and anger, and he shouted at the Creator. 'Go away. Leave me alone. I don't need you anymore. I am now powerful and you want to think of me as your little child. I am not your little child anymore. I can do anything that you can do. So just leave me alone.'

"'Alone?' said the Great Spirit. 'There is no alone. How can I leave you? We are one and cannot be apart.'

"These gentle, loving words only made False Face more angry. It seemed to him, in his anger, that the Lord was discrediting him in spite of all his long efforts and the remarkable knowledge and power that he had attained. It seemed to him that the Great Spirit was still claiming all power for himself. In his angry state, False Face determined to have a contest with the Lord of the Universe and he challenged Him:

"'I know you don't want these mountains moved, Lord. But I am going to move them against your will. Then you will see that I am something in my own right. You can pit your power against me if you wish, Lord!'

"'I do not pit anything against anything,' answered the Lord. 'This idea of a contest is a temporary dream. Wake up and come to me now and you will see that nothing is anything in its own right apart from all that is.'

"But False Face repeated his challenge: 'You are trying to take everything away from me, Lord. You cannot take this chance away. Do what you like. Oppose me if you like, but I am going to move these mountains anyway, knowing that you want them where they are, so that it will be clear that it is done by my will alone.'

"False Face waited there in the field, grim and determined, and there was nothing but silence. So he went about the contest. Though he strained with all his might, trying everything that he had learned and developed over the centuries, nothing happened. Nothing at all. There was only a soft breeze, and the mountains stood in the distance as always. He flew into a rage, cursing in a way that cannot be repeated and, when there was only silence, daring the Lord to respond. He called the Great Spirit a fake and a liar, claiming the Creator had pitted his Great Will against him in spite of promising he would not.

"Then an idea occurred to him. He would have his contest yet. He shouted at the Lord, daring the Lord to move the mountain while he tried to block Him with his own will as the Lord had done. He believed that if the Lord had neutralized his power then he could do the same to Him. But he also believed that the Lord might well want the mountains where they were, and would be unwilling to move them. In either case, nothing would happen. He craved to claim victory over the Lord and he felt sure he would win his dare. He shouted his challenge again. He clenched his fists and squinted his eyes and screamed into the sky; and before he could finish his sentence, he heard a trembling and a rumbling. He spun around to look just as the mountain was coming to his side. That was a mistake, for that caused the mountain to strike his face and break his nose.

"And at that the gentle voice of the Great Spirit was heard again: 'Now look what we have done to our beloved self. No matter. It is very temporary. We shall now set it right with our collective will, shall we?'

"False Face felt a moment of great pain, and then he had a sudden awareness. There was no contest. There had never been any contest. This was another of his countless lessons. But this was the ultimate lesson and he had arranged it—he and His Own Self—so that he could be free from the desire to be a separate, independent something in its own right. So that he could be free from being apart and alone."

Mad Bear leaned back in his chair and picked up his coffee. "But this is not one person," he went on, "this is a whole people. And this kind of look represents their humility and their awareness of their incompleteness." He turned away from me again, and now both of us stared at the face on the wall. "Just think what we have to look forward to. After all our learning and development, we are still going to come to that last great contest—that last big hurdle for the powerful ego. Isn't that something? But once you have made that last hurdle, that's it. Then you graduate and go on to a higher level."

I looked at the back of Mad Bear's head. I tried to imagine him at this "last big hurdle." I tried to picture him standing in such a field, engaged in such a contest—and coming out looking like False Face. He turned around and grinned at me as though he'd sensed my thoughts. "Looks like we're outa coffee," he said, holding his cup upside down. "This darn pot's too small. Whatya say we crank 'er up again and then get down to business? We gotta lot to talk about!"

WORDS TO KNOW

NOTE: When you write the definitions of the following words, make it a point to use at least three of them in conversation over the next day and three of them in your next writing assignment. Many times you'll find it difficult or impossible to use them in everyday speech or writing. What then is the point of defining them? Of learning them? At the very least, in all the following cases where you have unusual vocabulary terms to define, attempt to use them. How does attempting to use vocabulary that feels awkward or different change your view of your common speech and writing patterns? Learning how to use new vocabulary means just that—using the words. Write specifically how, where, when, and why you used the words and discuss with your class.

grotesque—

protruding—

Tuscarora—

perceptibly—

QUESTIONS

Create a simple Text Question, a simple You Question, and a simple Other Question. Once you have done that, answer your questions. Do the questions and answers interest you? Do they interest your classmates? Why or why not? Which questions would be more interesting, more complex if you combined them into Bi-Level Questions and answered them? Why? Revise you simple questions to create Bi-Level Questions.

WRITING ACTIVITIES

1. Write a one-sentence answer to one of your Bi-Level Questions. Share your answer with your classmates. How do they respond? What do you wish you had added to your writing? Why?
2. Write a one-paragraph answer to this question. Share your writing with your classmates. How do they respond? What do you wish you had added to your writing? Why?

GRAMMAR AND STYLE QUESTIONS

1. Look at the uses of punctuation in journalistic reading (e.g. "Pet Shop Fish") and a storytelling reading (e.g., "The Story of False Face"). How is the punctuation (commas, quotation marks) used stylistically? Use specific examples from the readings and cite how specific rules governing punctuation were followed or not followed to achieve certain stylistic effects.
2. One of the most difficult tasks for any new writer is to express time and timelines consistently and to match actions to those times and timelines. Take a paragraph from "The Story of False Face" that has a strong sense of either past, present or future tense, and rewrite it using a different verb tense (i.e., if it was written in the present tense, rewrite it in the past tense, and so forth). What is the effect of such a change? Were you consistent in your new selection of verb tense in your revision? And, if you had difficulty with consistency, without referring back to the text, restore the original tense and see how closely the paragraph matches how Boyd originally wrote it.

The African Fang Legends—Eboka

John Miller and Randall Koral, eds.

Among the Fang People in Northwestern Africa, a religious move-ment known as the Bwiti cult relies heavily on the powerful psy-chotropic properties of the eboka bush. Initiates into the cult ingest the plant in order to "see" the Bwiti, a divine spirit. Depending upon the quality of the hallucinatory visions, the initiate may be ad-mitted to Akum, the sect's inner circle. The original myth excerpted here reflects the religion's role as a response to the hardships im-posed by colonialism (" . . . the misery in which the blackman was living") as well as the belief that the Fang originally received eboka as a gift from the Pygmies.

—John Miller and Randall Koral

Introduction Like The Story of False Face, this piece uses narration and storytelling. However, it uses these modes of writing as a form of "real" history—something that will make you puzzle over what is real-ity and what is legend. Unlike Boyd's piece, no authorial voice enters the story to sort out the fact from fiction for you. The effect encourages you to see that reality is defined as much by the group as it is by the in-dividual—and how truly fragile and nonabsolute it is in either case.

Zame Ye Mebege (the last of the creator gods) gave us *eboka*. He saw the misery in which blackman was living. He thought how to help him. One day he looked down and saw a blackman, the Pygmy Bi-tumu, high in an Atanga tree, gathering its fruit. He made him fall. He died and Zame brought his spirit to him. Zame cut off the little fingers and the little toes of the cadaver of the Pygmy and planted them in various parts of the forest. The grew into the *eboka* bush.

THE VISION (NDEM EBOKA) OF NDONG ASSEKO

(Age 22; Clan Essabam; Unmarried)

When I ate *eboka* I found myself taken by it up a long road in a deep forest until I came to a barrier of black iron. At that barrier, unable to pass, I saw a crowd of black persons also unable to pass. In the distance beyond the barrier, it was very bright. I could see many colors in the air but the crowd of black people could not pass. Suddenly my father descended from above in the form of a bird. He gave to me then my *eboka* name, Onwan Misengue, and enabled me to fly up after him over the barrier of iron. As we proceeded the bird who was my father changed from black to white—first his tail feathers, then all his plumage. We came then to a river the color of blood in the midst of which was a great snake of three colors—blue, black, and red. It closed its gaping mouth so that we were able to pass over it. On the other side there was a crowd of people all in white. We passed through them and they shouted at us words of recognition until we arrived at another river—all white. This we crossed by means of a giant chain of gold. On the other side there were no trees but only a grassy upland. On the top of the hill was a round house made entirely of glass and built upon one post only. Within I saw a man, the hair on his head piled up in the form of a Bishop's hat. He had a star on his breast but on coming closer I saw that it was his heart in his chest beating. We moved around him and on the back of his neck there was a red cross tattooed. He had a long beard. Just then I looked up and saw a woman in the moon—a bayonet was piercing her heart from which a bright white fire was pouring forth. Then I felt a pain on my shoulder. My father told me to return to earth. I had gone far enough. If I went further I would not return.

THE VISION OF EMAN ELA

(Age 30; Clan Essamenyang; Married with One Wife)

When I ate the *eboka* very quickly my grandfather came to me. First he had black skin. Then he returned and he had white skin. It was he that gave me my *eboka* name. My grandmother then appeared in the same way. Because my grandfather was dead before I was born he asked me if I knew how I recognized him. It was through *eboka*. He then seized me by the hand and we found ourselves embarked on a grand route. I didn't have the sense of walking but just of floating along. We came to a table in that road. There we sat and my grandfather asked me all the reasons I had eaten *eboka*. He gave me others. Then my grandfather disappeared and suddenly a white spirit appeared before me. He grasped me by the arm and we floated along. Then we came to a crossroads. The road on which we were traveling was red. The other two routes were black and white. We passed over. Finally we arrived at a large house on a hill. It was built on one post. Within I found the wife of my mother's father. She gave me my *eboka* name a second time and also gave me the talent to play the *ngombi* harp. We passed on and finally arrived after passing over more crossroads at a great desert. There I saw descend from the sky— from the moon—a giant circle which came down and encircled the earth, as a rainbow of three colors—blue, red, and white. I began playing the *ngombi* under the rainbow and I heard the applause of men. I returned. All the *banzie* thought I had gone too far and was dead. Since then I have seen nothing in *eboka*. But each time I take it I hear the spirits who give the power to play the *ngombi*. I play what I hear from them. Only if I come into the chapel in a bad heart does *eboka* fail me.

WORDS TO KNOW

NOTE: When you write the definitions of the following words, make it a point to use at least three of them in conversation over the next day and three of them in your next writing assignment. Many times you'll find it difficult or impossible to use them in everyday speech or writing. What then is the point of defining them? Of learning them? At the very least, in all the following cases where you have unusual vocabulary terms to define, attempt to use them. How does attempting to use vocabulary that feels awkward or different change your view of your common speech and writing patterns? Learning how to use new vocabulary means just that—using the words. Write specifically how, where, when, and why you used the words and discuss with your class.

Zame Ye Mebege—

eboka—

Bitumu—

Atanga—

cadaver—

Onwan Misengue—

    bayonet—
    Essamenyang—
    ngombi—
    banzie—

QUESTIONS

Create a simple Text Question, a simple You Question, and a simple Other Question. Ask yourself the following to help you to generate ideas for composing each question:

1. Text Question—What are you asking about the text?
2. You Question—What does the text make you think about in your own life?
3. Other Question—What does the text make you think about in the world?

Now create a series of Bi-Level Questions based on this reading and your notes and answers to the above questions.

WRITING ACTIVITIES

1. Write for five minutes without stopping on the answer to one of your bi-level questions. Have someone else time you and record the time and that person's name at the top of the page on which you've written. Try doing this exercise by writing longhand, with a pen on paper.
2. Choose another of your Bi-Level Questions. This time, have someone time you, and write using your computer, typing without writing on paper first. Don't stop writing to correct anything until the five minutes are up—just keep writing. Does how you're writing (using a pen or using the computer) make a difference in what you write? Why or why not?
3. Bring both writing samples to class and share them with your classmates. How do they respond? What do you wish you had added to your writing? Why?

GRAMMAR AND STYLE QUESTIONS

1. One of the most difficult tasks for any new writer is to express time and timelines consistently and to match actions to those times and time-

lines. Take a paragraph from "The African Fang Legends" that has a strong sense of either past, present, or future tense, and rewrite it using a different verb tense (i.e., if it were written in the present tense, rewrite it in the past tense, and so forth). What is the effect of such a change? Were you consistent in your new selection of verb tense in your revision? And, if you had difficulty with consistency, without referring back to the text, restore the original tense and see how closely the paragraph matches how the author originally wrote it.

2. Look at the uses of punctuation from a journalistic reading and a storytelling reading. How is punctuation used stylistically? Use specific examples from the readings and cite how specific rules governing punctuation were followed or not followed to achieve certain stylistic effects.

3. Examine the use of specific forms of punctuation (commas, dashes, quotation marks) in three different readings. How are these specific forms of punctuation used to emphasize the tone each author established?

The End of Firpo in the World

George Saunders

The Comedy Central show South Park *(a strong favorite with kids, despite how many parents would love to protect them from its profanity and violence—but even more from its unflinching look behind the curtain at the great OZ of adult authority and knowledge in this country) has paved the way for a different kind of children's story, perhaps one closer to the grim reality provided here by George Saunders.*

Introduction As in The African Fang Legends, narration and storytelling are key literary elements in this story. But the reader of this story knows unequivocally that "The End of Firpo" is fiction (make-believe) in a conventional sense. How much do you trust Firpo (Cody) as a narrator, and why? Who does he remind you of, and why? The effect of using an unreliable narrator like Cody helps you to understand the difference between objectivity and subjectivity, and, in this case, between morality, immorality, and amorality.

The boy on the bike flew by the Chink's house, and the squatty-body's house, and the house where the dead guy had rotted for five days, remembering that the Chink had once called him nasty, and the squatty-body had once called the cops when he'd hit her cat with a lug nut on a string, and the chick in the dead guy's house had once asked if he, Cody, ever brushed his teeth. Someday when he'd completed the invention of his special miniaturizing ray he would shrink their houses and flush them down the shitter while in tiny voices all three begged for some sophisticated mercy, but he would only say, Sophisticated? When were you ever sophisticated to me? And from the toilet bowl they would say, Well yes, you're right, we were pretty mean, flush us down, we deserve it, but no, at the last minute he would pluck them out and place them in his lunchbox so he could send them on secret missions such as putting hideous boogers of assassination in Lester Finn's thermos if Lester Finn ever again asked him in Civics why his rear smelled like hot cotton with additional crap cling-ons.

It was a beautiful, sunny day and the aerobics class at the Rec had let out and cars were streaming out of the parking lot with sun glinting off their hoods, and he rode along on the sidewalk, racing the cars as they passed.

Here was a low hanging willow where you had to duck down, here was the place with the tilty sidewalk square that served as a ramp when you jerked hard on the handlebars, which he did, and the crowd went wild, and the announcers in the booth above the willow shook their heads and said, Wow, he takes that jump like there's no tomorrow while them other racers fret about it like tiny crying babies!

Were the Dalmeyers home?

Their gray car was still in the driveway.

He would need to make another lap.

Yesterday he had picked up a bright-red goalie pad and all three Dalmeyers had screamed at him, Not that pad Cody you dick, we never use those pads in the driveway because they get scuffed, you rectum, those are only for ice, were you born a rectal shitbrain or did you take special rectal shitbrain lessons, in rectal shitbrain lessons did they teach you how to ruin everybody's things?

Well yes, he had ruined a few Dalmeyer things in his life, he had yes pounded a railroad spike through a good new volleyball, he had yes secretly scraped a ski with a nail, he had yes given the Dalmeyer dog Rudy a cut on its leg with a shovel, but that had been an accident, he'd thrown the shovel at a rosebush and stupid Rudy had walked in front of it.

And the Dalmeyers had snatched away the goalie pad and paraded around the driveway making the nosehole sound, and when he tried to laugh to show he was a good sport he made the nosehole sound for real, and they totally cracked up, and Zane Dalmeyer said why didn't he take his trademark nosehole sound on Broadway so thousands could crap their pants laughing? And Eric Dalmeyer said hey if only he had like fifty different-sized noseholes that each made a different sound then he could play songs. And they laughed so hard at the idea of him playing songs on Broadway on his fifty different-sized noseholes that they fell to the driveway thrashing their idiotic Dalmeyer limbs, even Ginnie, the baby Dalmeyer, and ha ha ha that had been a laugh, that had been so funny he had almost gone around one two three four and smashed their cranial cavities with his off-brand gym shoes, which were another puzzling dilemmoid, because why did he have Arroes when every single Dalmeyer, even Ginnie, had the Nikes with the lights in the heel that lit up?

Fewer cars were coming by now from the Rec; the only ones that did were going faster, and he no longer tried to race them.

Oh, it would be revenge, sweet revenge, when he stuck the lozenge stolen from the wood shop up the Dalmeyers' water hose, and the next time they turned the hose on it exploded, and all the Dalmeyers even Dad Dalmeyer, stood around in their nice tan pants puzzling over it like them guys on "Nova." And the Dalmeyers were so stupid they would conclude that it had been a miracle, and would call some guys from a science lab to confirm the miracle, and one of the lab guys would flip the wooden lozenge into the air and say to Dad Dalmeyer, You know what, a very clever Einstein lives in your neighborhood and I suggest that in the future you lock this hose up, because in all probability this guy cannot be stopped. And he, Cody, would give the lab guy a wink and later, when they were walking away, the lab guy would say, Look, why not come live with us in the experimental space above our lab and help us discover some amazing compounds with the same science brain that thought up this brilliant lozenge, because, frankly, when we lab guys were your age, no way, this lozenge concept was totally beyond us, we were just playing with baby toys and doing baby math, but you, you're really something scientifically special.

And when the Dalmeyers came for a lab tour with a school group they would approach him with their big confident underwater watches and say wow oh boy had they ever missed the boat in terms of him, sorry, they were so very sorry, what was this beaker for, how did this burner work, was it really true that he had built a whole entire *T. Rex* from scratch and energized it by taming the miraculous power of cosmic thunder? And down in the basement the *T. Rex* would rear up its ugly head and want to have a Dalmeyer snack, but using his special system of codes, pounding on a heat pipe a different number of times for each alphabet letter, he would tell the *T. Rex*, No no no, don't eat a single Dalmeyer, although why not lift Eric Dalmeyer up just for the fun of it on the tip of your tremendous green snout and give him a lesson in what kind of power those crushing jaws would have if he, Cody, pounded out on the heat pipe Kill Kill Kill.

Pedalling wildly now, he passed into the strange and dangerous zone of three consecutive MonteVistas, and inside of each lived an old wop in a dago tee, and sometimes in the creepy trees there were menacing gorillas he took potshots at from bikeback, but not today, he was too busy with revenge to think about monkeys, and then he was out, into the light, coasting into a happier zone of forthright and elephantine BuenoVerdes that sat very honestly with big open eyes that were their second-story windows, and in his mind as he passed he said hello HELLO to the two elephants and they in turn said to him in kind Dumbo voices hey Cody HEY CODY.

The block was shaped something like South America and as he took the tight turn that was Cape Horn he looked across The Field to his small yellow house, which was neither MonteVista nor BuenoVerde, but predated the subdivision and smelled like cat pee and hamburger blood and had recently been christened by Ma's boyfriend Daryl, that dick, The House of FIRPO, FIRPO being the word Daryl used to describe anything he, Cody, did that was bad or dorky. Sometimes Mom and Daryl tried to pretend FIRPO was a lovey-dovey term by tousling his hair when they said it but other times they gave him a poke or pinch and sometimes when they thought he couldn't hear they whispered very darkly and meanly to one another FIRP attack in progress and he would go to his room and make the nosehole sound in his closet, after which they would come in and fine him a quarter for each nosehole sound they thought they had heard him make, which was often many, many more than he had actually really made.

Sometimes at night in his room Mom babied him by stroking his big wide head and saying he didn't have to pay all the quarters he owed for making the nosehole sound, but other times she said if he didn't knock it off and lose a few pounds how was he ever gonna get a date in junior high, because who wanted to date a big chubby nosehole snorter, and then he couldn't help it, it made him nervous to think of junior high, and he made the nosehole sound and she said, Very funny I hope you're amusing your own self because you're not amusing my ass one bit.

The Dalmeyer house now came into sight.

The Dalmeyer car was gone.

It was Go Time.

The decisive butt-kicking he was about to give the Dalmeyer hose would constitute the end of FIRPO in the world, and all, including Ma, would have to bow down before him, saying, Wow wow wow, do we ever stand corrected in terms of you, how could someone FIRPO hatch and execute such a daring manly plan?

The crowd was on its feet now, screaming his name, and he passed the Chink's house again, here was the driveway down which he must turn to cross the street to the Dalmeyers', but then oh crap he was going too fast and missed it, and the announcers in the booth above the willow gasped in pleasure at his sudden decisive decision to swerve across the newly sodded lawn of the squatty-body's house. His bike made a trough in the sod and went HUMPF over the curb, and as the white car struck him the boy and the bike flew together in a high comic arc across the street and impacted the oak on the opposite side with such violence that the bike wrapped around the tree and the boy flew back into the street.

Arghh arghh Daryl will be pissed and say Cody why are you bleeding like a stuck pig you little shit. There was something red wrong with his Arroes. At Payless when they bought the Arroes Mom said, If you squirm once more you're gonna be facedown on this carpet with my hand whacking your big fat ass. Daryl will say I buy you a good bike and what do you do, you ruin it. Ma will come up with a dish towel and start swiping at the blood and Daryl will say don't ruin that dish towel, he made his bed let him sleep in it, I'll hose him off in the yard, a little shivering won't kill him, he did the crime let him do the time. Or Ma might throw a fit like the night he slipped and fell in the school play, and Ms. Phillips said, Tell your mother, Cody, how you came to slip and fall during the school play so that everyone in the auditorium was looking at you instead of Julia who was at that time speaking her most important line.

And Mom said, Cody are you deaf?

And Ms. Phillips said, He slipped because when I told him to stay out of that mopped spot did he do it? No, he did not, he walked right through it on purpose and then down he went.

Which is exactly what he does at home, Mom said. Sometimes I think he's wired wrong.

And Ms. Phillips said, Well, today, Cody, you learned a valuable lesson which is if someone tells you don't do something, don't do it, because maybe that someone knows something you don't from having lived a longer time than you.

And Daryl said, Or maybe he liked falling on his butt in front of all his friends.

Now a white-haired stickman with no shirt was bending over him, touch touch touching him all over, like looking to see if he was wearing a bulletproof vest, doing some very nervous mouthbreathing, with a silver cross hanging down, and around his nipples were sprigs of white hair.

Oh boy, oh God, said the stickman. Say something, pal, can you talk?

And he tried to talk but nothing came and tried to move but nothing moved.

Oh God, said the stickman, don't go, pal, please say something, stay here with me now, we'll get through this.

What crazy teeth. What a stickman. The stickman's hands flipped around like nervous old-lady hands in movies where the river is rising and the men are away. What a Holy Roller. What a FIRPO. A Holy Roller FIRPO stickman with hairy nips and plus his breath smelled like coffee.

Listen, God loves you, said the stickman. You're going, O.K., I see you're going, but look, please don't go without knowing you are beautiful and loved. O.K.? Do you hear me? You are good, do you know that? God loves you. God loves you. He sent His son to die for you.

Oh the freaking FIRPO, why couldn't he just shut up? If the stickman thought he, Cody, was good, he must be FIRPO, because he, Cody, wasn't good, he was FIRPO, Mom had said so and Daryl had said so and even Mr. Dean in Science had told him to stop lying the time he tried to tell about seeing the falling star. The announcers in the booth above the willow began weeping as he sat on Mom's lap and said he was very sorry for having been such a FIRPO son and Mom said, Oh thank you, thank you, Cody, for finally admitting it, that makes it nice, and her smile was so sweet he closed his eyes and felt a certain urge to sort of shake things out and oh Christ dance.

You are beautiful, beautiful, the stickman kept saying, long after the boy had stopped thrashing, God loves you, you are beautiful in His sight.

WORDS TO KNOW:

NOTE: When you write the definitions of the following words, make it a point to use at least three of them in conversation over the next day and three of them in your next writing assignment. Many times you'll find it difficult or impossible to use them in everyday speech or writing. What then is the point of defining them? Of learning them? At the very least, in all the following cases where you have unusual vocabulary terms to define, attempt to use them. How does attempting to use vocabulary that feels awkward or different change your view of your common speech and writing patterns? Learning how to use new vocabulary means just that—using the words. Write specifically how, where, when, and why you used the words and discuss with your class.

miniaturizing—
squatty-body—
Firpo—
Holy Roller—

QUESTIONS

Look again at Williams's "Dragon." What is the purpose of the illustrations in that reading? What do such pictorial sources add to your understanding of a text? To your enjoyment of the text? Why? What pictorial sources could you gather to add to your understanding and enjoyment of this reading? Gather samples such as photos, drawings, or images.

WRITING ACTIVITIES

1. Create several Bi-Level Questions based on this text. This time, before you write, look at your collection of pictorial sources and choose your favorite picture and your favorite Bi-Level Question. Look at the question and look at the picture for several minutes and then write down all the ideas, words, phrases, thoughts that come to you from the question and the picture. Write for at least ten minutes without stopping except to look at your question and source again.
2. Try this same activity again with a second question and pictorial source.
3. Once you've finished, read over what you've written and look at how you could revise these two writings into one writing, incorporating the best parts of both of the original writings.
4. Share your third writing with your classmates. How do they respond? How specifically did you detail and use your pictorial source in your writing? What would you do differently if you were to revise further?

GRAMMAR AND STYLE QUESTIONS

1. Look at "exotic" punctuation (e.g., dashes, parentheses, exclamation points) and/or unusual phrasing within "Firpo" and discuss what effect the author's decisions regarding such punctuation and phrasing choices have on the reader. What does the use of grammar and style in this story tell you about the written word as opposed to the spoken word?

2. An important element of good usage is the concise and active expression of thoughts and ideas. Looking through "Firpo" and any other readings you have read so far, find specific concise, active, grammatical expressions, put them into your own words, and see how you can make them still more concise.

The Descent of the Gods

Serge Bramly

Serge Bramly's book is a great introduction to a little-known spiritual path. In no way a titillating anthropological curiosity, it is an opening to a way of life and belief that is followed by fifteen million Brazilians as well as millions more all across the Western hemisphere. Along with its sister religions of Vodun, Santería, and Ifa, Macumba—also known as Umbanda outside of Río—worships dieties from Africa. These religions entail complex philosophical concepts and spiritual discipline, yet are too often ignorantly labeled "primitive" and falsely relegated to a realm of fetish-dominated superstition. . . . Racial, political, and economic considerations have everything to do with the acceptance of a religion. When a belief system is denied respect its followers are denied power. The struggle for legalization of important religions of African origin has been a long one; challenges from Fundamentalists who call all other forms of worship "Deviltry" continue today. It's time to broaden the perspective: there are more Macumbeiros than Mormons. Freedom of religion must be recognized as a universal human right; unrestricted personal spiritual choice is a precondition for honorable interaction between peoples.

Renée Pinzón and Sin Soracco, *Macumba*

Introduction You're probably noticing a pattern in the readings you've read so far: all use some variation on the narrative style of writing. Serge Bramly uses a form of narrative that most closely relates to Boyd's style—an outsider sharing an interaction between him(her)self and another person—an incident, something that happened to them both—with you, the reader. The effect of Bramly showing you what happened to him when he went to the religious ceremony described in this reading will give you more of a sense of the physicality of Umbanda, and, in doing so, will give you more of a sense of its magic and its individuality even as you find yourself comparing and/or contrasting it to a religion with which you are more familiar.

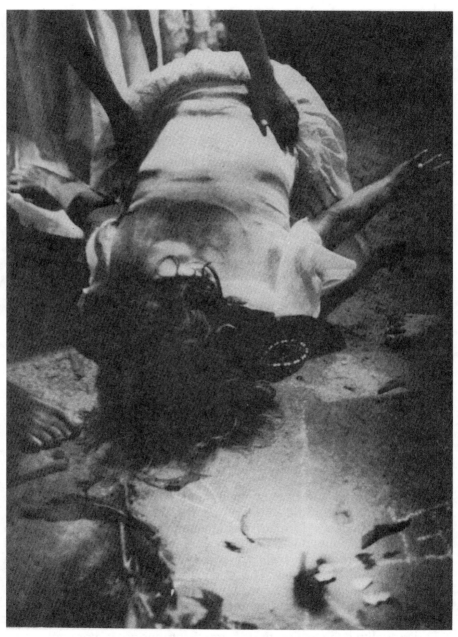

A medium in a trance salutes a magic diagram, a ponto riscado, on the floor of the ceremonial hall.

The smell of incense, candles and fresh-cut leaves . . . The walls, which have been papered with an odd design in pale blue and white, are covered with religious figures (Christ, Saint George slaying the dragon, etc.) rosaries and hand lettered signs—No Smoking, Respect the Law of Umbanda. The roof beams are hidden by a false ceiling made of thousands of tiny colored paper flags strung on thread. Here and there throughout the room candles burn in the sultry air. Outside, night is falling.

The large rectangular room is divided in two by a low, narrow barrier with an opening at the center. On one side of this divide the spectators, the faithful who have come to seek the help of Umbanda's gods, sit on long wooden benches—fifty-odd people of all ages and classes.

On the other side are the initiates—the mediums, "sons and daughters of the gods." The daughters of the gods are dressed in their ceremonial costumes: long pleated satin or cotton skirts, either white or blue, under which lie many layers of elaborate petticoats; puff-sleeved blouses appliquéd with lace; and innumerable glass bead necklaces in which are often entangled crosses or tin medallions. Immaculate white scarves have been wrapped around their heads like turbans. The mediums walk barefoot on the packed-earth floor, which has been strewn with green leaves.

At the far end of the room there is an alter with figures of saints, plaster statuettes, vases of flowers, candles, satin, ribbons, a crystal bowl, chipped glasses filled with clear water, flasks of perfume, a crucifix, and a large box of cigars. In a niche to the right of the alter there is a large grey mass—the vertebra of a whale.

The Brazilian friend who has invited me to attend the meeting leads me through the opening in the small room divider. I take off my sandals. I am introduced to the Mother of the Gods. Mother Maria-José is about fifty years old. Her features are delicate and energetic. She watches me with an amused curiosity. She is wearing the white ceremonial costume. After the usual polite exchange of formalities she welcomes me, saying that she is flattered to receive a foreigner in her terreiro. She asks that a chair be brought for me and sets me up in a corner near the altar, in the place of honor. And then she forgets all about me.

It is eight-thirty. Three men in shirts and pants, each carrying a drum, enter the room. The drums are long and cylindrical, narrow at the bottom and gaudily painted with bright colors.

The Mother comes and goes, speaking to each member of the congregation. She is giving her final instructions. The initiates line up along the walls, each holding a lighted candle. A drumroll is heard. The Mother's assistant, a man with a greying moustache, raises his arms to the sky; he is greeting the audience. He thanks his "Brothers and Sisters in Oxalá" for coming in such numbers. The initiates then pass before the Mother to make the ritual greeting of Umbanda with its theatrical, exaggerated gestures: the double accolade and then the handshake, elbows raised to the level of the head. "Saravá," they say, throwing themselves flat on their stomachs at her feet. She coldly helps them up. Then they greet one another. The ceremony has begun.

The voice of the assistant grows louder. Silence reigns over the audience. He prays:

> I greet the Ways of Umbanda,
> Saravá[1] Ogum, Iemanjá,
> Saravá Oxossi,
> Xangô and Oxalá![2]
> I salute the Ways of Quimbanda,
> the ways of the East,
> the Caboclos and the Pretos Velhos,
> I greet Exú and his family,
> and the family of souls,
> Saravá![3]

Everyone applauds. The drums begin to speak. The atmosphere changes imperceptibly. The Mother's assistant, who plays the part of Master of Ceremonies, calls out a name. He is summoning a god. The mediums and initiates sing to the glory of the god who has been named. They shift their weight from one foot to the other in time to the music. The songs are short—two or three stanzas. At the end of each song there is a burst of applause. The assistant summons another god. After a measure's rest the three drums launch a different rhythm and new songs begin.

Complicated diagrams are traced on the floor: words, flags and arrows overlap. The drawings are circular, and a lighted candle is placed in the center of each one.

---

[1]Saravá: ritual expression of greeting.

[2]Ogum, Iemanjá, Oxossi, Xangô and Oxalá; names of gods.

[3]The greeting is very important in Afro-Brazilian religions. Before a ceremony is begun, the faithful first greet all the gods and then each other. Each terreiro has its own particular gestures and expressions of greeting.

The dancers brace themselves. Their feet move faster and faster. They assemble in a circle around the Mother, who remains immobile in the center of the room. Her eyes are half-closed, and she seems to be looking at nothing.

She rests her weight on a knotted cane and smokes a broad pipe. The mediums dance and sing around her. They spin in the flickering light of the candles, turing endlessly as the beat accelerates. They summon the gods of Africa, imploring them with all their might to come quickly. Bending very low before the designs which have been traced into the earthen floor before the alter, they lament.

Suddenly a woman separates herself from the circle of dancers. Her turban poorly hides her blond hair. She gives a sharp cry, trembles, and nearly falls. She seems to be dizzy, and her eyes are upturned. The drums do not stop beating. She spins in the center of the room, her white skirt flying about her. She shouts again, and falls in ecstasy on one of the designs on the floor. All her limbs are shaking. The Mother comes toward her slowly and calmly. She picks her up and blows a pipeful of smoke in her face. She calms her by mumbling a prayer.

But from the other side of the room another woman advances. She has removed her turban, and her kinky hair seems to be standing on end. She is doubled over, and leans on a cane striped like a barber's sign. She drags herself along, muttering incomprehensible syllables. She is smoking a seasoned pipe. A bit of saliva shows at the corner of her lips. She breathes heavily. She walks right in front of me. Her voice is broken like the voice of an old man. Little by little almost all the mediums leave the ranks of the singers to dance in the center space of the terreiro. A man dances, gesticulating like a disjointed puppet: he laughs derisively, his head thrown back. A fat black woman with a thick cigar is drinking from the neck of a bottle of *cachaça*—50% sugar-cane liquor. She puts the bottle down in a corner and stands squarely, ready to greet all her companions. She grabs them around the waist and bluntly gives them the double hug. Then she blows a puff of her cigar smoke in their faces.

A man has fallen to the floor, nervous spasms rocking his whole body. The Mother picks him up and orders the musicians to change their rhythm. She slowly calms him down.

A woman in a trance leaves the ceremonial room through a small door hidden behind a curtain. She returns within seconds wearing a blue satin cape and an aluminum helmet that resembles a child's gladiator hat. She is carrying a large sword; She gives out blood-curdling shrieks and threatens everybody with her weapon.

Hands crossed behind her back, a young woman jumps up and down in place, rolling her eyes. A dancer accidentally bumps into her, but she doesn't even notice. Eyes open, she sees nothing: her mind is elsewhere. Suddenly her whole body goes limp and she bursts out laughing, her arms beating the air like the blades of a windmill. She mimes a strange dialogue. Not a sound can be heard; she is talking to an invisible other, punctuating her words with large, dramatic gestures.

At ten-thirty, on a signal from the Mother, the musicians stop playing. They exit with their drums. The singing continues. The mediums keep the beat by clapping their hands. About fifteen mediums are in a trance. Now they seem calmer. The Mother goes from one to the other, watching them, speaking to them. She whispers something to her assistant, after which he approaches the spectators and announces that the mediums are "ready to receive." One by one he ushers in all those who have come for help (requesting them first to remove their shoes), and guides them each to a different medium.

The woman with the cigar has sat down on the floor very close to me. Once again she has the bottle of cachaça in her hand. As she drinks, the liquor dribbles down her chin. A young, thin, athletic, well-dressed man is led up to her. He approaches timidly. He leans over and whispers at length into her ear. He is explaining his case. She pulls on her cigar, her eyes staring into nothingness. From time to time she asks a question, and he replies with embarrassment. She rises with surprising agility, takes his hands in her own and, without removing the cigar from her mouth, murmurs a prayer. Then she drops his hand and steps back. She walks toward him again, and strokes his face with her fingertips. She is like a hypnotist putting a patient to sleep. A few more magnetic moves and she begins to blow cigar smoke on him; first on his neck, then his shoulders, then his thighs. Finally she pronounces several sentences having to do with candles and red ribbons. The consultation is over. The young man leaves.

The same scene is repeated throughout the room. Those who have come seeking help recount their stories, the mediums perform a few steps and give their recommendations or prescribe a treatment to be followed. When all the visitors have left the Mother gathers the mediums around her. The songs and dancing are resumed (this time without the drums). The dancers are quieter now. The effects of the trance begin to wear off. The ceremony is over when all the mediums have returned to a normal state.

❖   ❖   ❖

WORDS TO KNOW

NOTE: When you write the definitions of the following words, make it a point to use at least three of them in conversation over the next day and three of them in your next writing assignment. Many times you'll find it difficult or impossible to use them in everyday speech or writing. What then is the point of defining them? Of learning them? At the very least, in all the following cases where you have unusual vocabulary terms to define, attempt to use them. How does attempting to use vocabulary that feels awkward or different change your view of your common speech and writing patterns? Learning how to use new vocabulary means just that—using the words. Write specifically how, where, when, and why you used the words and discuss with your class.

Umbanda—
initiates—
mediums—
appliqued—
vertebra—
terreiro—
Oxalá—
accolade—
Saravá—
Ogum—
Iemanjá—
Oxossi—
Xangô—
Quimbanda—
Caboclos—
Pretos Velhos—
Exú—
gesticulating—
cachaça—

QUESTIONS

Using the excerpt from *Macumba* as well as an excerpt from another of the readings in this text, create one of each of the three different types of Bi-Level Questions. Next, write your answers to the following questions: What other readings do you see to be related to the two you've chosen, and why? What are the major ideas they share? The specific details they share? Where do you see points of contrast?

WRITING ACTIVITIES

1. Select a text source outside this reader which relates to this reading as well as one other reading in this collection. Keep your selection to no more than three pages long. This text source can be a magazine, a Web page, a book, a newspaper, or magazine piece.
2. Write one sentence that states what you see to be the connection between the three readings or sources.
3. Write one sentence that states the main idea you have come up with after thinking over these three readings and what intrigued you about them. What point do you want to make about them, and why? (In other words, what important things do you want to say about them, and why?)
4. On which of your two sentences do you want to write one page, and why? Write your one page and be as detailed and specific as you can in your writing. Use specific examples whenever appropriate to illustrate your points.

GRAMMAR AND STYLE QUESTIONS

1. One of the best ways to learn grammar, in addition to learning the names and rules of grammatical elements, is to read other people's writing and determine how and why they write well. Take a grammatically imperfect piece of your own work, reread two or three readings from the readings you've read so far, and rewrite your piece afterwards. Is it grammatically better? Why or why not? What was the impact of seeing how other people put together words?
2. Compare and contrast reading by Bramly with the reading by Boyd. How do they use specific rules of grammar to get their points across? How does their use of grammar differ? What are the common features of both authors' writing? Cite specific rules of grammar and details in your answer.

There's a Man in the Habit of Hitting Me on the Head with an Umbrella

Fernando Sorrentino

Born in Buenos Aires in 1942, Sorrentino says of his stories, "I admire precision exceedingly, and conversely, I don't like ambiguity at all. In my stories, despite the strangeness of many situations, I try to make the images very concrete, very precise."

Introduction As with the story by George Saunders, you will find the narrator of this piece of fiction to be subjective and unreliable—not unlike people you know in real life. Perhaps even not unlike yourself. The effect of exposing you to so many variations on narration will be great detail and specificity in your own writing.

There's a man in the habit of hitting me on the head with an umbrella. It is five years to the day since he began hitting me on the head with his umbrella. At first I couldn't stand it; now I've grown accustomed to it.

I don't know his name. I know he's an ordinary man, with a plain suit, graying at the temples, and a nondescript face. I met him one sultry morning five years ago. I was sitting peacefully on a bench in Palermo Park, reading the newspaper in the shade of a tree. All of a sudden I felt something touch my head. It was this same man who now, as I write, automatically and impassively keeps striking me blows with his umbrella.

That first time I turned around full of indignation (I become terribly annoyed when I'm bothered while reading the paper); he went right on, calmly hitting me. I asked him if he were mad. He seemed not to hear me. I then threatened to call a policeman. Completely unruffled, he went on with what he was doing. After a few moments of hesitation—and seeing he was not about to back down—I stood up and gave him a terrific punch in the face. No doubt he is a weak man: I know that despite the force generated by my rage I do not hit all that hard. Still, breathing a tiny moan—the man fell to the ground. At once, making what seemed to be a great effort, he got up and again began hitting me over the head with the umbrella. His nose was bleeding, and I don't know why but at that moment I felt sorry for him, and my conscience troubled me for having struck him that way. Because, after all, the man was not hitting me very hard; he was really striking me quite soft and completely painless blows. Of course, such blows are terribly annoying. Everyone knows that when a fly settles on a person's forehead a person feels no pain; he feels annoyed. Well, that umbrella was a huge fly which, at regular intervals, kept settling on my head. Or, to be more precise, a fly the size of a bat.

At any rate, I could not stand that bat. Convinced that I was in the presence of a lunatic, I tried to get away. But the man followed me, in silence, without once letting up his blows. At this juncture, I began running (I may as well point out right here that there are few people as fast as I am). He set out after me, trying without luck to get in a whack or two. The man was gasping and gasping and panting so hard I thought if I kept him running like that my tormentor might sink dead on the spot.

For that reason I slowed to a walk. I looked at him. His face registered neither gratitude nor reproach. He just kept hitting me over the head with his umbrella. I thought of making my way to a police station and saying, "Officer, this man is hitting me over the head with an umbrella." It would have been unprecedented. The policeman would have stared at me suspiciously, asked for my papers, and begun questioning me with embarrassing questions. Probably he would have ended up arresting me.

I thought I'd best go home. I got onto the Number 67 bus. Not once letting up with his umbrella, the man got on behind me. I took the first seat. He stationed himself beside me, holding on to the strap with his left hand while with his right he kept swinging at me with his umbrella, implacable. The passengers began to exchange shy smiles. The driver was watching us in his mirror. Little by little, a fit of laughter, a growing convulsion, seized all the other riders. I was on fire with shame. My persecutor, completely unaffected by the uproar, went on hitting me.

I got off—we got off—at the Puente Pacífico. We continued on down Santa Fe Avenue. Everyone foolishly turned around to stare at us. I felt like saying to them, "What are you staring at, you idiots? Haven't you ever seen anyone whacking a man on the head with an umbrella before?" But it also occurred to me that they probably hadn't. Five or six kids began to follow us, shouting like a pack of wild Indians.

But I had a plan. Arriving home, I tried slamming the door in his face. I didn't manage it. With a firm hand—anticipating me—he grabbed the handle, there was a momentary struggle, and he entered with me.

Since then, he has continued hitting me on the head with his umbrella. As far as I know, he has never slept or had a bite to eat. All he does is hit me. He accompanies me in all my acts—even the most intimate ones. I remember, in the beginning, that the blows kept me from sleeping; I now believe it would be impossible to sleep without them.

Nevertheless, our relations have not always been good. Countless times, in all possible tones, I have asked him for an explanation. It's never been any use; in his quiet way he has gone on whacking me over the head with the umbrella. On several occasions, I have dealt him punches, kicks, and—God help me—even umbrella blows. He took these things meekly, as though they were all in a day's work. And this is exactly what is scariest about him: his quiet determination, his absence of hatred. In short, his inner conviction of carrying out a secret and superior mission.

Despite his apparent lack of physiological needs, I know when I hit him he feels the pain, I know he's weak, I know he's mortal. I also know a single shot would free me of him. What I don't know is whether when we're both dead he will go on hitting me on the head with his umbrella. Neither do I know whether the shot ought to be aimed at him or at me. In any case, this reasoning is pointless. I know full well I wouldn't dare kill either him or myself.

On the other hand, it recently occurred to me that I could not live without his blows. More and more frequently now I have a horrible premonition, I am distressed—deeply distressed—to think that perhaps when I most need him, this man will go away and I will no longer feel those soft blows of his umbrella that help me sleep so soundly.

WORDS TO KNOW

NOTE: When you write the definitions of the following words, make it a point to use at least three of them in conversation over the next day and three of them in your next writing assignment. Many times you'll find it difficult or impossible to use them in everyday speech or writing. What then is the point of defining them? Of learning them? At the very least, in all the following cases where you have unusual vocabulary terms to define, attempt to use them. How does attempting to use vocabulary that feels awkward or different change your view of your common speech and writing patterns? Learning how to use new vocabulary means just that—using the words. Write specifically how, where, when, and why you used the words and discuss with your class.

> nondescript—
> impassively—
> indignation—
> unruffled—
> implacable—
> Puente Pacífico—
> physiological—
> premonition—

QUESTIONS

Reread the story. Where does the beginning of the story turn into the middle of the story? Where does the middle of the story turn into the end of the story? How can you tell? Using the story, create one of each of the three different Bi-Level Questions. What pictorial images can you find that would accompany an answer to one of your Bi-Level Questions, and why?

WRITING ACTIVITIES

1. Take one of your Bi-Level Questions and write an answer to it. Be sure to include a reference to another text source in your answer as well as specific details from a pictorial source that you feel relates to the point of your writing.
2. Exchange your writing and sources with a classmate. What ideas did your classmate come up with that could add to yours? Together, come up with a new Bi-Level Question that combines your sources and writings. How do you both like the new writing? Does it go further than your individual writings did? Why or why not?
3. Take a copy of your joint writing home and revise and expand on your

central idea on the computer. Be sure to give your writing a beginning, a middle, and an end. Type "Introduction" as a heading to the beginning of the writing, "Body" as a heading to the middle of the writing, and "Conclusion" as a heading to the end of the writing. Use specific examples in your writing as well as specific details. Whenever appropriate, try using some of the new vocabulary you've been learning.

4. Share aloud with the rest of the class your joint writing as well as each of your new revisions on the joint writing. How do your classmates respond? What are they responding to and why? Which part of the two writings do your classmates like best: the beginning, the middle, or the end? Which do you and your partner like best? Why? What do you wish you had written differently, and why?

GRAMMAR AND STYLE QUESTIONS

1. Using a standard grammar reference (e.g., Strunk and White's *Elements of Style*), find three exceptions in Sorrentino's writing to any of the grammar and style rules such as a standard grammar and style reference has created, and discuss why Sorrentino may have broken those rules.

2. Look at "exotic" punctuation (e.g., dashes, parentheses, exclamation points) within Sorrentino's story and discuss what effect his use of these specific kinds of punctuation has on the reader. What does the use of grammar and style in this story tell you about the written word as opposed to the spoken word?

Collecting Kids' Stories of Past Lives

Edward Colimore

Birthmarks are important because they offer physical evidence for the link between past and present lives. One of Stevenson's cases is of an Indian boy who remembered being killed by a shotgun blast to his chest. On this boy's chest was an array of birthmarks that matched the pattern and location (verified by the autopsy report) of the fatal wounds. Another boy in India was born with stubs for fingers on only his right hand—an extremely rare condition. He remembered the life of boy who had his fingers cut off by the blades of a fodder chopping machine. One woman had three separate linear scarlike birthmarks on her back. As a child, she remembered the life of a woman who was killed by three blows to her back with an ax.

—Carol Bowman, *Children's Past Lives*

Introduction Edward Colimore's article about Carol Bowman, while it contains some storytelling elements, is journalistic—that is, it is a newspaper article, an example of reportage. The effect of this kind of writing, which includes some emphasis on some of the sensational aspects of cases of past-life regression, deliberately plays on certain emotional stances, beliefs, perspectives that you as readers have. Do you agree with her above quote? Why or why not?

Carol Bowman wasn't sure what to make of her son's deep fear of loud noises. Booming fireworks terrified him. The thumping diving board at an indoor pool made him howl and scream.

She told the stories to friend Norman Inge one afternoon as the two sat around a kitchen table with Bowman's son and daughter. Then, Inge, a hypnotherapist, suggested an experiment.

"Sit on your mom's lap," Inge told the 5-year-old boy. "Close your eyes and tell me what you see when you hear the loud noises that scare you."

Without being hypnotized, Chase Bowman began describing images from a bygone war—in present tense, as if he were there.

"I'm standing behind a rock," Chase said. "I'm carrying a long gun with a kind of sword at the end."

During the next 20 minutes, Bowman said, a freckled-faced boy who'd never shown an interest in war toys and movies detailed the hardships of a Civil War soldier.

He spoke in serious, mature tones beyond his years, she said. He sometimes tensed, took quick breaths and curled up in fear when talking about the tumult around him.

The experience changed Carol Bowman's life. She spent years researching a children's phenomenon that is now the subject of a book gaining international attention: *Children's Past Lives—How Past Life Memories Affect Your Child.*

It also led to the healing of her own children, she said. Chase so completely lost his fear of loud noises that now, at 14, he plays drums in a band. A severe chronic eczema—on his wrist—cleared up after the so-called past-life regression nine years ago.

What's more, in a similar experiment, Bowman's then 9-year-old daughter, Sarah, confronted her terror of house fires. She wound up describing a death in a blazing home in another lifetime—and lost her unnatural fears.

"I thought this has great potential for helping other children," said Bowman, whose book will be sold in England, Holland, Germany and Brazil, and is being translated into Chinese. "It was totally unexpected, the most fascinating thing I had ever experienced.

"I was on a completely different track, a stay-at-home mother, but this was a turning point in my life."

Bowman, a former Asheville, N.C., resident and paralegal who'd never researched or written a book before, soon found herself being interviewed on many nationally syndicated radio and television programs.

She told the story of her own healing through a past-life regression a year before her children's experiences. She said she had a severe lung ailment that cleared up after learning of two past lives where she had died—of consumption in the 19th century and in a gas chamber during World War II. Her belief in reincarnation had been broadened by Chase's and Sarah's regressions.

"I think our past-life experiences affect our personalities," said Bowman, 47, who now lives in Media, Delaware County. "We are a composite of everyone that we have been in the past. I think everyone has experienced a past life, but not everyone remembers it."

The idea of reincarnation is an old one. It's been embraced by several cultures and written about by many authors.

Barbara Lane, a clinical hypnotherapist whose book *Echoes From the Battlefield* documents the past-life descriptions of Civil War reenactors, believes in the "strong possibility" that the reenactors were remembering a real life under hypnosis.

But she theorized that the regression experiences also could be genetic memories, the life experiences of ancestors imprinted on genes and passed down.

Some people, Lane said, believe the experiences may be created by the mind from material read and forgotten, yet stored in the subconscious. Others think that regressed subjects are simply using their imagination—and familiarity with the period.

The Catholic Church rejects the notion of reincarnation, said a spokeswoman for the Archdiocese of Philadelphia. It believes that the body dies, but the soul is eternal and does not return to another body to live another life.

Nothing, Bowman said, adequately explains the past-life cases of children researched in her book. Many of them "remember" lives as members of other races or nationalities and sometimes speak another language, without ever having heard it before.

They're often too young to read or watch serious television documentaries, Bowman added, so they have nothing to draw on.

And some of them have birthmarks or birth defects corresponding to fatal wounds allegedly received in an earlier life, according to research by Ian Stevenson, a University of Virginia professor who wrote two volumes detailing 210 such cases.

Indeed, the past-life experiences of children appear to be "closer to the surface," said Bowman. ". . . This happens spontaneously in small children, 2-, 3-, and 4-year-olds, telling past memories without prompting from anyone—and whose parents had no belief in reincarnation.

"But there's no context for those memories in this culture, so they go unrecognized and unacknowledged."

Several months after his past-life recollections, Chase—in a matter-of-fact tone that caught his mother off-guard—began adding more detail to the life of his Civil War soldier.

"Mom, remember when I saw that I was a soldier with Norman?" he said, one morning during breakfast at their Media home.

"Yes," said Bowman, her heart pounding.

". . . Well, I was black," said Chase, then age 5. "There were black soldiers and white soldiers fighting together."

Three years later, with his "memory" triggered by fighting in the Persian Gulf War, the boy again recalled the life of the Civil War soldier, filling in additional information. This time, he described a happy life as a husband and father before the war, his longings for his family after entering the service—and his death on the battlefield.

"I'm behind the cannon," said Chase. "I'm hit. . . . I'm floating above the battlefield. I feel good that I'm done. I see the battle and the smoke below."

Because of her own past-life memories, Bowman said she was "primed to recognize the potential for helping all children."

Another parent, Tiiu Lutter of Springfield, Delaware County, told Bowman the story of her 2-year-old daughter who recalled dying in a car accident.

Lutter was driving over a bridge when little Liia said, "Mommy, this is just like where I died. . . . I was in my car, and it fell off the bridge into the water, and I died."

As Bowman studied each case, she repeatedly saw the same signs.

Whenever past-life memories had substance, the children often talked about them in a matter-of-fact tone.

They told their stories with consistent details.

They had knowledge beyond their experience.

And they exhibited corresponding behavior and traits, such as phobias, birthmarks or chronic physical conditions.

"When a child speaks so innocently and knowingly about living before, and so calmly describes what happens after death and on the journey to rebirth," Bowman said, "it is firsthand testimony to the truth that our souls never die."

She said she wrote her book as a guide for parents and psychologists, not to prove the existence of a past life.

"Healing and growth are the point," she said. "If you know the four signs, you can catch the magic moment" when a child speaks of a past life.

"The most important thing a parent can do is listen with an open mind," added Bowman. "Suspend your belief system while this is happening. Acknowledge your child. Don't cut them off. Let them talk about it."

❖   ❖   ❖

WORDS TO KNOW

NOTE: When you write the definitions of the following words, make it a point to use at least three of them in conversation over the next day and three of them in your next writing assignment. Many times you'll find it difficult or impossible to use them in everyday speech or writing. What then is the point of defining them? Of learning them? At the very least, in all the following cases where you have unusual vocabulary terms to define, attempt to use them. How does attempting to use vocabulary that feels awkward or different change your view of your common speech and writing patterns? Learning how to use new vocabulary means just that—using the words. Write specifically how, where, when, and why you used the words and discuss with your class.

hypnotherapist—

phenomenon—

eczema—

reincarnation—

reenactors—

traits—

phobias—

QUESTIONS

Visit Carol Bowman's Web site at www.childpastlives.org. Examine its content and explore related sites by clicking on the hyperlinks provided. What information intrigues you, and why? You've worked so far with creating Bi-Level Questions; now create Text/You/Other Questions. Develop at least three different Text/You/Other Questions related to this article's content and style.

WRITING ACTIVITIES

1. You will be writing on one of your Text/You/Other Questions for your activity. As a preliminary step, create a series of interview questions that you can ask your classmates that will relate to this reading in some way. What questions have you chosen for your interview questions and why? What does it mean to interview someone? Make your questions brief, but specific. Interview several of your classmates. Remember to ask "who, what, where, when, how, and why" questions rather than "yes or no" questions in order to get the most in-depth answers from your interview subjects. Write down everything that your classmates say in their answers. You may even wish to tape-record their answers.

2. Look over what you wrote down as their answers to your questions (and/or you can replay your tape and write down what you see to be significant quotes from your classmates. But remember, you must quote them exactly).

3. As you write in response to your Text/You/Other Question, see where you could include a brief quote or two from your classmates in your writing. How do their quotes add to your writing? What further ideas do they give you?

4. Share your writing with your class. Which writing stands out to you, and why?

GRAMMAR AND STYLE QUESTIONS

1. Look at the uses of punctuation in this journalistic reading and in a storytelling reading. How is the punctuation (commas, quotation marks) used stylistically? Use specific examples from the readings and cite how specific rules governing punctuation were followed or not followed to achieve certain stylistic effects.

2. Select another reading and compare and/or contrast it to this reading. What stylistic differences can you identify? Use specific examples from the readings and cite how certain rules governing grammar and style were followed or not followed to achieve certain stylistic effects.

Sri Venkateswara Swami Temple of Greater Chicago

Peruse the following information, obtained from a Web site, on a religious idol, Balaji, who is an incarnation of Vishnu. What value, if any, does such a site possess? What do you learn from the site versus what you already know? How does the layout appear the same or different from the print sources (books) you've read thus far in this reader? Visit this Web site to search for additional information you can find through exploring hyperlinks.

Introduction This reading contains a large number of what are certain to be completely new words to you. Don't be daunted; most can be defined from their context within the sentences in which they are used. The narrative is written using description and categorization. It very specifically details each and every single aspect of a religious idol, Balaji, one of the incarnations of Vishnu. Look carefully at how the writing ties details to point to purpose. It also structures the "beginning, middle, and end" of the narrative using the way a person's eyes travel over different aspects of religious statues, what they focus on, and why.

SRI VENKATESWARA SWAMI (BALAJI)

The presiding deity of the temple is Sri Venkateswara Swami, also known as Balaji in the northern parts of India. He is an incarnation of *Vishnu (Bhanvishvottara purana, Varaha purana*, etc.). The idol of the Lord is a majestic, beautiful and superbly executed one. All the qualities and attributes which are inherent in the nature of the Pervader and which are found in his manifestations are symbolized by the different qualities and attributes of His idol. Every feature, expression and ornamentation is of significance and is intended to be a fit object for meditation.

Four Arms:
The Lord's image has four arms, the upper right arm holds *Sudarsana Chakra* (discus) and right arm holds *Pancha-Janya* (Conch). The lower right hand is in *Varada hasta* (boon giving) pose and lower left hand is in *Katyavalambita* pose, turned inwards. Four represents fulfillment of manifestations in all spheres of existence, the four stages that may be found in every form of development of life. In the image it also represents dominion over four directions of space and thus absolute power.

Sankou (The Conch):
The conch is the symbol of origin of existence. It has the form of a multiple spiral evolving from one point into ever increasing spheres. It is associated with the element of water, the first compact element, and thus spoken of as born of the Casual waters. When blown, it produces a sound associated with the primeval sound *(AUM)* from which the creation evolved. The name of the conch Pancha-janya (born-of-five) also suggests the five elements (pancha *bhuta*).

Chakra *(The Discus):*
The discus is called 'Sudarsana' (Beauteous sight). It represents the Universal mind, the limitless power which invents and destroys all the spheres and forms of the universe, the nature of which is to revolve.

Kausthubha:
A brilliant gem called kausthubha ('born from the waters that surround the earth') adorns the chest of Balaji. This jewel represents consciousness which manifests itself in all that shines: the Sun, the Moon, Fire and Speech.

The Ear Rings:
Shaped like sea creatures *(makara)* the two ear rings represent the two methods of knowledge, intellectual knowledge *(sankhya)* and intuitive perception (yoga). Armlets and the Crown: Armlets are said to be the three aims of worldly life 'righteousness, success and pleasure'. The crown represents the unknowable reality.

Pitambara:
Golden veil seen worn by the Lord is said to represent the *Vedas* (the Hindu scriptures). 'The dark body shines through the thin golden veil just as divine reality shines through the sacred utterances of the Vedas'.

Yajnopavita:

The scared thread shown across the chest of the Lord is made of three threads said to be the three syllables of the sacred sound Aum. (A for *aadimatva* or creation, U for *uthkarsha* or sustenance and M for *miti* or limit).

SRI KANYAKA PARAMESHWARI

Sri Kanyaka Parmeshwari, Vasavi is incarnation of goddess Parvathi, divine consort and power of Lord Siva. Vasavi emphasizes virtues of love and character. She represents the importance of Education, Art, Music, Dance, being religious and offers freedom from temptations and protection from disruption of family traditions.

In a chaste young woman form right hand is in *Abhaya* (fear allaying) posture and left hand is in *Varadha* (boon giving) posture. She also appears with four arms. This form indicates end of incarnation and transition into form of Goddess *parvathi.*

SRI AYYAPPA

Ayyappa is also known as Sasta or Hariharaputra. He is son of Lord Siva and Mohini (Lord Vishnu in a delusory enchanting form). Siva is known as the God of destruction and Vishnu the God of sustenance. These two powers are said to be combined in Ayyappa. He destroys the low (tamasic) negative tendencies and promotes the pure cohesive (satvic) nature in the worshipper. The Lord is considered the God of constructive destruction, the Protector. He protects the spiritual wealth and power by maintaining the thought of godliness and destroys other thoughts pertaining to the worldly infatuations.

SRI SATYANARAYANA

Sri Satyanarayana Swami is also believed to be an incarnation of Vishnu and most of the characteristics attributed to Vishnu are also attributed to Him. He is worshipped in all Hindu households in a ceremony called Satyanarayana Vratam which is also celebrated at SVS temple annually. Hundreds of couples participate in this.

SRI LAKSHMI AND BHUDEVI

Along with divine consorts of Vishnu, Lakshmi appears with him in every one of his incarnations. When he appeared as *Vamana* she was *Kamala*, when he was *Parasurama* she was *Dharani*, when he was *Rama*, she was *Sita*, when he was *Krishna*, she was *Rukmini*. She is as inseparable from Vishnu as speech from meaning, knowledge from righteousness. Lakshmi according to *Bhagavatapurna*, was born out of the ocean of milk when gods and demons were churning it for nectar *(amruth)*. Lakshmi being known as goddess of wealth (wealth does not mean money alone, it includes all the nobler values of life, power of the mind, intellect, moral and ethical qualities etc.), the meaning behind the story is that wealth does not come to any one of its own accord, but has to be drawn out throughout self effort. This idea is well brought out in the allegory of the churning of the ocean of milk.

SRI ANJANEYA

Anjaneya (son of Anjani and Vayu) is depicted as an embodiment of devotion in the epic Ramayan. For all his services to Sri Rama he is said to have asked for only one thing in life. "Please give me the blessing that my affection for you should never diminish. Do not allow me to think of anything else. I want to live as long as your name is preserved among the sons of men. Let me be forever and forever be your devotee."

SIVA

Siva is worshipped in the form of Linga at the temple. Literally Siva means auspiciousness and Linga means a sign or symbol. Siva also means "one in whom the whole creation sleeps after dissolution. Siva is the embodiment of tamas, the centrifugal inertia, the tendency towards dispersion, toward disintegration and annihilation. When the universe expands indefinitely, it dissolves and gradually ceases to exist. That dispersion in the obscurity of the causal insubstantially is the end of all differentiation, of all places and time. Nothing that has existence can escape the process of destruction. Existence is only a stage of an expanding i.e., disintegrating universe. It is from destruction that creation again rises, hence destruction is the ultimate cause, the unmanifest origin of creation. Siva, the power of disintegration alone remains in the beginning and the end. The Linga installed in a temple is called achala Linga and is usually made of stone. It has three parts: the lowest part which is square is called Brahmabhaga and represents the Brahma the creator, the middle part which is octagonal is called Vishnubhaga represents Vishnu the sustainer. These two parts are embedded in the pedestal. The third, the Rudrabhaga which is cylindrical and projects outside the pedestal is the one to which worship is offered. Hence it is called Pujabhaga. Pujabhaga also contains certain lines, technically called 'Brahnasutra' without which Linga becomes unfit for worship.

Nandi (The Bull)
Nandi (the happy one) the bull on which Lord Siva rides is usually placed in front of a siva shrine. (Nandi will be installed at SVS temple in 1996). It represents virility and strength, the animal in man. Nandi is shown with the head turned away from the deity, but the gaze fixed on it. It is interpreted as 'jivatman' (the individual soul) with its animal nature pulling away from God but His grace pulling him back to Him.

PARVATI

Power of Siva is envisaged under three main aspects: A creative, all pervading active aspect called *Sakti*. A permanent, peaceful all pervading spatial aspect named Parvati, A destructive all pervading time aspect known as *Kali*. Parvati is described as daughter of *Parvata* (Stands for aakasa or either the fundamental substance of the universe) and *Menaka* (Stands for intelligence). Hence Parvati their offspring represents the conscious substance of the universe. That is why she is also called *Uma* (light or the bright one). At the subjective level Uma represents 'Brahmavidya' or spiritual wisdom, by which union with Siva or God is obtained.

GANAPATI

Ganapati or Ganesa, also known as Vighneswara or Vinayaka is the most popular of the Hindu deities worshipped by all sections of the Hindu society. No undertaking can get started without first worshipping him. This is because he is known as the Lord of Obstacles (Vighneswara or Vighnaraja). Ganapati stands for one of the basic concepts of Hindu mythological symbolism; the identity of the macrocosm and the microcosm or in religious terms the notion that man is the image of God. This notion of divinity of man and the immanence of God should be present before the mind whenever one begins anything, hence one should first bow to Ganesha. Ganapati is represented as an elephant headed man to express the unity of the small being, the microcosm i.e., man and the Great being, the macrocosm, pictured as an elephant. The man part of Ganapati, representing the manifest principle is inferior to the unmanifest, shown as the elephant. The elephant part therefore is the head.

The Mouse

The vehicle of *Ganapati* is the mouse *(Mushika)*. The mouse is the master of inside of everything. The all pervading *Atman* is the mouse that lives in the hole called intellect within the heart of every being. It is the real enjoyer of pleasures of all creatures. Like mouse, this self of all is a thief because unnoticed it steals all that people possess. It hides itself behind the inscrutable shapes of illusion, and no one knows that this inner ruler take for himself the pleasures people believe they enjoy.

SUBRAHYMANYA

The son of *Siva* and *Sakti* represents the highest state to which a spiritual aspirant can evolve. Etymologically the word *Subrahmanya* means one who tends the spiritual growth of the aspirants. He is also known as *Shanmukha* (Six faced), *Kumara, Skanda, Kartikeya, Velan* and *Murugan*. His weapon is a lance of dazzling brilliance with which this *Devasenapati* (commander of the army of Gods) vanquished any enemy. Symbolically the lance stands for knowledge and wisdom with which demons of ignorance can be destroyed. His vehicle is peacock. It is shown as belabouring a snake with one of its legs. Snake represents the cycle of the years, and the peacock is thus the killer of time. In cosmological terms. *Kumara* is identified with the solar energy which dwells in the higher sphere of the earth, beyond the sphere of air and gives rise to the cycle of the year *(Samvatsara-agni)*. He is thus the form of *Rudra* called *Nila-lohita* (Blue and Red).

REFERENCES

Dr. N. Ramesan, *The Tirumala Temple*, Tirumala Tirupati Devastanam.
Alain Danielou, *The Myths and Gods of India*, Inner Traditions International.
R. S. Nathan, *Symbolism in Hinduism*, Central Chinmaya Mission Trust.
Swami Harshananda, *Hindu Gods and Goddesses*, Sri Ramakrishna Mission.
George Mitchell, *The Hindu Temple, An Introduction to Its Meanings and Forms*.

WORDS TO KNOW

NOTE: When you write the definitions of the following words, make it a point to use at least three of them in conversation over the next day and three of them in your next writing assignment. Many times you'll find it difficult or impossible to use them in everyday speech or writing. What then is the point of defining them? Of learning them? At the very least, in all the following cases where you have unusual vocabulary terms to define, attempt to use them. How does attempting to use vocabulary that feels awkward or different change your view of your common speech and writing patterns? Learning how to use new vocabulary means just that—using the words. Write specifically how, where, when, and why you used the words and discuss with your class

deity—
Sudarsana Chakra—
Pancha-Janya—
Varada hasta—
Katyavalambita—
Aum—
kausthubha—
makara—
sankhya—
Vedas—
aadimatva—
uthkarsha—
miti—
Abhaya—
Varadha—
Parvathi—
Ayyappa—
Sasta—
Hariharaputra—
Lord Siva—
Mohini—
Sri Satyanarayana Swami—
Satyanarayana Vratam—
Lakshmi—
Vamana—
Kamala—

Parasurama—
Dharani—
Rama—
Sita—
Krishna—
Rukmini—
Bhagavatapurna—
amruth—
Anjaneya—
tamas—
centrifugal—
inertia—
dispersion—
annihilation—
differentiation—
unmanifest—
achala Linga—
Brahmabhaga—
Vishnubhaga—
Rudrabhaga—
Pujabhaga—
Brahnasutra—
Nandi—
jivatman—
Sakti—
Parvati—
aakasa—
Kali—
Menaka—
Uma—
Brahmavidya—
Ganapati or Ganesa—
Vighneswara—
Vinayaka—
macrocosm—
microcosm—
Mushika—
Subrahmanya—

Shanmukha—
Kumara—
Skanda—
Kartikeya—
Velan—
Murugan—
Devasenapati—
Samvatsara-agni—
Rudra—
Nila-lohita—

QUESTIONS

Go to a museum, church, or religious temple and select a religious object that includes lots of detail. Write down all the details you notice
about the object as specifically as you can. Furthermore, write down
the detail in the order in which your eye notices it. After each detail,
discuss either its impact on you (regardless of what you know about it
historically) or provide a historical explanation for the detail(s). Why
did you choose the object that you did? Using your selected object
(and being sure to get a picture of the piece), create several Text/
You/Other Questions.

WRITING ACTIVITIES

1. Answer one of your Text/You/Other Questions after you've decided
   what your main idea will be in your writing. Try beginning or introduc-
   ing your piece by focusing on a particular detail of your piece that will
   fascinate your readers and show (don't tell) why it will fascinate them.
2. If relevant and if you so desire, you may discuss a religious experience
   from your own life or a religious object from your own life. Be as detailed as you can in discussing it. Remember that your discussion including your religious experience and/or the religious object from your
   own life needs to connect in a meaningful way to your main idea, as
   well as connect to this reading and your selected religious object.
3. How long is your writing now? Does it seem harder to write just a sentence? Easier to write a page? Why?

GRAMMAR AND STYLE QUESTIONS

1. Examine the use of specific forms of punctuation in three different readings (you may choose any three readings you wish; feel free to choose from readings yet to be covered by your class). How are these specific punctuation choices used to emphasize the tone each author established?

2. Select a reading and compare and/or contrast it to this reading. What stylistic differences can you identify? Use specific examples from the readings and cite how certain rules governing grammar and style were followed or not followed to achieve certain stylistic effects.

The Three Day Grin

Thanhha Lai

Honoring your ancestors during Tet is hard work. You've got new clothes to buy, New Year's feasts to prepare, a smile to force. And for one Vietnamese daughter, there's the weight of tradition to carry from one generation to the next. . . . Surely I could not have been the only Vietnamese child who rebelled, despite the doctrine that every youngster with a drop of Vietnamese blood is a paragon of obedience. Adolescents are the same everywhere; they live for those moments of subversion.

—Thanhha Lai, "The Three Day Grin"

Introduction Thanhha Lai's piece is an interesting combination of journalism and narrative essay. As this article is about Lai and her family, it conveys a certain amount of intimacy to manipulate you as reader into both imagining yourself at this religious gathering and reminiscing and identifying with certain universal experiences all people share growing up under family customs and traditions—as well as family guilt.

I must thank the Buddha that Tet comes only once a year. Otherwise, my water-balloon cheeks, whose bones could support a mountain, would have exploded by now. More on these testimonial cheeks later. First let me explain Tet. It's the ebullient Vietnamese New Year's celebrated with the combined gusto of Christmas, New Year's Eve, Fourth of July, Thanksgiving, Easter, Halloween, Labor Day, Veterans Day, Valentine's Day and all the biggies' birthdays. It's a big deal. To recognize its importance, Vietnamese ancestors invented a slew of rituals, rules and regulations in its honor. Each family has a designated enforcer of tradition; in mine, it's my mother. She takes this task most seriously.

According to tradition, what happens the first three days of every lunar year determines your fate for the rest of the year. In this, the Year of the Mouse, the days of destiny fall on February 19, 20, and 21. These are the days when my cheeks and my wits are called into action.

Of course, the elaborate celebration doesn't just happen. One prepares for it, plans for it, stresses for it, lives for it—especially in Orange County, where approximately 150,000 Vietnamese live, making the community the largest outside of the native land. Here, holders of tradition are empowered, supporting one another in their determination to pass the past on to the future. This year, as in the past, my mother will have her rules for the first three days. No sweeping the floors, lest fortune go out with the dirt. No pouting, frowning, sneering or gossiping, lest it follow us all year. No relaying bad news, lest it interfere with our main preoccupation during Tet: smiling.

After Christmas, merchants throughout Westminster's Little Saigon usher in the Tet frenzy. Everywhere, you see bright red paper money to burn in honor of ancestors; bright red envelopes for li xi money (in which adults stuff crisp bills for youngsters who can still deliver well wishes in the native tongue); bright red packages of incense for the prayer tables; bright red fatty, sweet sausages for glutinous rice; and bright red dye for anything not already bright red. Red, of course, brings luck. Paper money, boosted by ancestral blessings, brings prosperity. These are the themes of Tet.

While my mother gets her house ready (my father has been missing in action in Vietnam since long ago), she also warns her six sons and three daughters to get ready. I am the youngest of nine children scattered throughout Southern California, so she can't actually inspect us until the fateful day. But she can call a lot. She insists that we wear only bright, clean, new clothes during the three precious days. She prefers red; green or yellow is tolerable. Forbidden are purple and black-morose colors meant for widows and starving poets. She reminds us to be happy, to smile upon greeting her, and to keep smiling for the next 72 hours.

Remember, if you're happy the first three days of the year, you'll be happy all year. These are the hours when I feel my cheeks swell, expanding until all that's visible is a balloon with lips and teeth. For whatever reason, the act of smiling has never tired my mouth, only my cheeks. They become so tight a caress might pop them.

The next step is carefully arranged, but every year my mother pretends it's as random as which child happens to show up first. It calls for one of her sons to appear at her door at exactly midnight bearing a branch from a tree resembling cay bo de, under which the

Buddha meditated and reached enlightenment. The branch brings good fortune into her home, so the bearer must be one whose astrological forecast is lucky for 1996.

My sisters and I are banished from selection. We're women, traditionally regarded as unlucky. Of course, in this politically correct side of the world, my mother doesn't actually say her daughters can't be the bearer of fortune. Instead, she hints for us to arrive a little late. This is peculiar for a mother who raised nine children on her own by juggling three jobs and dealing with the sexism ingrained in Vietnamese society. But tradition is tradition; she doesn't want to chance it, just in case our ancestors were right.

In selecting a son, my mother secretly consults three astrologists by mail, picking the prediction she likes best. I know because some years ago she let it slip that she knows how each of her children's lives will turn out each year because she has copies of their astrological fates. I imagine her selecting the most current picture of each child for the package, putting on her glasses and carefully printing each name behind each face, along with each date and time of birth. The pictures are used to detect physiognomy; birth information determines star alignment, or luck.

This year, she chooses my fourth-oldest brother. He just landed a full-time, full-benefits engineering job after three years in Southern California. He moved here because he fell in love, leaving a secure job in Texas. My mother's selection certainly was driven by luck, but I'm sure she also wants to make up for the years when she asked him to arrive a little late.

House in order, children in order, my mother is ready for Tet. She doesn't inspect her seven grandchildren—it's just assumed their parents will teach them well. During Tet no one questions my mother's authority, taste or wishes.

It is New Year's Eve 1994. I arrive at 12:30 A.M. having practiced my well wish, getting the tone and delivery just right. I've said the same thing for each of the last 20 years. It's as if my Vietnamese froze after I came to the United States at age 10. Holding my red li xi envelope, in which lies a crisp $100 bill, I approach my mother. She's inspecting me; her eyes travel from my puffy, salon-perfect Tet hair to my red-and-white Tet shoes, which match my new Tet skirt set.

"In this new year, I wish you all events as desired and your health rosy and strong."

"Fine, Fine, I, too, wish my youngest daughter much accomplishment in the new year and your fame shall ring forth throughout the land. In matters pertaining to love, a smoldering contentment will envelop my youngest daughter and she will be ready for marriage."

Cheers ring out around us; my cheeks reluctantly lift. My mother is watching, smiling to set an example. My cheeks lift higher. She nods in approval. Everybody is smiling and nodding in approval. If we do this right, for the rest of the year we all will be unwaveringly happy.

I hand her the red envelope. She smiles and nods, tucking my envelope into the stack in her palm. I do not get one back. My li xi years are over. In my family, after a certain age, usually the age when you should have children, the envelopes stop coming. They are forwarded to your children. If you have not managed to get married and have children, you get nothing. At 30, I now hand out the darling red pouches.

The li xi logic goes like this: water rushes downward; leaves fall downward; tears drop downward; so li xi also goes downward, from older to younger. I had some good years, when my mother and siblings, all older, lavished me with crisp bills. In the case of my mother, she has reached an age when she can defy nature, a salmon of sorts.

I follow protocol. I approach my oldest brother. Smiling.

"In this new year, I wish you all events as desired and your health rosy and strong."

"Ah, very good. I, too, wish you a splendid year filled with good health and success. Your heart shall find tenderness and settle."

Next oldest brother. Smiling.

"In this new year, I wish you all events as desired and your health rosy and strong."

"Beautifully said. You are the poet of the family. Get married."

Next brother. My cheeks are up.

"In this new year, I wish you all events as desired and your health rosy and strong."

"OK. You, too."

Next brother. Then the next. Then the youngest. I keep smiling. I approach my sisters. Smiling. Then my nieces and nephews surround me, wishing me good health and happiness in their broken Vietnamese. Out go red envelopes.

The little ones run off. Still smiling, I'm finally able to notice my mother's handiwork. Familiar decorations in red and gold shine in the living room. Gold silk covers the ancestral prayer table, on which sit black-and-white photographs of both sets of my grandparents. A smaller portrait of my father is set farther back. My mother manages to look at my father's photograph only once a year. The man in the photograph is so young at 37—the last image we have of him.

Two red strips, each with four ancient Vietnamese words sewn in gold thread, hang behind the prayer table. The words are from a riddle poem my mother wrote in her youth. The riddle is impossible to translate, its meaning hidden in the subtext. I can tell you the words speak of honor and tradition.

Sticks of incense already fill the golden lotus bowl. I step up and add mine; my mother watches to be certain I bow three times. This is the one time when smiling is discouraged.

I turn toward the kitchen table; my cheeks automatically expand. Set on a red tablecloth are Tet foods so familiar that just the sight of the colorful arrangements bring back taste and smell, feelings and occasions.

As usual, the centerpiece is banh chung, a square, light green salty rice cake first created by a prince to symbolize the people of Vietnam. He used basic ingredients that every person can afford—glutinous rice, mung beans and pork—and the cake has become legendary for its democratic spirit. The light green coloring comes from being wrapped in banana leaves and boiled.

Banh chung's square shape represents the land on which people toiled and grew the ingredients. As years passed, it came to symbolize the shape of the earth. It was created before people got the idea the earth had a shape, way before science. When I look at the cake, I think, "Who am I to question these Tet rituals and rules and regulations that predate science?" Yes, it is true that my mother told me and my sisters when we were young not to be the first to touch the floor in the new year. That honor belonged to a boy; the lucky factor, you remember. Yes, our neighbor in Vietnam secretly arranged for my two oldest brothers to carry pails of water past her house, then "accidentally" spill them on her porch. It was believed that water rushed in money. And yes, our other neighbor screamed with pleasure when one of my brothers, as a toddler, wandered into her living room the first day of the year and pooped on her tile—an omen thought to bring in gold. I'm beginning to think maybe these beliefs, well, superstitions, have lasted this long for good reasons.

Immediately surrounding the banh chung are plates of red glutinous rice, pork rolls, yellow gooey rice, sweet sausage, thickened mung bean sweet soup, glass noodles topped with vegetables and shrimp, dried bamboo chicken soup. On the outer rim, closest to reach, sit arrangements of confections that ache the tooth on sight. The Vietnamese can turn anything into a sweet munchie by pan-frying it with white sugar until the sugar melts and forms a crust: lotus seeds, ginger, coconut, persimmon, pear, squash. No wonder we're so happy during Tet—consider the sugar high.

At an end table, in a crystal bowl, watermelon seeds the size of pinkie nails reign supreme, shimmering in their new dyed red coat. Eating them leaves red fingertips, red lips and red tongue-luck that won't wash off until days after the festivities.

I eye the food and forget the nervousness I endured while selecting three Tet outfits. I forget about driving around and around until I can arrive late enough. I forget that as a girl I used to sabotage my mother's rules—each year getting out of bed and touching my feet to the forbidden ground right at midnight, before any boy could bring fortune to our house. If my mother knew, she would blame me for the fall of Saigon.

I reach for a lotus seed. Sweet, crunchy and powdery. I smile. I reach for a dyed-pink strip of coconut. Fatty and sweet. I smile brighter, bribed by the promise of gluttony.

It's 3 A.M. We've eaten. We've exchanged well wishes. We're still smiling. Three of my brothers pack up their families to return home. Work awaits in the morning, a Monday. The rest of us have managed to schedule floating holidays and time off. No one dares mention that if one works on the first three days, one labors all year long. It's secretly hoped that luck will be lenient in this solar-calendar culture.

In Vietnam, the country shuts down for Tet. No convenience stores, no last-minute shopping. Merchants give their goods away rather than be caught selling near the eve. They want to be at home, regally relaxed, praying for a prosperous new year. At midnight, cities light up with firecrackers, burned in every house to oust old spirits and welcome new ones. I don't mean sparkling, cutesy fireworks; I mean Chinese-copy red firecrackers the size of a roll of quarters. They're sold 20 to a string, and they are as loud as bombs. The deafening noise starts in the morning of the first day; at times, smoke thickens at street level and forces people up to balconies to breathe.

Nothing so dramatic happens now in my house. We leave the noisemaking to Tet festival organizers, who import enough firecrackers to create another Big Bang. We welcome the new year quietly, smile endlessly, and eat and eat and eat.

Day four of the new year, I return to real life. Stomach a little plumper, cheeks definitely more expansive. I start the process of massaging them back to size. Palms flat on cheeks, around and around. The motion reminds me of chewing, around and around, all those flavors, all three days. I think maybe it's a fair trade after all. I'm learning to cook some of the best food there is. I truly enjoy the family reunion Tet occasions. Who knows, one future Tet I might be checking my own children's cheeks for the right degree of tautness. I might arrange an ancestral prayer table similar to my mother's. Both sets of my children's grandparents would reign supreme. And as I bow to portraits of my young father and, I hope, a mother who lives many Tets beyond today, I'm certain I'll ache for her rules.

WORDS TO KNOW

NOTE: When you write the definitions of the following words, make it a point to use at least three of them in conversation over the next day and three of them in your next writing assignment. Many times you'll find it difficult or impossible to use them in everyday speech or writing. What then is the point of defining them? Of learning them? At the very least, in all the following cases where you have unusual vocabulary terms to define, attempt to use them. How does attempting to use vocabulary that feels awkward or different change your view of your common speech and writing patterns? Learning how to use new vocabulary means just that—using the words. Write specifically how, where, when, and why you used the words and discuss with your class.

testimonial—
Tet—
ebullient—
slew—
usher—
li xi—
glutinous—
cay bo de—
ingrained—
physiognomy—
alignment—
smoldering—
subtext—

banh chung—
mung beans—

QUESTIONS

Create a series of Bi-Level and Text/You/Other Questions based on this reading. Then create a series based on using this reading in combination with another reading in this text or outside of this text. What are the major issues in this short narrative? What details seemed the most vivid to you and why?

WRITING ACTIVITIES

1. Choose one of your Text/You/Other Questions and modify it to include some reference to either a family or religious custom you've experienced.
2. Write a response to your question, using the kind of specific detail that Lai uses—that is, colors, gestures, objects, food, people's quirky characteristics, what you see when you walk down the street, and so forth. Include specific quotes that family members, you, or other people involved in the custom actually say or said. Remember to put quotation marks around what people actually say or said and to start a new paragraph every time a different person speaks.
3. In the last reading, you concentrated on choosing a specific detail to begin your writing and capture your reader's attention. Now see how you can focus even more specific details into the middle or "body" of your writing. While the beginning of your writing is to "whet your reader's appetite" and show them what your main point or idea is, the body of your writing gives you the opportunity to expand, embellish, paint the full details and specific examples that illustrate the "picture" of your idea.
4. Include in your writing details of the history or origin behind certain events, incidents, gestures, behaviors, and so forth, as Lai does.
5. Exchange your writing with one of your writing classmates. What is that person's response and why? Based on your writing partner's reaction, what would you revise about the writing, and why?
6. Rewrite some part of the writing on the spot based on your writing partner's suggestions.
7. Decide whose piece of writing you would like to share aloud with the rest of your class.

8. Read both the original version and revised version to your class. What is the response, and why?

GRAMMAR AND STYLE QUESTIONS

1. Choose wordy, general expressions from your own writing, including writing done for exercises in this book, and revise them to make them concise, active expressions that are correct grammatically. What changes did you make in terms of grammar and style, and why?

2. One of the most difficult tasks for any new writer is to express time and timelines consistently and to match actions to those times and timelines. Take a paragraph from Lai's reading that has a strong sense of either past, present, or future tense, and rewrite it using a different verb tense (i.e., if it was written in the present tense, rewrite it in the past tense, and so forth). What is the effect of such a change? Were you consistent in your new selection of verb tense in your revision? And, if you had difficulty with consistency, without referring back to the text, restore the original tense and see how closely the paragraph matches how the author originally wrote it.

3. One of the best ways to learn grammar, in addition to learning the names and rules of grammatical elements, is to read other people's writing and determine how and why they write well. Take a grammatically imperfect piece of your own work, read two or three readings from *Turning the Century* (you may select any reading from this reader, but be sure to include Lai's reading as one of them), and rewrite your piece afterwards. Is it grammatically better? Why or why not? What was the impact of seeing how other people put together words?

From Baroque to Ultra-Baroque

Ichiro Ono

I, who am in the position to shoot, click the shutter at the contact point between the desire to make the whole thing simple and ordered and the desire to let it rage intricately and without limit. My desire to shoot something that truly attracts me means I want to capture it as it is and bring it back without inserting my personal feelings, if possible.

—Ichiro Ono, "From Baroque to Ultra-Baroque"

Introduction This piece uses a travelogue style and exposition to convey added meaning to the sampling of the photographs that accompany this essay, that are the reason for the essay. When you take a picture of something, you literally take it out of its natural setting and context and can hang it in space, or wherever you want. What does that do to the image? What about to the language that accompanies the image (whether written or oral)?

What images does one conjure up when one hears the word "Mexico"? A man in a sombrero playing a guitar, lovely women in colorful dress, and traditional cuisine such as corn tamales? Or, residents of Mexico City suffering from air pollution, Chiapas farmers standing tall with firearms held high, or the crises in the currency? Or, for those with an artistic bent, it may be the pyramids of the Aztec and the Maya, the revolutionary frescos of Rivera and Siqueiros, Frida Kahlo, or Buñuel.

Whatever comes to mind, I think that pious, Catholic, baroque churches shining with gold may be unfamiliar as images of Mexico.

Art styles from all over the world poured in to Mexico in the colonial era of the sixteenth to early nineteenth centuries, reflecting the age of ocean trade. The term "baroque" originally referred to an irregular pearl, and the baroque style, imported from Europe during the mid-seventeenth century, was an extravagant departure from the sober, restrained styles of the Renaissance. Fused with ancient native American sensibility while absorbing other influences from the sea-trading world that collected in Mexico, the baroque style evolved and commenced to tightly pack the architecture with so much ornamentation that we could describe it as a kind of "gap-ophobia." This is "ultra-baroque," meaning, in other words, the baroque of the baroque.

It was in the 18th century that ultra-baroque reached its peak. During the mid-seventeenth century, due to restrictions placed on immigration from Spain, the power of new generations born in Mexico of Spanish lineage, called "criollos," and those of mixed European and Indian blood called "mestizos" began to rise. Consequently, Mexican architecture developed to reflect the tastes of those citizens who had attained economic power and had become patrons of the church; seeking after visible splendor became a primary interest. This set the groundwork to encourage the exploding popularity of the baroque style.

In the latter half of the seventeenth century, an architecture with the added originality of the indigenous culture appeared. Good examples are the Chapel of the Rosary in Puebla and the Church of Santo Domingo in Oaxaca. While the intermingling of bloodlines went on, some of the native Indian culture was absorbed into colonial society, and in ecclesiastical decoration the European baroque model came to take on a Mexican coloration, carrying vestiges of thousands of years of indigenous culture, including the sophisticated civilizations of the Mayas and Aztecs. These traditions may be glimpsed in a statue of a dark-complexioned Mary, or an Indian-looking angel peering out from a brilliantly colored jungle, or a saint whose head has been cut off as if he were a sacrificial offering, or a lively expression of suffering using the blood of animals.

Originally, the architectural styles introduced to Mexico after the conquest were regional Spanish types reflecting the seven-century history of Islamic domination in Spain, rather than pure Renaissance, Mannerist, or baroque. It seems to me that the oriental, Moorish taste imported with the Spanish inspired the creativity of the indigenous craftsmen in Mexico and contributed to the revival of the sensibilities of their ancestors.

The elaborately ornamented ultra-baroque churches in Mexico have an extremely simple architectural structure. While Europe's baroque style pursues dramatic spatial structure in three-dimensional depth, Mexican ultra-baroque pursues the supremacy of two-dimensional ornamentation to completely fill the overall surface. At that time in Europe, churches were built according to varied architectural plans, but in Mexico church plans are nearly identical if they fall within the same era. They applied a simple basic structure, which had a history of many successful examples, and the total effort concentrated on the visible areas while invisible areas were simplified.

"The Day of the Dead" in early November is the best time to observe that the ultra-baroque sensibility is alive among the people of Mexico even today. We can clearly see where Indian ceremonies to honor the dead are united with Western baroque festivity. Flowers and candies are everywhere, and all the streets and villages welcome the souls of the dead by competing with ornaments and colors.

We can see Mexican sensibilities in the statues of saints created by unknown craftsmen. Christ's rope-tied hands, his bruised legs, his face looking almost ecstatic. A beautiful Mary, sympathetic; and adorable infant, innocent angels. Their expressions are natural and even sensual. They have professional stylists who change their wigs and clothing, so the hair on the head of Christ switches between straight and curled. The religion here is not a silent praying in the deep bottom of one's mind, but is an intense experience directly stimulating to one's feelings. In the New World, these gaudy churches and lovely statues of Mary were aimed at impressing the absoluteness of Christianity upon the indigenous people and making newcomers contribute money for the greater glorification of God's home, to secure a place in heaven by enhancing their social positions on earth.

There is a theory that regions which embrace cultures that exhibit extravagant ornamentation are often riddled with earthquakes. Certainly the region from Mexico to Guatemala has suffered from major earthquakes. In Sicily, Catania, and Noto, which were rebuilt after being destroyed by eruptions from Mt. Etna, are magnificent baroque cities. Antigua in Guatemala was a city as large as Mexico City or Lima and served as the capital of a governor-generalcy during the colonial era, but in the seventeenth century, recurrent great earthquakes brought it to ruin. Today, when we visit Antigua, ruins of the churches are scattered around, even in the woods outside of town, and we can muse on the prosperity of bygone days. I wonder what the baroque ornamentation remaining here and there in the ruined churches could tell us. The people must have known that the next earthquake would again reduce them to rubble. Even so, people ornamented the houses of God even more gorgeously when they were rebuilt. I wonder if it was because they sought God's help where destruction could visit at any time, and were driven by a desire to fill their world with beauty.

During the time I studied architecture in college, I spent a lot of time traveling seeking encounters with architecture. This was because I wanted to encounter an architecture that would energize my creativity. At first; I thought that such architecture would exist at the contact point of Eastern and Western cultures. So I trekked across only the Eurasian landmass, and it was a long time before I made a different journey to encounter the Mexican ultra-baroque. The extravagantly ornamented Mexican baroque would seem to be the absolute opposite of simple Japanese architecture. However, it seems to me that the essence hidden in the expression has something in common with some examples in Japanese temple architecture.

Even though I may be exploring the baroque, I do not want to take pictures of Western Europe's orthodox architectural styles. Like modern architecture, they do not stir my blood, nor am I interested in vernacular architecture. In short, modern universality and local folkloric traditions are not what appeal to me in themselves; my interest is in how to convey the aspects of ultra-baroque, established by the layers of struggle between the two, through my own consolidation. The traditional power of the indigenous people rages beyond the rules of western European architecture and the strictures of Catholicism even while attending to those rules. A thrill arises from the realization that destruction starts out from the details while at the same time the forces of integration continue on.

I, who am in the position to shoot, click the shutter at the contact point between the desire to make the whole thing simple and ordered and the desire to let it rage intricately and without limit. My desire to shoot something that truly attracts me means that I want to capture it as it is and bring it back without inserting my personal feelings, if possible. For me the act of shooting a photograph has the same import as the activity involved in collecting objects, such as by buying one's favorite chinaware or a gold-leafed statue of Mary. It might be better to say that I am a collector rather than a photographer.

Church of Santo Domingo, Oaxaca

Day of the Dead

Cemetery, Night of the Day of the Dead

WORDS TO KNOW

NOTE: When you write the definitions of the following words, make it a point to use at least three of them in conversation over the next day and three of them in your next writing assignment. Many times you'll find it difficult or impossible to use them in everyday speech or writing. What then is the point of defining them? Of learning them? At the very least, in all the following cases where you have unusual vocabulary terms to define, attempt to use them. How does attempting to use vocabulary that feels awkward or different change your view of your common speech and writing patterns? Learning how to use new vocabulary means just that—using the words. Write specifically how, where, when, and why you used the words and discuss with your class.

sombrero—
tamales—
Chiapas—
Aztec—
Maya—
Rivera—
Siqueiros—
Frida Kahlo—
Buñuel—
pious—
baroque—
extravagant—
Renaissance—
gapophobia—
criollos—
mestizos—
Puebla—
Oaxaca—
intermingling—
ecclesiastical—
vestiges—
indigenous—
Mannerist—

Moorish—
Catania—
Noto—
Mt. Etna—
Antigua—

QUESTIONS

Pay careful attention to the photographs that follow this reading—examine the intricate detail of the scenes and objects therein. What do you see? Which has the greatest impact on you and why? To what extent do the photographs go with the reading—are they integral to or simply an accompaniment to the reading? Create a Text/You/Other Question using the photographs here as well as another pictorial source. Why did you choose what you chose?

WRITING ACTIVITIES

1. Revise your Text/You/Other Question to also include an additional reading.
2. Use as many specific details as you can in writing your "answer" to your question. Remember to have a one-two sentence main point that you want to get across to your reader and get it across in the first one or two sentences of your writing.
3. Revise your writing to save your main point until the final paragraph of your writing (keep your writing to no more than one page). Which do you like better? Why?
4. Try using a single sentence or phrase from Ono's essay somewhere in your writing. Put quotation marks around the phrase or sentence. Where did you decide to put the quote, and why? What does it do to and/or for your writing to use another author's quote to accompany what you've written?
5. In response to questions following other readings, you practiced using specific details to catch your reader's attention in the introduction and the body. Now use them in the end or "conclusion" to your one-page writing.
6. Discuss with your writing partner, and then with your class, the difference in the choice and quality of the details you use in each of the three parts of your writing. Do the choice and quality make a difference? Why?

GRAMMAR AND STYLE QUESTIONS

1. Compare and contrast Ono's reading with another author's reading. You may preview readings the class has not yet read or review past readings to select your choice. How do these two authors use specific grammatical forms to get their points across? How does their use of grammar to get their points across differ? What are the common features of both? Use specific rules of grammar and details in your answer.

2. Look at the uses of punctuation in a journalistic reading and a story-telling reading. How would you categorize Ono's reading based on punctuation and style? How is punctuation (commas, quotation marks, for instance) used stylistically? Use specific examples from the reading and cite how specific rules governing punctuation were followed or not followed to achieve certain stylistic effects.

Heaven's Gate:
A Twee Paradise for Wimps

Cintra Wilson

There's a lot of tawdry, melodramatic harshness to be reckoned with on planet Earth, but that's the whole point, right?

—Cintra Wilson

Introduction Cintra Wilson has written this editorial essay for the Sunday paper. In addition to vivid detail and small bits of narrative, both personal and historical, Wilson uses sarcasm and humor in her essay— she gives it a voice that clearly speaks to you. How does she do this? Look at her vocabulary. What effect does "talk" have on writing? How can you use it in your own writing for heightened effect and impact?

"Nobody KNOWS the difference between fantasy and reality anymore, it's frightening," remarked my lawyer. I was looking at a front-page *New York Times* article about urban Russians beating each other's heads into mush with hammers over issues of "witchcraft." Thirty-nine dead because the Mothership would make no stopover trip to Rancho Santa Fe to pick up its crew members physically. Less than a thousand days until the ball drops on the new millennium, and people are already flapping out of their skins, either metaphorically or with their heads in plastic bags.

I had a big paranormal experience involving death and spaceships when I was 17, and a few more nifty shamanistic trips later on. Had I been a more organized human being, I now feel certain that I could have parlayed that haze of information into the foundations of a New Religion, and gotten 40 or 50 people to walk around me and think I'm Jesus. The world has always been irrational and desperate in regards to God. Higher Truth, be it Catholic or "Star

Trek," is elusive and elite to people who don't feel worthy or trusting of any instinctual knowledge—from their own minds and hearts—of what "God" might be, what "Higher Knowledge" might be. God is Love, clean and simple, but what ELSE? The ways we can screw up the ensuing answer are boundless.

I watched my aunt tumble headfirst into regions of Scientology so twisted and foreign, nobody from the "outside" could talk to her anymore. I've seen people become Christian so hard they alienated all their friends. I've been warned against wearing black hats or eating coconut, for fear of offending the mighty African Orishas. I find this idea theoretically absurd, but I still don't do either.

A cult's best tactic is making the people in it feel that their life in the Real Reality, the Other Place, is going to be much more fabulous and privileged, and they will be Huge Players who will have the slobbering respect of anybody who is really popular on Earth NOW— politicians, movie stars, investment bankers. "You have a very special role to play in God's big circus, you're the Main Ballerina," they will tell you. "The reason you feel so uncomfortable all the time is because you're so metaphysically superior. Rejoice!" Here they ply you with a twee flavor of reality: Gardens of Disney Abundance, Boundless Wonder, Pulsating Love. Sentient Leaders waiting to generously escort you into the Light. Abandon the body and live like a sexless Sun God, surrounded by lots of beeping lights and unicorns with long, silky rainbow-colored hair.

When I think about The 39 Dead in Rancho Santa Fe, I think of a bunch of well-meaning, good-hearted losers and sci-fi geek misfits who worked hard and were nice to each other and wanted to renounce all of the complicated things of the world that don't really make any sense: sex, for example, and Mean People and Super-Rich people. They all probably really loved Marshall Herff Applewhite, ashamed closet homosexual and musical theater failure, and Herff was a real success for the first time in his life. The Heaven's Gate Web site is full of easy hooks that anybody who hated high school or was discouraged by corporate world domination could eat straight out of the Mylar bag: Do you feel totally dissatisfied? Do you hate this life and want to shed this state and blossom as a more enlightened entity?

Well, duh.

You're going to have to abandon everyone you know and be an outcast. We're your REAL family now, they say. Who hasn't yearned for their "REAL" family? The families we are assigned are invariably a pain in the ass; we all have the gnawing pain of a sense that nobody understands our deeper selves. Cults and religions make people feel less alone; therein lies the opiate.

This world doesn't make sense to people who are guileless and without Edge, who are unwilling to grow sufficient Fangs in order to do combat with corrupt influences and other ungentle realities. There is a lot of tawdry, melodramatic harshness to be reckoned with on planet Earth, but that's the whole point, right? It's a kind of spiritual boot camp where both the rewards and the punishments are huge, and there is no linear cause or effect to anything. How good you are does not dictate how rich you are or how happy you are or how successful or well loved. Those are all different avenues that need to be worked on simultaneously in a carefully balanced web of personal multi-tasking, and it's horrendously difficult, and there're no super-clear guidelines, although people will say it's in the Bible or the Koran or what have you.

I keep remembering this Joseph Campbell point, whenever I hear about any religion eschewing all of the distasteful elements of belonging to the human world. I think of St. George, in Campbell's words, "needing to become sufficiently terrible to slay the dragon."

There are coarse vibrational elements on spaceship Earth. If you were a higher force of benevolence and mercy, would you send a cub into the wild with no teeth? We NEED some of our disgraceful elements of vice and sin. We NEEDED to murder Caligula. We NEED to have sex with each other. We need morphine and wine, and tobacco and crazy dancing. Sure, everything might be more advanced if we could all just cut it out and walk around respectfully stroking one another in a fraternal fashion and be completely in tune with the Higher Will of a purely wonderful intelligence, free of crime and shame and depression and starvation and sickness and war, but the whole point of this planet is we HAVE the capacity to improve things drastically and bring them around to the point where people won't want to kill themselves and become little gray pod boys in space.

You only need to go to a local aquarium or zoo to know that there could never be anything so wondrous as the proliferation of life on Earth, the incredibly complex and interdependent matrix of nature that is already right here. If you're not stoned on the ecology that exists in your own back yard, no Garden Planet full of custard pastries and dimpled cherubim and talking rabbits is going to rock your world, either. This place is a fixer-upper, at this point, but fer gosh sakes, there's so much stuff here worth preserving. Those who bail out are cheating the zebras and the water rats and the manatees of their rightful champions and spokespersons. Only absolute Wimps would sucker out in a blaze of barbiturates, instead of hanging around and helping and seeing how interesting this place gets in the next handful of years.

We can always use more gentle little furry animals like Applewhite and his shorn eunuchs in the world. They've deprived us of their positive energies and kooky ideas, and it's a tragedy as great as losing another species of fish.

WORDS TO KNOW

NOTE: When you write the definitions of the following words, make it a point to use at least three of them in conversation over the next day and three of them in your next writing assignment. Many times you'll find it difficult or impossible to use them in everyday speech or writing. What then is the point of defining them? Of learning them? At the very least, in all the following cases where you have unusual vocabulary terms to define, attempt to use them. How does attempting to use vocabulary that feels awkward or different change your view of your common speech and writing patterns? Learning how to use new vocabulary means just that—using the words. Write specifically how, where, when, and why you used the words and discuss with your class

> millennium—
> metaphorically—
> Scientology—
> twee—
> Marshall Herff Applewhite—
> Mylar—
> opiate—
> eschewing—
> Caligula—
> proliferation—
> cherubim—

QUESTIONS

Pay particular attention to Wilson's tone in her essay. How would you describe her attitude? Or, better put, if she were reading this piece aloud, how do you think her tone of voice would sound? After thinking about the different subjects she discusses and the manner in which she discusses them, create a series of Bi-Level Questions for discussion with your classmates and a series of Text/You/Other Questions for your writing activities. Remember to include other sources, text and pictorial, as part of your questions.

WRITING ACTIVITIES

1. Read through your collection of writings and notice what tone, if any, you have used in your writings. Is it the same for each piece? Where do you see the tone? Identify specific words and phrases. How could you develop more of a tone? More variety in your tone?

2. After you choose the question you want to answer, think about what words you could use in your writing to convey the tone that will best match the point you want to get across. Look at some of Wilson's choices of words: twee; well, duh. Use words that convey a sense of you speaking and living in your writing.

3. Write a least a page, using specific details and sources, a beginning, middle, and end, and a "tone of voice."

4. Exchange your writing with a classmate. What do you hear in the writings? Compare and contrast your current writings with previous writings. Which do you like better and why? Share your discussion with the rest of your class.

GRAMMAR AND STYLE QUESTIONS

1. Examine the use of punctuation and/or stylistic word choices in three different readings (include Wilson's essay as one of your choices). How are specific punctuation and stylistic word choices (slang, for instance) used to emphasize the tone each author establishes?

2. Select a text reading and a reading originally published on the Internet. Analyze these examples, and as you do, compare and contrast their purpose, audience, and effectiveness. Which makes more of an impact on you and why? How are they similar or different stylistically, and why? How do differences in style affect you and why? Use specific examples from the readings and cite how specific rules of grammar were followed or not followed to achieve certain stylistic effects.

Out of All Them Bright Stars

Nancy Kress

Award-winning science fiction writer Nancy Kress talks about her short story "Out of All Them Bright Stars":

"Most science fiction concerns the doings of characters directly involved in the center of whatever action is altering their environment. This makes sense: the center of the action is where the interesting stuff happens.

"The great majority of us, however, are not at the center of history. We don't avert war, we don't start war, we don't discover radical truths, we don't go where no man has gone before. At the moment of First Contact with an alien race, we will have been at the dentist.

"I wanted to write a story about a character whom history happens to, not the other way around. She stands at the center of no story but her own.

"Maybe that's enough. Or maybe not."

—Nancy Kress

Introduction Again, you will find yourself faced with an unreliable narrator in this fiction story. The effect here is to force you to pin down how you know when to believe someone's story—what details are objective? Subjective? Real? How does this apply to your own writing?

So I'm filling the catsup bottles at the end of the night, and I'm listening to the radio Charlie has stuck up on top of a moveable panel in the ceiling, when the door opens and one of them walks in. I know right away it's one of them—no chance to make a mistake about *that*—even though it's got on a nice-cut suit and a brim hat like Humphrey Bogart used to wear in *Casablanca*. But there's nobody with it, no professor from the college or government men like on the

TV show from the college or even any students. It's all alone. And we're a long way out the highway from the college.

It stands in the doorway, blinking a little, with rain dripping off its hat. Kathy, who's supposed to be cleaning the coffee machine behind the counter, freezes and stares with one hand still holding the used filter up in the air like she's never going to move again. Just then Charlie calls out from the kitchen, "Hey Kathy, you ask anybody who won the Trifecta?" and she doesn't even answer him. Just goes on staring with her mouth open like she's thinking of screaming but forgot how. And the old couple in the corner booth, the only ones left from the crowd after the movie got out, stop chewing their chocolate cream pie and stare too. Kathy closes her mouth and opens it again and a noise comes out like "Uh—errrgh . . ."

Well, that made me annoyed. Maybe she tried to say "ugh" and maybe she didn't, but here it is standing in the doorway with rain falling around it in little drops and we're staring like it's a clothes dummy and not a customer. So I think that's not right and maybe we're even making it feel a little bad, *I* wouldn't like Kathy staring at me like that, and I dry my hands on my towel and go over.

"Yes, sir, can I help you?" I say.

"Table for one," it says, like Charlie's was some nice steak house in town. But I suppose that's the kind of place the government people mostly take them to. And besides, its voice is polite and easy to understand, with a sort of accent but not as bad as some we get from the college. I can tell what it's saying. I lead him to a booth in the corner opposite the old couple, who come in every Friday night and haven't left a tip yet.

He sits down slowly. I notice he keeps his hands on his lap, but I can't tell if that's because he doesn't know what to do with them or he thinks I won't want to see them. But I've seen the close-ups on TV—they don't look so weird to me like they do to some. Charlie says they make his stomach turn, but I can't see it. You'd think he'd of seen worse meat in Vietnam. He talks enough like he did, on and on and on, and sometimes we even believe him.

I say, "Coffee, sir?"

He makes a sort of movement with his eyes. I can't tell what the movement means, but he says in that polite voice, "No, thank you. I am unable to drink coffee," and I think that's a good thing because I suddenly remember that Kathy's got the filter out. But then he says, "May I have a green salad, please? With no dressing, please."

The rain is still dripping off his hat. I figure the government people never told him to take off his hat in a restaurant, and for some reason it tickles me and makes me feel real bold. This polite blue guy isn't going to bother anybody, and that fool Charlie was just spouting off his mouth again.

"The salad's not too fresh, sir," I say, experimental-like, just to see what he'll say next. And it's the truth—the salad is left over from yesterday. But the guy answers like I asked something else.

"What is your name?" he says, so polite I know he's really curious and not starting anything. And what could he start anyway, blue and with those hands? Still, you never know.

"Sally," I say. "Sally Gourley."

"I am John," he says, and makes that movement with his eyes again. All of a sudden it tickles me—"John!" For this blue guy! So I laugh, and right away I feel sorry, like I might have hurt his feelings or something. How could you tell?

"Hey, I'm sorry," I say, and he takes off his hat. He does it real slow, like taking off the hat is important and means something, but all there is underneath is a bald blue head. Nothing weird like with the hands.

"Do not apologize," John says. "I have another name, of course, but in my own language."

"What is it?" I say, bold as brass, because all of a sudden I picture myself telling all this to my sister Mary Ellen and her listening real hard.

John makes some noise with his mouth, and I feel my own mouth open because it's not a word he says at all, it's a beautiful sound, like a bird call only sadder. It's just that I wasn't expecting it, that beautiful sound right here in Charlie's diner. It surprised me, coming out of that bald blue head. That's all it was: surprise.

I don't say anything. John looks at me and says, "It has a meaning that can be translated. It means—" but before he can say what it means Charlie comes charging out of the kitchen, Kathy right behind him. He's still got the racing form in one hand, like he's been studying the Trifecta, and he pushes right up against the booth and looks red and furious. Then I see the old couple scuttling out the door, their jackets clutched to their fronts, and the chocolate cream pie not half-eaten on their plates. I see they're going to stiff me for the check, but before I can stop them Charlie grabs my arm and squeezes so hard his nails slice into my skin.

"What the hell do you think you're doing?" he says right to me. Not so much as a look at John, but Kathy can't stop looking and her fist is pushed up to her mouth.

I drag my arm away and rub it. Once I saw Charlie push his wife so hard she went down and hit her head and had to have four stitches. It was me that drove her to the emergency room.

Charlie says again, "What the hell do you think you're doing?"

"I'm serving my table. He wants a salad. Large." I can't remember if John'd said a large or a small salad, but I figure a large order would make Charlie feel better. But Charlie doesn't want to feel better.

"You get him out of here," Charlie hisses. He still doesn't look at John. "You hear me, Sally? You get him *out*. The government says I gotta serve spics and niggers but it don't say I gotta serve him!"

I look at John. He's putting on his hat, ramming it onto his bald head, and half standing in the booth. He can't get out because Charlie and me are both in the way. I expect John to look mad or upset, but except that he's holding the muscles of his face in some different way I can't see any change of expression. But I figure he's got to feel something bad and all of a sudden I'm mad at Charlie, who's a bully and who's got the feelings of a scumbag. I open my mouth to tell him so, plus one or two other little things I been saving up, when the door flies open and in bursts four men, and damn if they aren't *all* wearing hats like Humphrey Bogart in *Casablanca*. As soon as the first guy sees John, his walk changes and he comes over slower but more purposeful like, and then he's talking to John and to Charlie in a sincere voice like a TV anchorman giving out the news.

I see the situation now belongs to him, so I go back to the catsup bottles. I'm still plenty burned though, about Charlie manhandling me and about Kathy rushing so stupid into the kitchen to get Charlie. She's a flake and always has been.

Charlie is scowling and nodding. The harder he scowls, the nicer the government guy's voice gets. Pretty soon the government guy is smiling sweet as pie. Charlie slinks back into the kitchen, and the four men move toward the door with John in the middle of them like some high school football huddle. Next to the real men he looks stranger than he did before, and I see how really flat his face is. But then when the huddle's right opposite the table with my catsup bottles John breaks away and comes over to me.

"I'm sorry, Sally Gourley," he says. And then, "I seldom have the chance to show our friendliness to an ordinary Earth person. I make so little difference!"

Well, that throws me. His voice sounds so sad, and besides I never thought of myself as an ordinary Earth person. Who would? So I just shrug and wipe off a catsup bottle with my towel. But then John does a weird thing. He just touches my arm where Charlie squeezed it, just touches it with the palm of one of those hands. And the palm's not slimy at all—dry, and sort of cool, and I don't jump or anything. Instead I remember that beautiful noise when he said his other name. Then he goes out with three of the men and the door bangs behind them on a gust of rain because Charlie never fixed the air-stop from when some kids horsing around broke it last spring.

The fourth man stays and questions me: what did the alien say? what did I say? I tell him, but then he starts asking the exact same questions all over again, like he didn't believe me the first time, and that gets me mad. Also he has this snotty voice, and I see how his eyebrows move when I slip once and accidentally say "he don't." I might not know what John's muscles mean but I sure the hell can read those eyebrows. So I get miffed and pretty soon he leaves and the door bangs behind him.

I finish the catsup and mustard bottles and Kathy finishes the coffee machine. The radio in the ceiling plays something instrumental, no words, real sad. Kathy and me start to wash down the booths with disinfectant, and because we're doing the same work together and nobody comes in, I finally say to her, "It's funny."

She says, "What's funny?"

"Charlie called that guy 'him' right off. 'I don't got to serve him,' he said. And I thought of him as 'it' at first, least until I had a name to use. But Charlie's the one who threw him out."

Kathy swipes at the back of her booth. "And Charlie's right. That thing scared me half to death, coming in here like that. And where there's food being served, too." She snorts and sprays on more disinfectant.

Well, she's a flake. Always has been.

"*The National Enquirer,*" Kathy goes on, "told how they have all this firepower up there in the big ship that hasn't landed yet. My husband says they could blow us all to smithereens, they're so powerful. I don't know why they even came here. *We* don't want them. I don't even know why they came, all that way."

"They want to make a difference," I say, but Kathy barrels on ahead, not listening.

"The Pentagon will hold them off, it doesn't matter what weapons they got up there or how much they insist on seeing about our defenses, the Pentagon won't let them get any toeholds on Earth. That's what my husband says. Blue bastards."

I say, "Will you please shut up?"

She gives me a dirty look and flounces off. I don't care. None of it is anything to me. Only standing there with the disinfectant in my hand, looking at the dark windows and listening to the music wordless and slow on the radio, I remember that touch on my arm, so light and cool. And I think, they didn't come here with any firepower to blow us all to smithereens. I just don't believe it. But then why did they come? Why come all that way from another star to walk into Charlie's diner and order a green salad with no dressing from an ordinary Earth person?

Charlie comes out with his keys to unlock the cash register and go over the tapes. I remember the old couple who stiffed me and I curse myself. Only pie and coffee, but it still comes off my salary. The radio in the ceiling starts playing something else, not the sad song, but nothing sappy neither. It's a love song, about some guy giving and getting treated like dirt. I don't like it.

"Charlie," I say, "What did those government men say to you?"

He looks up from his tapes and scowls. "What do you care?"

"I just want to know."

"And maybe I don't want you to know," he says, and smiles nasty like. Me asking him has put him in a better mood, the creep. All of a sudden I remember what his wife said when she got the stitches, "The only way to get something from Charlie is to let him smack me around a little, and then ask him when I'm down. He'll give me anything when I'm down. He gives me shit if he thinks I'm on top."

I do the rest of the clean-up without saying anything. Charlie swears at the night's take—I know from my tips that it's not much. Kathy teases her hair in front of the mirror behind doughnuts and pies, and I put down the breakfast menus. But all the time I'm thinking, and I don't much like my thoughts.

Charlie locks up and we all leave. Outside it's stopped raining but it's still misty and soft, real pretty but too cold. I pull my sweater around myself and in the parking lot, after Kathy's gone, I say, "Charlie."

He stops walking toward his truck. "Yeah?"

I lick my lips. They're all of a sudden dry. It's an experiment, like, what I'm going to say. It's an experiment.

"Charlie. What if those government men hadn't come just then and the . . . blue guy hadn't been willing to leave? What would you have done?"

"What do you care?"

I shrug. "I don't care. Just curious. It's *your* place."

"Damn right it's my place!" I could see him scowl, through the mist. "I'd of squashed him flat!"

"And then what? After you squashed him flat, what if the men came in and made a stink?"

"Too bad. It's be too late then, huh?" He laughs and I can see how he's seeing it: the blue guy bleeding on the linoleum and Charlie standing over him, dusting his hands together.

Charlie laughs again and goes off to his truck, whistling. He has a little bounce in his step. He's still seeing it all, almost like it really *had* happened. Over his shoulder he calls to me, "They're built like wimps. Or girls. All bone, no muscle. Even *you* must have seen that," and his voice is cheerful. It doesn't have any anger in it, or hatred, or anything but a sort of friendliness. I hear him whistle some more, until the truck engine starts up and he peels out of the parking lot, laying rubber, like a kid.

I unlock my Chevy. But before I get in, I look up at the sky. Which is really stupid because of course I can't see anything, with all the mists and clouds. No stars.

Maybe Kathy's right. Maybe they do want to blow us all to smithereens. I don't think so, but what the hell difference does it ever make what I think? And all at once I'm furious at John, furiously mad, as furious as I've ever been in my life.

Why does he have to come here, with his bird calls and his politeness? Why can't they all go someplace else beside here? There must be lots of other places the can go, out of all them bright stars up there behind the clouds. They don't need to come here, here where I need this job and so that means I need Charlie. He's a bully, but I want to look at him and see nothing else but a bully. Nothing else but that. That's all I want to see in Charlie, in the government men—just small-time bullies, nothing special, not a mirror of anything, not a future of anything. Just Charlie. That's all. I won't see nothing else.

I won't.

"I make so little difference," he says.

Yeah. Sure.

WORDS TO KNOW

NOTE: When you write the definitions of the following words, make it a point to use at least three of them in conversation over the next day and three of them in your next writing assignment. Many times you'll find it difficult or impossible to use them in everyday speech or writing. What then is the point of defining them? Of learning them? At the very least, in all the following cases where you have unusual vocabulary terms to define, attempt to use them. How does attempting to use vocabulary that feels awkward or different change your view of your common speech and writing patterns? Learning how to use new vocabulary means just that—using the words. Write specifically how, where, when, and why you used the words and discuss with your class.

Humphrey Bogart—
Trifecta—
Casablanca—
air-stop—
peels out—

QUESTIONS

Remembering that this reading is fiction, how real do you see the world of "Out of All Them Bright Stars" to be and why? What part is/seems unreal and how do you make the determination about where to draw the line? How do you feel after reading this story? How do you think you are supposed to feel and why? Create a series of Text/You/Other Questions, each of which brings together three or more of the readings you've read so far in this reader, and which in some way sums up important points and ideas at which you have arrived based on the readings about religion and spirituality.

WRITING ACTIVITIES

1. As usual, choose your most challenging question on which to write.
2. Think about particular spiritual and/or religious ideas or beliefs you have, how they have been affected by these readings, and why. Write for five to ten minutes on these ideas and/or beliefs.
3. Compile your sources (you may want to return to sources you've already worked with, or choose new ones—either way, you want to cover new ground in using them in your writing), make notes, and decide which notes you will use in what parts of your paper.
4. Using all the elements you've practiced with so far, write a two-page paper on your question. Incorporate your text sources, pictorial sources, vivid details, quotations, incidents from your personal experience, definitions, and tone.
5. Begin your paper with a challenge to your reader; end your paper with a challenge to your reader. There are plenty of things we should do; that's easy to point out. But as Kress's story shows us, there are other

things that we do do. Why? Will we ever change? Why or why not? So then what?

6. Share your questions and writings as a class. Which are the most interesting, the most insightful, the most challenging? Why? Ask some students to read their first writings, followed by their newest writings. How have students' writing progressed? Give them detailed feedback.

GRAMMAR AND STYLE QUESTIONS

1. Examine the use of punctuation in three different readings (including Kress's story). How is punctuation used to emphasize the tone each author has established?

2. Compare and contrast Kress's story to one of the readings originally published on the Internet. Analyze these examples. How are they similar or different stylistically? Use specific examples from the readings and cite how rules of grammar and style were followed or not followed to achieve certain stylistic effects.

FASHION VICTIMS, FASHION PLATES, OR FASHION SCHOLARS?

Tattooed Charms

Diane L. Umemoto

Inflight magazines are in the business of creating an image of a place for you, to thrill you as you're flying to that place. Whether or not the image is accurate or realistic isn't the point; it's whether or not it's romantic and plays on some collective unconscious image the majority of people share about that given place. Sometimes that means an ugly stereotype, other times a blissful dream—real romantic visions all share that double-sided weapon.

Introduction The effect of this type of mood writing is to make you anticipate reaching and discovering a new destination. This reading is written as an article, an article found in a glossy inflight airline magazine. Would you know this if you weren't told it? Why or why not? Which sections are designed to put you in a particular mood? How would it feel if you were reading this piece on a plane headed somewhere versus in a reader during a required college writing course?

The gilded image of the late spirit doctor, Luang Pu Sri Chantr, glows softly in the half light. Before him a white-robed figure, lips stained red with the betel mixture he is chewing, fingers prayer beads and mumbles incoherently. The crowd shuffles patiently. A moment or two later, the robed man looks up and, without removing the lump of betel from his cheek, lights a cigarette. Disciples sitting at his feet move closer, for they know the body of their master is now inhabited by the spirit of the dead teacher whose image watches benignly from the altar. He is ready to bestow advice and curative blessings.

Luang Pu Sri Chantr—for the medium is called by the name of the spirit—is a healer and guidance counselor, not a fortune-teller. Each week dozens of applicants come to this rude wooden hall in the outskirts of Bangkok for a few minutes of advice and encourage-

Tattooed Japanese Postman, nineteenth century
Hand-tinted color albumen print (photoreproduction) From *Japan*, Volume VI, 1897.
The Mariners' Museum Reseach Library and Archives DS809 B87.
    The history of tattooing in Japan is long and complex. More than 1,500 years ago, Chinese travelers noted that Japanese men and women were heavily tattooed. In the Middle Ages, tattoos were used in Japan to mark criminals. In the late eighteenth century, in an attempt to purge the general public of certain cultural excesses, the government effectively banned certain types of painting, theater, and dress. Many Japanese responded by replacing their outlawed kimonos with elaborate, colorful tattooed "body suits."

ment. Khun Worachak has opened a small restaurant which is not doing well; the medium counsels patience. A young woman is having marital problems; a boy wants to know how he can get the attention of a girl; an old woman hopes the touch of the medium's foot will relieve the pain of an arthritic shoulder. After each consultation the teacher, or *acharn,* as he is called in Thai, dips a stick in sooty ink and draws a talisman on the applicant's forehead. One of his disciples then makes the charm permanent by symbolically tattooing the design with invisible sesame oil. A dab of gold leaf completes the process, and the applicant departs fortified with a modicum of divine protection.

Tattooing with invisible oil is a way of bending to social convention. In Bangkok, the middle and upper classes frown on tattoos, magical or otherwise. A tattooed woman would be absolutely outrageous. But the young men of the lower classes are under no such restrictions, and many of those present have their chests, backs and arms covered with tattoos—as does the medium himself.

Given the size of his clientele, the medium has developed mass-production techniques. He has had rubber stamps made with the required designs—a small stylized Buddha image, for example. Each week, the medium stamps a design, usually part of a larger diagram, on the boy's body. He utters the sacred formula necessary to give the tattoo magical power. The boy then goes over to one of the medium's disciples to have the design tattooed in permanent ink.

While this assembly-line method ensures uniformly high design quality, it is certainly not the traditional method of giving magical tattoos. Among the Thai peoples—including the Shans of Upper Burma and the Lao—there have always been specialists in the art of tattooing. Such men draw and tattoo the designs themselves, all the while muttering sacred spells that make the charm effective. In their eyes, it would be unthinkable to use stamped designs, much less let an untrained novice do the sacred tattooing.

Nor would commercial inks used in Bangkok meet with the approval of a traditional specialist. To make the charm truly effective, great care should be taken in making the ink. The base of home-made ink is soot for black, vermilion for red. Each specialist has his own recipe. One ancient recipe from Laos insists that the soot must come from burning lard and be mixed with the bile of a wild bull, bear or pig. And that's just the base.

Certain special charms need special added ingredients in the ink. Among the Shans, for instance, a recipe for a love charm includes dried gekko skin. Gekkos are noisy lizards that live in the rafters and are said to bring good luck to the house where they stay. What could be more appropriate for a charm aimed at domestic bliss? On the other end of the scale, some inks used in very potent aggressive charms are said to include a small amount of human corpse fluid!

Both the tattooer and the boy receiving the charm know they are taking part in a sacred ritual. There is no place here for the tipsy sailor sauntering into a seaside tattoo parlor to have a buxom blonde or "I love mom" emblazoned on his chest. When a boy approaches Luang Pu Sri Chantr, or perhaps a Buddhist monk trained in the arts of beneficial magic, he does so with reverence. He is not, after all, asking the master to draw a clever picture, but rather to help him gain protection from the spirit world. In this sense, every magical tattoo specialist is a spirit medium.

The day chosen for tattooing is likely to be an auspicious day of the week, when the "spirits are strong." Tuesday and Saturday are good days, though the best of all is the fifth day of the fifth lunar month. When the time has come, the young man presents a small offering to the master. The master, in turn, first pays homage to the great tattoo teachers of the past, then concentrates his mind religiously, and sets to work.

The instrument he uses is a long graceful wooden shaft. At one end of the shaft is a sharply pointed bronze or steel tip with deep crosswise slits that hold the ink. The tattoo master works quickly, tracing over the design with a series of punctures so close together that the dots fade into a rough line. Inexperience shows here. Luang Pu Sri Chantr's young disciples often fail to make the punctures close enough together, so that the newly tattooed lines look more like a series of dots. Skillful artisans, on the other hand, have been known to execute as many as fifteen figures in little over half an hour. During the entire process, the traditional tattoo master chants special incantations to make the charm effective.

Aside from these magic spells the design itself must carry some powerful meaning. The most primitive designs are animals, both real and mythical, which have special qualities. Just as men like to carry tigers' teeth for bravery, or lucky rabbits' feet, so we find pictures of mythical lions, wild boar, dragons, or eagles traced on the bodies of the Thai. Perhaps some of the wonderful powers of these wild beasts will be magically transferred to the man who wears their image. But what could be the remarkable qualities of the humble lizard, whose tattooed figure is one of the most common in Bangkok? Lizards are among the most ancient symbols in Southeast Asia, found even on pottery made three thousand years ago. Here, where life centered around the waterways, lizards and serpents were worshipped as river gods. Although its religious power has no doubt decreased over the centuries, the little lizard remains an ancient and powerful talisman.

Two hundred thousand years ago the worship of the natural world was joined in Southeast Asia by the great religions of India, Hinduism and Buddhism. With them came the idea that images of Hindu gods and heroes, or of the Lord Buddha, could give even greater protection than animal charms. Luang Pu Sri Chantr, in fact, totally rejects animal figures, believing them to be of a lower, or less spiritual order. Instead of a tiger or a dragon, his preferred tattoo for invulnerability is a small stylized Buddha image repeated sev-

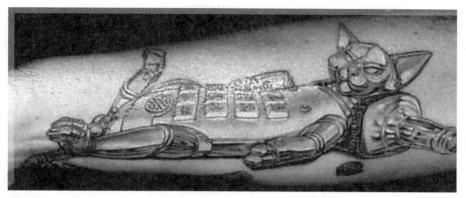

Image of cyber-cat that is also a cellular phone lounging against a whiskey bottle taken from the Richmond Tattoo Arts Festival '98 Photo Album.

eral times across the chest or back. More spectacular is the popular image of the white monkey general, Hanuman, superhero of the Indian *Ramayana* epic.

The magical spells, called *gatha,* that are spoken by the tattoo master are often tattooed onto the skin for good measure. Even the letters themselves are considered sacred, for instead of Thai, the Khmer (Khom) alphabet is used. This is because holy Buddhist scriptures came to the Thai people by way of the Khmer civilization to the east. Since holy books were written in this script, people came to believe that the ancient letters had magical properties in themselves. Using the Khom alphabet adds to the effectiveness of the charm.

Another extremely popular motif is a letter or number topped with a conical zigzag flourish, called an *unalom.* This has been related both to the mystical Hindu syllable *om* and to the traditional curled tuft of hair between the eyebrows of the Lord Buddha. It has become the fashion among some of Bangkok's youth to tattoo a single *unalom* on the Adam's apple.

Often men have their entire chest and back covered with letters and symbols meticulously built up into a mystical diagram. These diagrams, or *yantras,* protect the wearer from evil influences. These *yantras* are also printed on special jackets for people who do not wish to be tattooed. A temple on the popular resort island of Phuket in southern Thailand dispenses printed *yantras* for different purposes, such as protecting one's body, financial affairs, house or car.

According to Thai belief, different parts of the body are worthy of different degrees of respect. The head, which is the seat of the soul, is the most sacred, while the feet, in constant contact with dirt, are least respected. The tattoo master must choose the right sort of tattoo for each part of the body. *Yantra* are very holy, beneficial tattoos, often given by Buddhist monks. They can be drawn on the chest or upper back. In fact, a man might even shave his head to have a mystical diagram or Buddha image tattooed on the crown. Such a tattoo is thought to prevent his head from harm and to make him be well-liked by other people.

Nowadays it is not very common, at least in Bangkok, to be tattooed below the waist. This was not always the case. Among the Shans, Lao and Burmese, the area between the waist and the knees was once so densely filled with tattoos that the wearer seemed to be clad in tight-fitting trousers. These tattoos, now found only on a few old men in north or northeastern Thailand, were strictly decorative. Because of the great pain involved in receiving so many tattoos, this decoration was considered an indispensable sign of masculinity. Without leg tattoos a young man could not hope to gain favor with the girls.

But in the twentieth century, those people who have their thighs tattooed are likely to have aggressive intentions. One design that was popular as a thigh tattoo and is still one of the most popular Thai amulets—worn below the waist—is a lively phallus animated with legs and tail. It is one of the many tattoos that is supposed to make the wearer invulnerable to knives and bullets.

Delving into the mysticism and magic of tattoos can be a dangerous sport. If the tattoo master isn't very careful, he can conceivably create a design whose magical power is too strong for the person receiving it. Weak-minded people, they say, can be driven mad by certain designs of ancient sages or demons. To keep this from happening, a tattoo master may purposely leave out part of the design—the last syllable of the written charm, say—to weaken its effect.

Very few masters, of course, know the necessary drugs and incantations for the most powerful tattoos. Both the recipient and tattoo master have to have strong stomachs as well, since either human flesh or corpse fluid, as mentioned earlier, is involved in the attendant rites. Shway Yoe, writing of nineteenth century Shans, reported that some tattooers made the patient chew the raw flesh of a man who had been hanged, while the powerful figure was being tattooed on his chest. This unusual rite produced a kind of superman with enormous strength and the ability to jump to great heights. Unfortunately, no body was considered strong enough to sustain this power, and the superman, so rumor had it, would usually become so dangerous and wild that he would have to be killed in his sleep. One such pathetic giant was only saved by having the magical figure tattooed out with a rusty nail and sacred medicines administered by a holy ascetic.

When the tattooing is finished, the young man once more performs a ritual to ask the nonhuman powers to make his charm effective. These powers, once invoked, enter the body through pricks in the skin at the top of the skull made with the tattoo needle.

But what is to keep the power of the charm from disappearing once the boy has left his tattoo master? Like all amulets, tattooed charms must be carefully maintained. The young man takes home with him a number of incantations to help maintain the charm's effectiveness, and a number of taboos to keep it from being destroyed.

During the final rites, the tattoo master may demonstrate the effectiveness of a tattoo for invulnerability. In this case, the young man will be face down on the floor as the master brandishes a bamboo knife, showing how sharp the point is. After uttering the appropriate magic formula, he will stab the knife into the protected area. Invariably, the point of the knife is broken and the skin unpierced. One hardy anthropologist, B. J. Terwiel, who underwent this ceremony, claims he could "hardly feel the impact of the knife." Terwiel speculates that the point of the knife may have been broken before the thrust. On the other hand, a doctor operating in northern Thailand, where extensive leg tattoos can still be found, mentioned that she had broken many an injection needle on a tattooed hip.

But does Terwiel feel invulnerable? "I personally do not feel invulnerable," he writes, "but the same goes for many Thais." The Thais would not be so adamant. They would be more likely to agree with another, gentler assessment of the efficacy of tattoos: Sometimes they work and sometimes they don't. But they are the best protection one has.

WORDS TO KNOW

NOTE: When you write the definitions of the following words, make it a point to use at least three of them in conversation over the next day and three of them in your next writing assignment. Many times you'll find it difficult or impossible to use them in everyday speech or writing. What then is the point of defining them? Of learning them? At the very least, in all the following cases where you have unusual vocabulary terms to define, attempt to use them. How does attempting to use vocabulary that feels awkward or different change your view of your common speech and writing patterns? Learning how to use new vocabulary means just that—using the words. Write specifically how, where, when, and why you used the words and discuss with your class.

Luang Pu Sri Chantr—
betel—
incoherently—
acharn—
talisman—
modicum—
Shans—
Lao—
gekkos—
unalom—
Ramayana—
gatha—
Khmer—
Om—
yantras—
Phuket—

QUESTIONS

List all the situations in which you find tattoos. What would you say about the range of examples you've listed? Have you ever wanted to get a tattoo? Why or why not? What would the design be? What would it represent? You've worked throughout the first part of this reader using the Text/You/Other Question–building method. Now it's time for you to practice creating questions using the Three-Layered Question-building method.

Refer to the notes you wrote as you read "Tattooed Charms." Using the Three-Layered Question builder, create a question based on "Tattooed Charms" that includes the necessary three parts:

1. The Quotation that catches your attention.
2. A Sentence/Comment that shows why you are calling attention to that quotation.
3. The Question you want to ask.

Ask yourself the following to help you to generate ideas for composing your Three-Layered Question:

1. The Quotation—Does it capture your attention? Why?
2. A Sentence/Comment—What is interesting about the quotation? Why are you calling attention to it? Why is it worth examining more closely? To what does it relate?
3. The Question—What larger issue do you want to ask about? What is the point you want to get across? To explore?

Now create a series of Three-Layered Questions based on this reading, using this method.

WRITING ACTIVITIES

1. Select your most challenging question on which to write.
2. Write for at least five minutes without stopping.
3. Exchange your writing with one of your classmates, and read through each other's questions and writings.
4. After you've read through them, together create a new Three-Layered Question and writing that incorporates aspects of both of your original writings. Which do you like best and why?
5. Take the new writing home and elaborate on what you've written by finding a text source and a pictorial source from which you can include details and references in your new writing.
6. Bring your new writings to class and work with them again to incorporate them into a new Three-Layered Question and writing.
7. Share this new writing with your classmates. How do they respond, and why? What specific feedback do they give you? What specific feedback did you find important? Why?

GRAMMAR AND STYLE QUESTIONS

1. One of the best ways to learn grammar, in addition to learning the names and rules of grammatical elements, is to read other people's writing and determine how and why they write well. Take a grammatically imperfect piece of your own work, select and read or reread any two or three readings from this reader (including "Tattooed Charms"), and rewrite your piece afterwards. Is it grammatically better? Why or why not? What was the impact of seeing how these other writers put together words?

2. An important element of good usage is the concise and active expression of thoughts and ideas. Looking through this reading, find concise, active, grammatical expressions and/or phrases, put them into your own words, and see how you can make them still more concise.

3. Now take wordy, general grammatical expressions from writing you've done based on this reading, and revise them to make them concise, active grammatical expressions and/or phrases.

Weight for me

Kaz Cooke

Writer/cartoonist Kaz Cooke is one of Australia's most popular multimedia authors and has written four other books. "Special bonus fact," she screams from the back of Real Gorgeous, *from which this reading comes, "You are not your buttocks." "Are you terrified of Mint Milanos? What the hell is a liposome anyway? Do you have hips?" She even provides you with a Body Police Quiz.*

Introduction The clue to the mode of writing featured in this reading lies in the dual career listed for writer Kaz Cooke: writer/cartoonist. This reading mixes category with definition with examples with statistics and research—you'll find many of the forms of writing you will use in academic essays. The other clue lies in the connection of the word "multimedia" to this writer. If you guessed this means writing mixed with drawings and pictures, you're right. The effect of combining pictures with words here is very deliberate: Using humor, Cooke wants to catch you off guard about your complicity in perpetuating the problems women face about their bodies—regardless of whether you're a man or a woman.

Food As a Sin

"Oh, I musn't," "Oh, I really shouldn't," "It will go straight to my hips." I guess we're just not encouraged to say, "Oh, no. I couldn't possibly. It would go straight to the production of skin cells, my central nervous system, and my toenail growth." (Normal body functioning accounts for 70 percent of daily energy expenditure.)

British *Slimmer* magazine has a "Shapescope" astrology column which in one month tells Aquarians that they have a body like an intricate machine and should not neglect their health (as if) and Scorpios they are going to meet someone new so they'd better lose weight. Pisces must say "no" to temptation in October. In fact there is an awful lot about temptation: Librans should only have romance as a temptation if they lose weight; Aries need willpower; Geminis need determination *and* willpower (they're not eating for two, after all); and Leos shouldn't be giving in to tasty tidbits. Virgos, too, must not give in to temptation.

Australian *Cleo* magazine's survey "Love, Sex and the Dieting Woman" found that 67 percent of women feel guilty every day about eating.

According to diet lore, "indulging" or "giving in to temptation" is a "sin." (Strangling a few people is a sin. Invading East Timor is a sin. "Ethnic cleansing" is a sin. Testing nuclear weapons in the Pacific is a sin. I'm sorry, but eating doesn't quite make the grade.)

Australian *Who Weekly* magazine, which has run many stories about eating disorders, kicked off 1994 with its front-cover screamer "Diet Winners and Sinners of the Year: Here's the Scoop on Who Got Fat, Who Got Fit and How They Did It."

English comedian Jennifer Saunders says, "I'm completely neurotic about [weight]. I've always been overweight. Actually I haven't always been overweight. I started as soon as I became this moody sort of schoolgirl . . . I put on weight and then dieted at school. Cup of soup for lunch and then you'd go across to the shop and buy six Mars Bars. No-one's teaching you anything: you should just eat normally. Just be sane about it. Not like these neurotic people who go, 'Well, that's a bit naughty isn't it what you're eating?' Naughty! I'm eating! It's food. I'm EATING IT! . . . I KNOW I'M BEING NAUGHTY. EATING FOOD IS WRONG ALTOGETHER."

Seven thousand respondents to a *Mirabella* magazine survey revealed that those who were extremely overweight ate the most candy but, at 47 percent, the dangerously *underweight* ate more cakes and cookies than anyone else. The most craved foods were chocolate and ice cream. Chocolate is seen as the biggest sin and so consequently it is the biggest craving.

The Gender Gap: Show Us Your Portion

Traditionally food is served in its best and largest proportions to the men: as a reward for status, as fuel for hunting. Biscuits, like handkerchiefs, come in "man size." Little children in countries where there is not enough food will have more chance of survival if they are boys: they are given more food. Having a smaller portion used to be seen as ladylike, dainty, mysterious. Fanatical Christian girls were praised in years gone by for refusing to eat, fainting, and having hal-

FOOD IS NOT THE DEVIL: PROOF

← quite pointy

FIG 1: BEELZEBUB

FIG 2: THE MUSHROOM

lucinations (visions from the Lord). Their wasted bodies were seen as proof that they could live on faith alone. To be thin and deprived was to be "good."

Food As a Reward

Eating is often associated with reward in our society—an ice cream for being good, candies after eating our "greens," a celebratory meal, a birthday cake. Food gets mixed up with love or with comfort and security for some people. Cooking is often an act of love and nourishment from a parent or lover and it becomes symbolic of being cared for and protected.

The smell or appearance of food "induces an anticipatory increase in insulin (blood sugar), and in appetite," say Peter Dally and Joan Gomez, authors of *Understanding Anorexia and Obesity*. "The pleasurable feelings associated with the beginning of a meal are due to endorphins, self-made opiates which give a sense of well-being. For most people the endorphin concentration falls away quickly as the meal progresses."

Food Pornography

The glossy, full-colour pictures of chocolate cakes and fruit custard flans in magazines that also carry diets are a forbidden realm but an irresistible one. One ice cream is described in sexual advertising as "wicked." Another is "to die for." Denial of food is strongly linked to an obsession with it. Some anorexics and bulimics throw elaborate dinner parties, worship food, become "foodies." They cannot eat it or absorb it but they must be near it. It's a kind of masochistic torture.

Food Obsession

Most diet books encourage the food obsession. Margaret O'Sullivan's *The Heavenly Body Diet* suggests that women keep a "food diary."

"It's absolutely essential," she said while promoting her book. "It takes me no more than three minutes and I do it in bed at night or during the commercial breaks when I'm watching television." She, too, talks of "keeping your weight under control" by counting calories weekly rather than daily. This she sees as an incredible freedom! "If you indulge every now and again you simply take extra care on the other days." This hardly revolutionary idea, along with its boring calorie-counting obsession, was promoted on almost a full page of a Sydney newspaper.

Maybe it started with that weirdo Bible story. I mean, a woman eats an apple—one little apple! And the next thing you know everyone's chucked out of the Garden of Eden and all the evils of the earth, including lawyers and public transport ticket inspectors, famine and pestilence, are visited upon the earth by a vengeful and furious all-powerful God. No wonder women feel guilty about eating. Thankfully Eve wasn't offered a piece of black forest cake by that old snakie thing or we'd all be pulverised into atoms.

NUTRITION

Healthy Eating

In 1994 the top-selling products at American supermarkets were carbonated drinks, candy, soups, chips, and snacks. I hope you were not expecting them to be unprocessed bran, kelp by-products, and agar-agar. No, Americans are more your sort of Cocoa Puffs nutritionists. Together, we eat almost 22 billion fast-food meals a year.

So, if we assume that we should not be drinking 8 quarts of Coke and having a lardburger every couple of hours, how *should* we be eating?

The Victorian Health Promotion Foundation's Eating Behavior Project suggests some ideas for healthier eating:

- Give yourself permission to eat.
- "Legalise" all foods without feeling guilt.
- Avoid counting calories.
- Use hunger as the cue for eating, not the time of day or habit.
- Eat small meals about every three to five hours.
- Trust your food choices—eat anything you want, forbid nothing.
- Sit down while eating.
- Don't hide away and eat alone—create a pleasant environment and table to eat at.
- Focus your senses on food, its colour, smell, texture, and taste. (They also mention sounds, but if your food is singing, put it away.)
- Notice how your body reacts to certain foods.

There are not many rules for healthy eating, but here they are:

- Don't diet: ever.
- Eat what your body wants you to.
- Vary your food so you don't get bored.
- Don't stick popcorn up your nose.
- Don't trust food advertising.
- Know where your food comes from.
- Don't use added salt.
- Eat fresh food whenever possible.
- Eat as much organically produced food as you can afford.
- If you get into a food fight, make sure you have the custard.

The Food Groups

Forget the old four food groups you learned years ago—they have been modified. Modified, hell, nutrition's a completely different beastie.

Don't take any notice of the magazine that said, "Peruse your plate and leave something on it. There's no reason to eat all the food you're served just because it's there. Your main course arrives with chicken, roast pumpkin and green beans. Eat two of the three choices and leave the third one after a little taste." Noooooooooooo! Eat some of all three!

Your body needs regular hits of the following things: water; vitamins A, C, D, E, K, and B complex; calcium; iron; folic acid; magnesium; iron; zinc; phosphorus; potassium; sodium (no need to add it, it's in most foods already); sulphur; iodine; complex carbohydrates;

protein; essential fatty acids; and fibre. The key is in eating a *variety* of foods to get all the goodies.

Generally, we tend to have too much fat, alcohol, sugar, salt, and animal protein and not enough green leafy things, vegetables, fruit, bread, and grains.

DAILY NEEDS

Meats and meat alternatives—including fish, the odd egg, nuts, seeds—once a day (go easy on the salami!), twice for a woman who is pregnant, for extra iron, zinc, and protein.

Milk and dairy products—including cheese and yoghurt—2 serves (this could be a glass of milk and a small tub of yoghurt). Pregnant women need 3 serves for extra protein and calcium.

Veggies—you know, the stuff at the vegetable market. Go wild and eat lots but have at least 4 serves of different veggies a day. Lentils and legumes are included here.

Fruit—"An apple a day . . ." Fresh is best—three different types a day.

Breads and cereal—important for fibre. Include rice and pasta. Go for it with 5 and preferably more serves a day. (Not so difficult when a serve is a slice of bread or half a cup of cereal.) Pregnant and active women may need 7 to 8 serves a day. Very active adults and growing teenagers can need up to 9 to 12 serves a day (preferably whole-meal).

And remember, a cakie a day keeps the madness away. This is a loose guide only: you don't want to be weighing bits of food and counting up slices and generally getting obsessed with it. Food is not mathematics. Life is too short to weigh lentils.

I like this idea the best: Many nutritionists just divide the food groups into three sections: eat less fat, oil, and sugar; eat moderate amounts of meat, fish, poultry, eggs, and dairy foods; and eat lots of fruit, vegetables, legumes, bread, and cereals. How simple is that?

You'll find that this is probably what your body is asking for once it settles down anyway. You'll be lying there and your body will say, "I'd like some spinach and something kind of crunchy, maybe in a more lurid shade of orange." "A carrot?" you'll inquire. "That's it," the body will say. "I'll have a couple of those carroty things and something red and round and deliciously squishy that explodes in your mouth." "I believe that's what they refer to in intellectual circles as a cherry tomato," you'll reply. "And I want a cheese sandwich and a Junior Mint. Later I may toy with leeks."

If somebody hassles you about eating too much, or eating between meals, strike them repeatedly with this book.

Osteoporosis

This is a deficiency disease. The bones lose minerals, particularly calcium, and become brittle and weak, often causing stooping and breaking bones in old age. The decline in bone strength tends to speed up after menopause. Technically, the term refers to people who have lost 50 to 75 percent of their original bone material. Although generally we are told, especially by dairy organisations, that dairy-food calcium intake is the key to protecting ourselves, excessive animal protein consumption, including milk consumption, has been linked to osteoporosis.

The average measurable bone loss in a woman meat-eater at 65 years old in America is 35 percent. The average rate for her vegetarian sister at the same age: 7 percent. It seems that the more animal protein we eat (including that from fish), the more calcium our bodies lose.

Unchallenged research shows that even very high calcium intakes are cancelled out by high animal protein consumption. Bantu women have a dangerously low calcium intake by our standards, but they eat virtually no animal protein. Their osteoporosis rate is very low. This doesn't mean we should stop taking in calcium: we still need it. But it would seem that rather than simply eating more dairy products, we should be eating less protein supplied by meat.

Physical activity from a young age is also linked to low rates of osteoporosis, so get dancing.

FURTHER INFORMATION

To know more in detail about which foods have which goodies, ring your regional or state health department and get them to send you some nutritional information. A visit to a dietician or a good book on different foods might also be useful. Be careful where your books or pamphlets come from. Industry organisations will be very biased in favour of their own products.

The National Center for Nutrition and Dietetics
216 West Jackson Boulevard
Suite 800
Chicago, IL 60606
Phone: (312)899-0040

They can send you pamphlets and books and answer your questions (although you're not supposed to ask about baseball scores).

Most public hospitals and women's health centres employ nutritionists you can go to see.

FURTHER READING

Dr. Phyllis Butow, Jillian Ball, and Fiona Place, *When Eating Is Everything: How to Overcome Your Eating Problems and Change Your Life* (New York: Doubleday, 1991).

Jane Brody, *Jane Brody's Nutrition Book: A Lifetime Guide to Eating Better for Better Health and Weight Control* (New York: Ballantine, 1987).

John Robbins, *Diet for a New America: How Your Food Choices Affect Your Health, Happiness and the Future of Life on Earth* (N.H.: Stillpoint, 1987). A brilliant book about what we eat and how it is produced, and a healthier and saner way to eat for ourselves and the planet. (For instance, 64 percent of U.S. cropland is used to grow animal feed: only 2 percent is for fruits and vegetables.)

Jane Brody and Judith E. Brown, *Everywoman's Guide to Nutrition* (Minneapolis: University of Minnesota Press, 1990).

Carlton Fredericks, *The Columbia Encyclopedia of Women's Nutrition* (New York: Putnam, 1989).

Gary Null, *The Vegetarian Handbook* (New York: St. Martin's Press, 1987).

WORDS TO KNOW

NOTE: When you write the definitions of the following words, make it a point to use at least three of them in conversation over the next day and three of them in your next writing assignment. Many times you'll find it difficult or impossible to use them in everyday speech or writing. What then is the point of defining them? Of learning them? At the very least, in all the following cases where you have unusual vocabulary terms to define, attempt to use them. How does attempting to use vocabulary that feels awkward or different change your view of your common speech and writing patterns? Learning how to use new vocabulary means just that—using the words. Write specifically how, where, when, and why you used the words and discuss with your class.

    Timor—
    neurotic—
    anticipatory—
    insulin—

anorexia—
obesity—
endorphin—
tizz—
choccy—
bulimics—
masochistic—
pulverized—
folic acid—
magnesium—
zinc—
phosphorous—
potassium—
sodium—
sulphur—
iodine—
complex carbohydrates—
essential fatty acids—
lentils—
legumes—
osteoporosis—

QUESTIONS

Look at how the cartoon goes with the writing itself. Are they necessary together? Why or why not? What do they add? What is the tone of
this piece and where specifically do you hear the tone the strongest?
What did you already know before reading the piece? What new information did you learn? Create two or three new Three-Layered Questions based on this reading.

WRITING ACTIVITIES

1. Choose one of your new Three-Layered Questions. To what extent are
   any of your questions based on the assumption that Cooke's facts and
   figures are accurate? How do you know?
2. Before you write on your question, do some of your own research on a
   selected portion of Cooke's text. Check knowledgeable sources for con-

firmation of her information. What sources did you use to confirm or disprove what she says and why? Make a list of these sources and bring them to your class.

3. Share your source lists. What makes you and your classmates confident in your choice of supporting evidence sources and why? On which facts was Cooke right? Wrong? Which are a matter of opinion?

4. Now go back and modify your question as necessary. Once you have a new question, write on that Three-Layered Question for at least ten minutes without stopping. Where did it get difficult to continue writing and why?

5. Try creating a writing as Cooke does, using interactive media. You may wish to draw something to accompany the writing, or even design a writing on the computer using sound bytes or clip art, for instance.

6. "Perform" your writing for your class. What is the response and why? Are your additional media choices integral to your writing? How would you revise them to make them so if they are not?

GRAMMAR AND STYLE QUESTIONS

1. Select a reading from the Internet to compare and contrast with Kaz Cooke's reading. Analyze these examples. What is the difference in style, and why? Use specific examples from the readings and cite how specific rules of grammar were followed or not followed to achieve certain stylistic effects.

2. Using a standard grammar reference (e.g., Strunk and White's *Elements of Style*), find three exceptions (from any of the readings in this reader, including Kaz Cooke's piece) to any of the grammar and style rules such a standard reference has created, and discuss why the authors broke those grammar and style rules.

Excerpts, Interviews, and Photos from Art on the Edge of Fashion

In discussing the Art on the Edge of Fashion back in February of 1997, Curator of the Arizona State University Art Museum Heather Sealy Lineberry asks why so many artists today make work incorporating or examining clothes, appearance, and fashion. She says of the artists in Art on the Edge of Fashion that they are trying to pin down the nature of identity. "This process is complicated by our rapidly changing world and becomes intensified as we approach the end of the Millennium. Curiously all of the artists in the exhibition insist on using hand techniques traditionally associated with clothing at some point in their artistic process. As new technologies mushroom, and fewer objects around us are hand-made, it is as if they need a physical and psychological grounding to define identity."

Introduction This particular collection of readings was obtained from an Internet site and uses the format of an interview, marked by the interviewer's and the interviewee's initials over each paragraph spoken by that particular person. It also uses brief reviews of the various performance art productions as well as accompanying pictures of the costumes and performances to give you a sense of how the visuals and the words fit together.

MZ: What is the concept of the exhibition?

HL: Art on the Edge of Fashion presents the work of eight contemporary artists who all utilize the familiar and prevalent visual language of clothing and appearance. Many of the pieces in the exhibition actually take the form of clothing, although they are not meant to be "clothing." They are completely unwearable because of their size, materials, or distortions. The artists use clothing forms to examine issues of identity, particularly gender, and to examine the societal forces that dictate the way we look. Sociologists

Photo by Kim Adams

have demonstrated that we read people quickly and easily based on their appearance, on their clothing, hair, skin color and tone, and body shape. The work in this exhibition questions quick assumptions based on appearance, and scrutinizes the forces, like fashion, that determine appearance and so indicate identity.

For example, Beverly Semmes makes dresses that resemble cocktail dresses or sweet high-waisted dresses with Peter Pan collars. But they are huge. They hang on the wall and drape down onto the floor. She mocks the styles and stereotypes of women and their clothing, and the strangely shaped clothes that we drape and squeeze onto our bodies. On the other hand, Semmes also empowers the image of women by creating these massive dresses that free the body from constraint and seem best suited for Amazons.

MZ: Why organize this exhibition now?

APRIL FLANDERS, ANNETTE FOSTER and ANGELA BETTRIDGE—"An Affected Appearance" was a ceremony/performance dealing with clothing and female relationships. The piece explored the issues of clothing as armor with which to face the world. There were five parts to the work. "Periodical Strutting" involved costume and dance. "Tic-Tac Coat" featured one dancer wearing a coat covered with boxes of orange Tic Tacs. Another dancer opened all the boxes and turned the first dancer upside down. They were followed by a woman in a business suit and heels who picked up all the Tic-Tacs. "Woman in the Mirror" featured two dancers facing each other as if they were looking in a mirror. As the "real person" examined her body in the mirror, the other person stuffed squishy material into her outfit. "Layer Piece" had one dancer wearing many layers of clothing. Another dancer slowly cut the clothing off the first dancer to reveal her painted nude body. "Feminine Products" featured a dancer wearing a skirt and top made entirely of feminine products and a pair of cowboy boots. She moved around on stage and finally pulled out a fabricated rubber-band gun and shot tampons into the air.

HL: This question basically started my research: Why are so many artists today making work incorporating or examining clothes, appearance, and fashion? In addition to the eight selected artists, there are many others across the country, and I can think of a number of art students at ASU who are dealing with these same issues and forms.

Like many contemporary artists, the artists in Art on the Edge of Fashion are trying to pin down the nature of identity. This process is complicated by our rapidly changing world and becomes intensified as we approach the end of the Millennium. Curiously all of the artists in the exhibition insist on using hand techniques traditionally associated with clothing at some point in their artistic process. As new technologies mushroom, and fewer objects around us are hand-made, it is as if they need a physical and psychological grounding to define identity.

MZ: Why at this Museum?

HL: The ASU Art Museum has a long tradition of collecting and showing handmade objects, specifically craft. Recently we have expanded our programming to include new media and new approaches to art-making. The artists in this exhibition span those two concerns. They recognize the power of materials and processes on the artists, during making, and on the viewer. Many of the pieces in the show are made, at least in part, from very familiar media—fabric like that which we sleep under, eat off of and wear. But the artists freely make use of other media for their final presentations and are not afraid of new media. The show includes sculpture, photographs, installations, performance, and video. The artists seem to recognize few barriers and use whatever they can to convey their content.

WORDS TO KNOW

NOTE: When you write the definitions of the following words, make it a point to use at least three of them in conversation over the next day and three of them in your next writing assignment. Many times you'll find it difficult or impossible to use them in everyday speech or writing. What then is the point of defining them? Of learning them? At the very least, in all the following cases where you have unusual vocabulary terms to define, attempt to use them. How does attempting to use vocabulary that feels awkward or different change your view of your common speech and writing patterns? Learning how to use new vocabulary means just that—using the words. Write specifically how, where, when, and why you used the words and discuss with your class

> curators—
> prevalent—
> dictate—
> sociologists—
> scrutinizes—
> constraint—
> Amazons—
> privy—
> periscopes—

QUESTIONS

How long does it take you to figure out the point of this reading and why? How essential are the photographs? The words? Why? How did the combination of pictures and words make you look again at objects you might take for granted? Why? Create a series of Three-Layered Questions based on this reading.

WRITING ACTIVITIES

1. Select one of your Three-Layered Questions and answer it. Don't do any research, just write. Simply use what you know as of this moment and what you know from the reading.
2. Now add another photograph and short reading to the Art on the Edge of Fashion collection that you just read, and give the whole package to one of your classmates to write his or her answer/response. Keep a copy of the package to write about for yourself.
3. Create a Three-Layered Question based on the package and write your answer/essay to it.
4. Compare and contrast your answer to your classmate's. What was the result?
5. Add an aspect to the package, either pictures, words, or both that would require both you and your classmate writing on this package to incorporate research in your writing.

6. Test the "truth" and "up-to-dateness" of the source that you used from which to get your research. How do you test it for validity? How do you make that research an integral part of your writing? Revise what you wrote to include this kind of analysis of your sources.

7. What was your point or main idea when you started? What happened to your point as you revised? Did it change or not? Why?

8. Share one of your writings with your classmates. What comments/suggestions do they have for you? Which did you feel were important and why?

GRAMMAR AND STYLE QUESTIONS

1. Select a text reading and a reading from the Internet (include these excerpts from "Art on the Edge of Fashion"). You may even wish to compare and contrast this Internet example to other readings originally published on the Internet, such as those you've read in this reader. Analyze these examples. What is the difference in style and word choice, and why? Use specific examples from the readings and cite how specific rules of grammar and style were followed or not followed to achieve certain stylistic effects.

2. Using a standard grammar reference (e.g., Strunk and White's *Elements of Style*), find three exceptions (from any of the readings in this reader) to the rules such a standard reference has created, and discuss why the authors broke those rules. Include these excerpts from "Art on the Edge of Fashion" as part of your choices. How does a writer's choice of audience affect his or her adherence to standard rules of grammar? Use specific examples from specific readings in writing your answer.

What the Indian Means to America

Luther Standing Bear

Luther Standing Bear (1868–1947), a member of a Teton Sioux tribe, attended the government Indian school at Carlyle, Pennsylvania, and later worked in jobs ranging from storekeeper to minister to performer in Buffalo Bill's Wild West Show. Having lived during and observed first hand the forcible removal of Indians to reservations during the rapid expansion of the West, Standing Bear found the government practices untenable. Author of My People the Sioux *(1928),* My Indian Boyhood *(1931),* Stories of the Sioux *(1934), and* Land of the Spotted Eagle *(1933), Luther Standing Bear had a career that spans the spectrum of true irony. Among other professions, he worked as a storekeeper, a minister, and a performer in Buffalo Bill's Wild West Show.*

Introduction Luther Standing Bear writes his essay using historical references, but he also uses a style of presenting details that could be described as functioning like a camera lens. His word choices move over the landscape that you take for granted and focus on images about which you have developed tired stereotypes, whether you realize it or not. As he does this, he also tells you little stories, making full use of tone of voice, attitude, and mood. You feel as if he is speaking right to you.

The feathered and blanketed figure of the American Indian has come to symbolize the American continent. He is the man who through centuries has been moulded and sculpted by the same hand that shaped its mountains, forests, and plains, and marked the course of its rivers.

The American Indian is of the soil, whether it be the region of forests, plains, pueblos, or mesas. He fits into the landscape, for the hand that fashioned the continent also fashioned the man for his surroundings. He once grew as naturally as the wild sunflowers; he belongs just as the buffalo belonged with a physique that fitted, the man developed fitting skills—crafts which today are called American. And the body had a son, also formed and moulded by the same master hand of harmony. Out of the Indian approach to existence there came a great freedom—an intense and absorbing love for nature; a respect for life; enduring faith in a Supreme Power; and principles of truth, honesty, generosity, equity, and brotherhood as a guide to mundane relations. . . .

The white man does not understand the Indian for the reason that he does not understand America. He is too far removed from its formative processes. The roots of the tree of his life have not yet grasped the rock and soil. The white man is still troubled with primitive fears; he still has in his consciousness the perils of this frontier continent, some of its fastnesses not yet having yielded to his questing footsteps and inquiring eyes. He shudders still with the memory of the loss of his forefathers upon its scorching deserts and forbidding mountaintops. The man from Europe is still a foreigner and an alien. And he still hates the man who questioned his path across the continent.

But in the Indian the spirit of the land is still vested; it will be until other men are able to divine and meet its rhythm. Men must be born and reborn to belong. Their bodies must be formed of the dust of their forefathers' bones.

The attempted transformation of the Indian by the white man and the chaos that has resulted are but the fruits of the white man's disobedience of a fundamental and spiritual law. The pressure that has been brought to bear upon the native people, since the cessation of armed conflict, in the attempt to force conformity of custom and habit has caused a reaction more destructive than war, and the injury has not only affected the Indian, but has extended to the white population as well. Tyranny, stupidity, and lack of vision have brought about the situation now alluded to as the "Indian Problem."

There is, I insist, no Indian problem as created by the Indian himself. Every problem that exists today in regard to the native population is due to the white man's cast of mind, which is unable, at least reluctant, to seek understanding and achieve adjustment in a new and a significant environment into which it has so recently come.

The white man excused his presence here by saying that he has been guided by the will of his God; and in so saying absolved himself of all responsibility for his appearance in a land occupied by other men.

Then, too, his law was a written law; his divine decalogue reposed in a book. And what better proof that his advent into this country and his subsequent acts were the result of divine will! He brought the Word! There ensued a blind worship of written history, of books, of the written word, that has divided the spoken word of its power and sacredness. The written word became established as a criterion of the superior man—a symbol of emotional fineness. The man who could write his name on a piece of paper, whether or not he possessed the spiritual fineness to honor those words in speech, was by some miraculous formula a more highly developed and sensitized person than the one who had never had a pen in hand, but whose spoken word was inviolable and whose sense of honor and truth was paramount. With false reasoning was the quality of human character measured by man's ability to make with an implement a mark upon paper. But granting this mode of reasoning be correct and just, then where are to be placed the thousands of illiterate whites who are unable to read and write? Are they, too, "savages"? Is not humanness a matter of heart and mind, and is it not evident in the form of relationship with men? Is not kindness more powerful than arrogance; and truth more powerful than the sword?

True, the white man brought great change. But the varied fruits of his civilization, though highly colored and inviting, are sickening and deadening. And if it be the part of civilization to maim, rob, and thwart, then what is progress? . . .

After subjugation, after dispossession, there was cast the last abuse upon the people who so entirely resented their wrongs and punishments, and that was the stamping and labeling of them as savages. To make this label stick has been the task of the white race and the greatest salve that it has been able to apply to its sore and troubled conscience now hardened through the habitual practice of injustice.

But all the years of calling the Indian a savage has never made him one; all the denial of his virtues has never taken them from him; and the very resistance he has made to save the things inalienably his has been his saving strength—that which will stand him in need when justice does make its belated appearance and he undertakes rehabilitation.

All sorts of feeble excuses are heard for the continued subjection of the Indian. One of the most common is that he is not yet ready to accept the society of the white man—that he is not yet ready to mingle as a social entity.

This, I maintain, is beside the question. The matter is not one of making over the external Indian into the likeness of the white race— a process detrimental to both races. Who can say that the white man's way is better for the Indian? Where resides the human judgment with the competence to weigh and value Indian ideals and spiritual concepts; or substitute for them other values?

Then, has the white man's social order been so harmonious and ideal as to merit the respect of the Indian, and for that matter the thinking class of the white race? Is it wise to urge upon the Indian a foreign social form? Let none but the Indian answer! Rather, let the white brother face about and cast his mental eye upon a new angle of vision. Let him look upon the Indian world as a human world; then let him see to it that human rights be accorded to the Indians. And this for the purpose of retaining for his own order of society a measure of humanity. . . .

The spiritual health and existence of the Indian was maintained by song, magic, ritual, dance, symbolism, oratory (or council), design, handicraft, and folk-story.

Manifestly, to check or thwart this expression is to bring about spiritual decline. And it is in this condition of decline that the Indian people are today. There is but a feeble effort among the Sioux to keep alive their traditional songs and dances, while among other tribes there is but a half-hearted attempt to offset the influence of the Government school and at the same time recover from the crushing and stifling regime of the Indian Bureau.

One has but to speak of Indian verse to receive uncomprehending and unbelieving glances. Yet the Indian loved verse and into this mode of expression went his deepest feelings. Only a few ardent and advanced students seem interested; nevertheless, they have given in book form enough Indian translations to set forth the character and quality of Indian verse.

Oratory receives a little better understanding on the part of the white public, owing to the fact that oratorical complications include those of Indian orators.

Hard as it seemingly is for the white man's ear to sense the differences, Indian songs are as varied as the many emotions which inspire them, for no two of them are alike. For instance, the Song of Victory is spirited and the notes high and remindful of an unrestrained hunter or warrior riding exultantly over the prairies. On the other hand, the song of the *Cano unye* is solemn and full of urge, for it is meant to inspire the young men to deeds of valor. Then there are the songs of death and the spiritual songs which are connected with the ceremony of initiation. These are full of the spirit of praise and worship, and so strong are some of these invocations that the very air seems as if surcharged with the presence of the Big Holy.

The Indian loved to worship. From birth to death he revered his surroundings. He considered himself born in the luxurious lap of Mother Earth and no place was to him humble. There was nothing between him and the Big Holy. The contact was immediate and personal, and the blessings of Wakan Tanka flowed over the Indian like rain showered from the sky. Wakan Tanka was not aloof, apart, and ever seeking to quell evil forces. He did not punish the animals and the birds, and likewise He did not punish man. He was not a punishing God. For there was never a question as to the supremacy of an evil power over and above the power of Good. There was but one ruling power and that was *Good.*

Of course, none but an adoring one could dance for days with his face to the sacred sun, and that time is all but done. We cannot have back the days of the buffalo and the beaver; we cannot win back our clean blood-stream and superb health, and we can never again expect the beautiful *rapport* we once had with Nature. The springs and lakes have dried and the mountains are bare of forests. The plow has changed the face of the world. Wi-wila is dead! No more may we heal our sick and comfort our dying with a strength founded on faith, for even the animals now fear us, and fear supplants faith.

And the Indian wants to dance! It is his way of expressing devotion, of communing with unseen power, and in keeping his tribal identity. When the Lakota heart was filled with high emotion, he danced. When he felt the benediction of the warming rays of the sun, he danced. When his blood ran hot with success of the hunt or chase, he danced. When his heart was filled with pity for the orphan, the lonely father, or bereaved mother, he danced. All the joys and exaltations of life, all his gratefulness and thankfulness, all his acknowledgments of the mysterious power that guided life, and all his aspirations for a better life, culminated in one great dance—the Sun Dance.

When the Indian has forgotten the music of his forefathers, when the sound of the tomtom is no more, when noisy jazz has drowned the melody of the flute, he will be a dead Indian. When the memory of his heroes are no longer told in story, and he forsakes the beautiful white buckskin for factory shoddy, he will be dead. When from him has been taken all that is his, all that he has visioned in nature, all that has come to him from infinite sources, he then, truly, will be a dead Indian. His spirit will be gone, and though he walk crowded streets, he will, in truth, be—*dead!*

But all this must not perish; it must live, to the end that America shall be educated no longer to regard native production of whatever tribe—folk-story, basketry, pottery, dance, song, poetry—as curios, and native artists as curiosities. For who but the man indigenous to the soil could produce its song, story, and folk-tale; who but the man who loved the dust beneath his feet could shape it and put it into undying, ceramic form; who but he who loved the reeds that grew beside still waters, and the damp roots of shrub and tree, could save it from seasonal death, and with almost superhuman patience weave it into enduring objects of beauty—into timeless art!

Regarding the "civilization" that has been thrust upon me since the days of reservation, it has not added one whit to my sense of justice; to my reverence for the rights of life; to my love for truth, honesty, and generosity; nor to my faith in Wakan Tanka—God of the Lakotas. For after all the great religions have been preached and expounded, or have been revealed by brilliant scholars, or have been written in books and embellished in fine language with finer covers, man—all man—is still confronted with the Great Mystery.

So if today I had a young mind to direct, to start on the journey of life, and I was faced with the duty of choosing between the natural way of my forefathers and that of the white man's present way of civilization, I would, for its welfare, unhesitatingly set that child's feet in the path of my forefathers. I would raise him to be an Indian!

WORDS TO KNOW

NOTE: When you write the definitions of the following words, make it a point to use at least three of them in conversation over the next day and three of them in your next writing assignment. Many times you'll find it difficult or impossible to use them in everyday speech or writing. What then is the point of defining them? Of learning them? At the very least, in all the following cases where you have unusual vocabulary terms to define, attempt to use them. How does attempting to use vocabulary that feels awkward or different change your view of your common speech and writing patterns? Learning how to use new vocabulary means just that—using the words. Write specifically how, where, when, and why you used the words and discuss with your class.

Teton Sioux—
pueblos—
mesas—
equity—
mundane—
formative—
fastnesses—
vested—
cessation—
tyranny—
absolved—
decalogue—
paramount—
maim—
thwart—
inalienably—
subjection—
manifestly—
regime—
oratory—
exultantly—
Cano unye—
Wakan Tanka—
rapport—
Wi-wila—

QUESTIONS

What assumptions does Standing Bear make about America and things American? What do you find interesting about those assumptions? This time, when you create your Three-Layered Questions, see how you can include either another reading from this segment of the anthology, or one of the readings from the previous part on spirituality.

WRITING ACTIVITIES

1. This time, before you choose a question, make a list of specific images of Indians. Be as detailed as you can about what these images are and where you saw these images.

2. Choose one of your Three-Layered Questions and write on that question for a page without stopping.

3. What did you discover your point was? Did you already know what you wanted to say regardless of the images you used to detail your writing, or did you let the images affect your point in some way?

4. Share your writing with your classmates. Did they feel you were detailed enough? Why or why not? Did you feel you were detailed enough? Why or why not?

5. Ask this question of yourself and of your classmates: Are you affected more by words or by pictures (images), and why?

GRAMMAR AND STYLE QUESTIONS

1. One of the most difficult tasks for any new writer is to express time and timelines consistently to match actions to those times and timelines. Take a paragraph from Standing Bear's reading that has a strong sense of either past, present, or future tense, and rewrite it using a different verb tense (i.e. if it was written in the present tense, rewrite it in the past tense, and so forth). What is the effect of such a change? Were you consistent in your new selection of verb tense in your revision? And, if you had difficulty with consistency without referring back to the text, restore the original tense and see how closely the paragraph matches how Standing Bear originally wrote it.

2. Look at the uses of punctuation from a journalistic reading and a storytelling reading. How would you categorize Standing Bear's piece, and why? How is punctuation used stylistically? Use specific examples from the readings and cite how specific rules governing punctuation were followed or not followed to achieve certain stylistic effects.

Charlie: *Peripheral Realist* and *Misty: Formal Expansionist*

Burton Silver and Heather Busch

Near the bottom of the copyright page of Why Cats Paint *reads the statement: "*Why Cats Paint *is a registered international experiment in inter-species morphic resonance and is designed to test the hypothesis of formative causation." At the top of the page reads the following quote by Einstein: "In order for something to be so, we first have to think it."*

Introduction You may have been exposed to this type of weighty verbiage in film criticism and art reviews. But you should enjoy this writing because it provides an excellent example of how words can allow you to take something absolutely seriously and get others to do so in the process—even if your seriousness is covering a great, big, fat joke. Or even if your seriousness is deadly serious. Many people take their pets very seriously. How seriously are you supposed to take this writing and why? What words give you clues?

CHARLIE

Peripheral Realist

When Charlie, (Charlie Erwin Schrödinger Jones), was six months old he was inadvertently shut inside a refrigerator for five hours. Somehow that event seems to have been a turning point in his life—transforming him virtually overnight into a prolific painter. Many human artists have attributed the sudden urge to express themselves artistically to an emotionally shattering event in their early lives. Both Van Gogh and Picasso suffered pre-pubescent claustrophobic traumas, and it seems possible that Charlie became totally

The Wild Side, 1991. Acrylic on enamel, 63 x 101 cm. Collection of the artist. Cats use their peripheral vision far more than we realize. This is why they will suddenly look intently in one direction when there seems to us to be nothing there at all. What they are doing of course, is using their more color and movement specific peripheral vision to study objects looking sideways at them. (You can tell which side by noting the direction of the tail tip—it points in the opposite direction to the side of vision). Charlie has just completed an impressionistic work in which the dishtowel appears as a major motif, and he can be seen checking his subject peripherally.

fixated with painting on the refrigerator after being 'punished' by it, in the same way as Picasso's early experience may have been responsible for what Robert Hughes has described as " . . . the intensity with which he could project his fear of women . . ."[1] In both cases, their work seems more of an exercise designed to explore, and thereby come to terms with, the object of their disaffection, rather than to celebrate its existence. Of course, their paintings may express a degree of triumphal ascendancy on occasions, but if this suggests celebration, it applies to the successful subjugation of the object rather than to the object itself.

This is not to say that much of Charlie's work fails to consider other objects or states, any more than one would suggest Picasso deals exclusively with subjects that stir his misogynistic tendencies. But we must recognize the fact that, whatever Charlie chooses to paint, he paints it on the refrigerator—the cause of his trauma. One suggestion is that he may simply prefer its smooth surface because it suits his technique, but there are other smooth surfaces, such as the dishwasher and kitchen cupboards to choose from. Another possibility, put forward by psychologist Lyn Ng of the Animal Esthetics Department at Stanford, is that he is marking the refrigerator as a way of asking to be fed. However, Charlie's food is kept in the refrigerator in the cellar, besides which, he meows very loudly when he is hungry.

By painting on the refrigerator, Charlie is most likely doing one of two things. Firstly, he could be trying to change the physical appearance of the original trauma object (which he is forced to live with), thus disguising it and rendering it less powerful, in much the same way as Picasso applied cubist abstractions to female nudes for similar reasons. Alternately, he could be attempting to 'move' the offending trauma object by painting a motif from another part of the room onto it and then, by looking at it peripherally, make it appear to move suddenly into relation to the original position of the motif. Either way, he is able to gain power over it, which must surely be why he paints it.

MISTY

Formal Expansionist

Misty's popularity as a painter is due mainly to the figurative nature of her images. The elegant, bi-colored forms that sometimes extend up to ten meters in length, are immediately evocative and invite a

---

[1]Hughes, Robert. *The Shock of the New*. London, Thames & Hudson, 1991.

wide range of projective interpretations. In a recent work, *A Little Lavish Leaping* the surface is heavily built up with short black verticals to produce an elongated curvilinear mass that is at once dense yet strongly nuanced with movement. Tension gathers at the base and builds upwards, flowing to a release (or is it a curtailment?) in the upper ovoidal form. What is so exciting about a work like this, apart from the obvious technical excellence, is its strength of imagery which, when combined with contextual uncertainty, encourages a high degree of varying interpretation.

For example, the cat's owner, Zenia Woolf, feels that the work concerns an incident in which her four-year-old son deliberately squirted Misty with the hose from the balcony. To her, each pink area describes the typical arched body of a cat as it leaps to avoid danger while the long black shape clearly represents the water

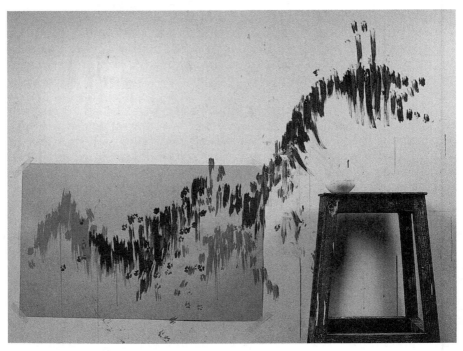

A Little Lavish Leaping, 1993. Acrylic on card and wall. 120 x170 cm. Preserved *in situ* North York, Toronto. Misty's paintings are greatly valued for their strong yet ambiguous imagery which, combined with contextual uncertainty, allow for a great richness of interpretation. The power of this sort of cat art lies in its very incomprehensibility which enables it to provoke and intrigue.

snaking down from above and following the cat after its first strike, to hit it again—now more heavy and wet. Woolf feels sure the cat knew the work could not be understood if left within the confines of the canvas and when Misty was unable to mark higher than she could leap, meowed insistently for the stool to be moved so that she could complete the work. To her owner, the purpose of the cat's painting was to depict the distressing incident as clearly as she could in the hope that the owner would constrain the child from torturing her again in the future.

However, Michael Dover of the Orion Art Gallery in North York, who titled the work, has a different interpretation. He feels that it is too easy to find traumatic incidents in a cat's recent experience and use them as a context within which to interpret its art. For example, he correctly points out that Misty travelled in the Woolf's car to visit friends in Port Credit just a week before the painting was completed. On the return journey the son pulled her tail and was scratched on the wrist. Should we, he wonders, be interested in the fact that the form of the work almost perfectly describes that fifteen-mile stretch of coastline between Port Credit and Toronto, finishing with the shape of Center Island? Certainly, cats have a remarkable sense of direction but Misty wouldn't know that bird's-eye view unless she'd flown over it or had a long discussion with a local hawk!

Dover prefers to tackle the work from a more useful, functional standpoint and feels that it clearly describes some important aspects of feline leaping strategy. The curved black lines describe the path of the leap itself. It begins with the crouched form of the cat ready to spring in the upper right quadrant and follows it down to the pink impact-position below, from which it leaps again, to land with out-stretched paws, in the next position.

Local art critic Emma Way agrees, but insists the cat is leaping in the other direction and that the pink areas describe the crucial spring-off points which dictate the success of the leap. Others have seen a dinosaur galloping to the right and there are those who favor a squirrel jumping down to the left. In the end we can never be sure just what Misty intended. The important thing is that we don't stop trying to understand.

WORDS TO KNOW

NOTE: When you write the definitions of the following words, make it a point to use at least three of them in conversation over the next day and three of them in your next writing assignment. Many times you'll find it difficult or impossible to use them in everyday speech or writing. What then is the point of defining them? Of learning them? At the very least, in all the following cases where you have unusual vocabulary terms to define, attempt to use them. How does attempting to use vocabulary that feels awkward or different change your view of your common speech and writing patterns? Learning how to use new vocabulary means just that—using the words. Write specifically how, where, when, and why you used the words and discuss with your class.

> prepubescent—
> claustrophobic—
> disaffection—
> ascendancy—
> subjugation—
> misogynistic—
> spontaneity—
> motif—
> elongated—
> curvilinear—
> curtailment—

QUESTIONS

Think about how this reading challenges your notions of art and who can make art. Again, from where do your definitions originate? How seriously are we meant to take this text and why? Create a series of Three-Layered Questions based on this reading which also incorporate one reading each from each of the other segments in this anthology.

WRITING ACTIVITIES

1. Select one of your Three-Layered Questions and exchange that question with a classmate for one of his or her questions on which to write.
2. Write on that question for five to ten minutes without stopping.

3. Transfer your longhand writing onto a computer (if you wrote in longhand).

4. Cut and paste different parts of your writing into a different order from what you see to be the original, traditional, and/or appropriate beginning, middle, and end.

5. How do you like your new version? What makes the inversion jumble in the order of your sentences, your paragraphs right or wrong? Appropriate or not appropriate? Why?

6. Exchange what you wrote aloud with the rest of your classmates. Even try reading what you wrote in backwards order. What works even better than it did in forwards order and why?

GRAMMAR AND STYLE QUESTIONS

1. Compare and contrast this reading with the segments from "Art on the Edge of Fashion." What specific choices in grammatical construction do the authors make and how do the authors use these choices to serve their literary purposes? Compare and contrast their choices. Use specific rules of grammar and details from the readings in your answer.

2. Using a standard grammar reference (i.e. Strunk and White's *Elements of Style*), find three exceptions (from any of the readings in this reader including this segment from *Why Cats Paint*) to any of the grammar and style rules such a standard reference has created, and discuss why your selected authors broke those rules.

Courtly Vision

Bharati Mukherjee

Born and educated in Calcutta, Mukerjee is part of the new wave of modern women writers charging onto the battlegrounds of the literary world. She has won Guggenheim, National Endowment for the Arts, and Woodrow Wilson fellowships.

Introduction Bharati Mukerjee's piece is a short-short story. Her language is descriptive and filled with images and detail. What makes her use of art terms and visuals different than that of the authors of *Why Cats Paint* (the previous reading)? How seriously are you supposed to take her descriptions? How do you know?

Jahanara Begum stands behind a marble grille in her palace at Fatchpur-Sikri.

Count Barthelmy, an adventurer from beyond frozen oceans, crouches in a lust-darkened arbor. His chest—a tear-shaped fleck of rust—lifts away from the gray, flat trunk of a mango tree. He is swathed in the coarse, quaint clothes of his cool-weather country. Jacket, pantaloons, shawl, swell and cave in ardent pleats. He holds a peacock's feather to his lips. His face is colored in admonitory pink. The feather is dusty aqua, broken-spined. His white-gloved hand pillows a likeness of the Begum, painted on a grain of rice by Basawan, the prized court artist. Two red-eyed parrots gouge the patina of grass at the adventurer's feet; their buoyant, fluffy breasts caricature the breasts of Moghul virgins. The Count is posed full-front; the self-worshipful body of a man who has tamed thirteen rivers and seven seas. Dainty thighs bulge with wayward expectancy. The head twists savagely upward at an angle unreckoned except in death, anywhere but here. In profile the lone prismatic eye betrays the madman and insomniac.

On the terrace of Jahanara Begum's palace, a slave girl kneels; her forearms, starry with jewels, strain toward the fluted handle of a decanter. Two bored eunuchs squat on their fleshy haunches, awaiting their wine. Her simple subservience hints at malevolent dreams, of snake venom rubbed into the wine cups or daggers concealed between young breasts, and the eunuchs are menaced, their faces pendulous with premonition.

In her capacious chamber the Begum waits, perhaps for death from the serving-girl, for ravishing, or merely the curtain of fire from the setting sun. The chamber is open on two sides, the desert breeze stiffens her veil into a gauzy disc. A wild peacock, its fanned-out feathers beaten back by the same breeze, cringes on the bit of marble floor visible behind her head. Around the Begum, retainers conduct their inefficient chores. One, her pursed navel bare, slackens her grip on a *morchal* of plumes; another stumbles, biceps clenched, under the burden of a gold hookah bowl studded with translucent rubies and emeralds; a third stoops, her back an eerie, writhing arc, to straighten a low table littered with cosmetics in jewelled pillboxes. The Begum is a tall, rigid figure as she stands behind a marble grille. From her fists, which she holds in front of her like tiny shields, sprouts a closed, upright lotus bloom. Her gaze slips upward, past the drunken gamblers on the roof-terraces, to the skyline where fugitive cranes pass behind a blue cloud.

Oh, beauteous and beguiling Begum, has your slave-girl apprised the Count of the consequences of a night of bliss?

Under Jahanara Begum's window, in a courtyard cooled with fountains into whose basin slaves have scattered rose petals, sit Fathers Aquaviva and Henriques, ingenuous Portuguese priests. They have dogged the emperor through inclement scenery. Now they pause in the emperor's famed, new capital, eyes closed, abstemious hands held like ledges over their brows to divert the sullen desert breeze. Their faces seem porous; the late afternoon has slipped through the skin and distended the chins and cheeks. Before their blank, radiant gazes, seven itinerant jugglers heap themselves into a shuddering pyramid. A courtier sits with the priests on a divan covered with brocaded silk. He too is blind to the courage of gymnasts. He is distracted by the wondrous paintings the priests have spread out on the arabesques of the rug at their feet. Mother and Child. Child and Mother. The Moghul courtier—child of Islam, ruler of Hindus—finds the motif repetitive. What comforting failure of the imagination these priests are offering. What precarious boundaries set on life's playful fecundity. He hears the Fathers murmur. They are devising stratagems on a minor scale. They want to trick the emperor into kissing Christ, who on each huge somber canvas is a bright, white, healthy baby. The giant figures seem to him simple and innocuous, not complicated and infuriating like the Hindu icons hidden in the hills. In the meantime his eyes draw comfort from the unclad angels who watch over the Madonna to protect her from heathens like him. Soft-fleshed, flying women. He will order the court artists to paint him a harem of winged women on a single poppy seed.

The emperor will not kiss Christ tonight. He is at the head of his army, riding a piebald horse out of his new walled city. He occupies the foreground of that agate-colored paper, a handsome young man in a sun-yellow *jama* Under the *jama* his shoulders pulsate to the canny violent rhythm of his mount. Behind him in a thick choking diagonal stream follow his soldiers. They scramble and spill on the sandy terrain; spiky desert grass slashes their jaunty uniforms of muslin. Tiny, exhilarated profiles crowd the battlements. In the women's palace, tinier figures flit from patterned window grille, to grille. The citizens have begun to celebrate. Grandfathers leading children by the wrists are singing of the emperor's victories over invisible rebels. Shopkeepers, coy behind their taut paunches, give away their syrupy sweets. Even the mystics with their haggard, numinous faces have allowed themselves to be distracted by yet another parade.

So the confident emperor departs.

The Moghul evening into which he drags his men with the promise of unimaginable satisfactions is grayish gold with the late afternoon, winter light. It spills down the rims of stylized rocks that clog the high horizon. The light is charged with unusual excitement and it discovers the immense intimacy of darkness, the erotic shadowiness of the cave-deep arbor in which the Count crouches and waits. The foliage of the mango tree yields sudden, bountiful shapes. Excessive, unruly life—monkeys, serpents, herons, thieves naked to the waist—bloom and burgeon on its branches. The thieves, their torsos pushing through clusters of leaves, run rapacious fingers on their dagger blades.

They do not discern the Count. The Count does not overhear the priests. Adventurers all, they guard from each other the common courtesy of their subterfuge. They sniff the desert air and the air seems full of portents. In the remote horizon three guards impale three calm, emaciated men. Behind the low wall of a *namaz* platform, two courtiers quarrel, while a small boy sneaks up and unties their horses. A line of stealthy women prostrate themselves and pray at the doorway of a temple in a patch of browning foliage. Over all these details floats three elegant whorls of cloud, whorls in the manner of Chinese painting, imitated diligently by men who long for rain.

The emperor leaves his capital, applauded by flatterers and loyal citizens. Just before riding off the tablet's edge into enemy territory, he twists back on his saddle and shouts a last-minute confidence to his favorite court-painter. He is caught in reflective profile, the quarter-arc of his mustache suggests a man who had permitted his second thoughts to confirm his spontaneous judgments.

Give me total vision, commands the emperor. His voice hisses above the hoarse calls of the camels. *You, Basawan, who can paint my Begum on a grain of rice, see what you can do with the infinite vistas the size of my opened hand. Hide nothing from me, my co-wanderer. Tell me how my new capital will fail, will turn to dust and these marbled terraces be home to jackals and infidels. Tell me who to fear and who to kill but tell it to me in a way that makes me smile. Transport me through dense fort walls and stone grilles and into the hearts of men.*

> "Emperor on Horseback Leaves Walled City"
> Painting on Paper, 24 cms x 25.8 cms
> Painter Unknown. No superscription
> c. 1584 A.D.
> Lot No. SLM 4027-66
> Est. Price $750

WORDS TO KNOW

NOTE: When you write the definitions of the following words, make it a point to use at least three of them in conversation over the next day and three of them in your next writing assignment. Many times you'll find it difficult or impossible to use them in everyday speech or writing. What then is the point of defining them? Of learning them? At the very least, in all the following cases where you have unusual vocabulary terms to define, attempt to use them. How does attempting to use vocabulary that feels awkward or different change your view of your common speech and writing patterns? Learning how to use new vocabulary means just that—using the words. Write specifically how, where, when, and why you used the words and discuss with your class.

grille—
Fatehpur-Sikri—
arbor—
pantaloons—
ardent—
admonitory—
Begum—
Basawan—
gouge—
patina—
caricature—
Moghul—
prismatic—
insomniac—
terrace—
decanter—
subservience—
malevolence—
menaced—
pendulous—
premonition—
capacious—
morchal—
hookah—
translucent—
beguiling—
inclement—
abstemious—
porous—
itinerant—
arabesques—
precarious—
strategems—
innocuous—
rapacious—
subterfuge—
namaz—

QUESTIONS

List all the things you see this story to be about and why. What is the power of art? What forms does art take? Keeping in mind your art-related writings that you did in the previous segment of this anthology, create a set of Three-Layered Questions that involve this reading and those other art-related readings. Shape your questions around an image, a picture, a person, any source that does not include words.

WRITING ACTIVITIES

1. Choose one of your Three-Layered Questions and answer it using as much specific detail as you possibly can—only reveal your main idea through the details themselves.
2. Now answer that same question only use words that are as general, vague, abstract as possible. Make sure that you tell, not show, your main idea. Which version works best for you, and why?
3. Exchange your two writings with your class. What differences do they notice? How do those differences compare and contrast to the differences that you notice?
4. Limit yourself to a page for either writing. Then limit yourself to a paragraph. Finally, limit yourself to a sentence. Which works best? Which was hardest? Why?

GRAMMAR AND STYLE QUESTIONS

1. Look at "exotic" punctuation (e.g., dashes, parentheses, exclamation points) as well as any unusual word choices and/or style markers (e.g., italics, boldface type) within any of the readings in this book (including "Courtly Vision,") and discuss what effect the authors' use of these kinds of punctuation has on the reader. What does the use of grammar and style tell you about the written word as opposed to the spoken word?
2. One of the most difficult tasks for any new writer is to express time and timelines consistently and to match actions to those times and timelines. Take a paragraph from "Courtly Vision" that has a strong sense of either past, present, or future tense, and rewrite it using a different verb tense (i.e., if it was written in the present tense, rewrite it in the past tense, and so forth). What is the effect of such a change? Were you consistent in your new selection of verb tense in your revision? And, if you had difficulty with consistency, without referring back to the text, restore the original tense and see how closely the paragraph matches how the author originally wrote it.

Miss Snake Charmer Queen/ The Rattlesnake Round-Up

Beverly Stoeltje

Whether the competition is for the title of Miss Universe or the Crooked Tree Cashew Queen, these contests showcase values, concepts, and behavior that exist at the center of a group's sense of itself and exhibit values of morality, gender, and place. We live in a world where everyone seems to be watching satellite television and drinking Coke; it is also a world where making, claiming, and maintaining local identity and culture is increasingly important. The beauty contest stage is where these identities and cultures can be—and frequently are—made public and visible.

—Collen Ballerino Cohen, Richard Wilk, and Beverly Stoeltje

Introduction Beverly Stoeltje is an academic writer and researcher, which is apparent in her scientific manner of taking apart and analyzing a pop culture event—the Rattlesnake Round-Up Beauty Contest. She uses symbolic analysis of seemingly ordinary or trivial events. Additionally, she uses quotation marks for a particular purpose—can you tell what that is?

MISS SNAKE CHARMER QUEEN/ THE RATTLESNAKE ROUND-UP

From the beginning we should be aware that this event is embedded in the Rattlesnake Round-Up, a local community festival occurring annually in February. Every annual celebration has a stated purpose and a specific symbol (Stoeltje 1992). The rattlesnake serves that function in Sweetwater, a small town located in northwest Texas where the residents are engaged in agriculture and small business. The Round-Up is organized by the Jaycees of Sweetwater, the local chapter of the nation-wide organization of young business-men. Many of the Jaycees grow beards or mustaches for the Round-Up and wear cowboy hats, jeans, boots, and red vests decorated with a rattlesnake image during the event. One of their activities is guiding out-of-town visitors, some of whom are wealthy tourists, on rattlesnake hunts. At some point prior to the Round-Up all of the contestants in the beauty pageant are taken out on a hunt together.

The Round-Up gathers thousands of snakes together in the City Auditorium for viewing, milking, butchering, and eating. When the Round-Up begins, the snakes are brought to the City Auditorium and placed in "pits," circular bins constructed with waist-high solid fences that permit easy viewing. The live snakes maintain a constant, low-level buzz with their rattles and a stench that no amount of "air-freshener" can affect. Throughout the day the Jaycees organize demonstrations in which the venom is "milked" from snakes, snakes are "handled," and snakes are skinned, butchered, cooked, and eaten. Snake products for sale include belts, hat bands, wallets, belt buckles, paper weights and translucent toilet seats with fangs inside them.

Whether one associates snakes with the serpent of the Garden of Eden, bearing knowledge and connoting evil, or with the phallic symbolism so pervasive in popular culture, or with the murky unconscious, snakes reverberate with symbolic messages suggesting the power and danger of sexuality. The concentration of so many rattlesnakes inside a single building and the "handling" and "milking" demonstrations, in which a man holds a snake between his legs and squeezes venom out of the snake's mouth with his hands, creates an atmosphere saturated with sexual potency and subtle messages of danger represented by the rattlesnake's venom.

Male and female symbolism come together when the winner of the Miss Snake Charmer contest enters the pit to "handle" a rattlesnake. The rules of the Miss Snake Charmer pageant require that the Queen must go to the Round-Up where the rattlesnakes are gathered together, enter "the pit" with the rattlesnakes and demonstrate for the crowd that she can handle a rattlesnake. A dramatic contrast to the queen on the pageant stage, the queen in the rattlesnake pit must confront the challenge of the snake in her hand.

WORDS TO KNOW

NOTE: When you write the definitions of the following words, make it a point to use at least three of them in conversation over the next day and three of them in your next writing assignment. Many times you'll find it difficult or impossible to use them in everyday speech or writing. What then is the point of defining them? Of learning them? At the very least, in all the following cases where you have unusual vocabulary terms to define, attempt to use them. How does attempting to use vocabulary that feels awkward or different change your view of your common speech and writing patterns? Learning how to use new vocabulary means just that—using the words. Write specifically how, where, when, and why you used the words and discuss with your class

Jaycees—
phallic—
murky—
saturated—

QUESTIONS

Analyze and comment on the introductory statement that precedes this reading. What, if any, interaction have you had with a beauty contest? What specific images do you remember from beauty contests that you've seen? How do you envision the contest you've just read about? Create a series of Three-Layered Questions which incorporate any of the earlier readings with this one.

WRITING ACTIVITIES

1. Gather a series of beauty contest images, either from a magazine, newspaper, or film/video clip. You may even want to tape something off the news or a pageant show.
2. Find a way to incorporate what you've gathered for image sources into your question and revise the question.
3. Write at least a page on that question, using specific detail and creating an attention-getting introduction and an even more attention-getting conclusion.
4. Find a print source and take a one-phrase–one-sentence quote from that source to include somewhere in your paper.

5. How do your sources affect the tone of your paper?
6. How many people, when you shared your readings aloud, took a stand for or against beauty contests? Why? Were you one of them? Why?

GRAMMAR AND STYLE QUESTIONS

1. One of the best ways to learn grammar, in addition to learning the names and rules of grammatical elements, is to read other people's writing. Take a grammatically imperfect piece of your own work, read two or three readings from this reader (including this piece by Stoeltje), and rewrite your piece afterwards. Is it grammatically better? Why or why not? What was the impact of seeing how other people put together words?
2. An important element of good usage is the concise and active expression of thoughts and ideas. Looking through any three readings, including Stoeltje's, find concise, active, grammatical expressions, put them into your own words, and see how you can make them still more concise.

Our People Say . . .

African Proverbs

Proverbs pack layers of cultural and social meaning and context into a short sentence or phrase. They also let you know whether you are part of a particular group or not.

Introduction Proverbs are nearly always a sentence long (with certain exceptions). Do fewer words mean there's less meaning? How do you tell how much a phrase or a sentence is communicating and whether you need to say more? What parts of these proverbs indicate their cultural origin?

Proverbs are central to African culture and tradition. A good African proverb will make you smile and nod your head in appreciation. It may even make you laugh out loud. It will definitely make you think. A proverb is never explained to the listener. If you can't understand it, it is time for you to spend some time listening to the elders in your village. If you have forgotten where your village is, then remember this—"the disobedient fowl obeys in a pot of soup."

We invite you to enjoy those that follow and to contribute to this growing archive.

In time we will set up a form to make it easy for you to add to this list but for now please email your favorite proverbs to *africa@pobox.com.*

- The disobedient fowl obeys in a pot of soup (Benin–Nigeria).
- The crocodile does not die under the water so that we can call the monkey to celebrate its funeral (Akan).
- When two elephants fight it is the grass that suffers (Uganda).
- The frog does not jump in the daytime without reason (Nigeria).

- One goat cannot carry another goat's tail (Nigeria).
- The family is like the forest, if you are outside it is dense, if you are inside you see that each tree has its own position (Akan).
- It is the woman whose child has been eaten by a witch who best knows the evils of witchcraft (Nigeria).
- The hunter does not rub himself in oil and lie by the fire to sleep (Nigeria).
- The hunter in pursuit of an elephant does not stop to throw stones at birds (Uganda).
- If all seeds that fall were to grow, then no one could follow the path under the trees (Akan).
- Even the mightiest eagle comes down to the tree tops to rest (Uganda).
- A tiger does not have to proclaim its tigritude (Wole Soyinka-Nigeria).
- Before you ask a man for clothes, look at the clothes that he is wearing (Yoruba, Nigeria).
- As long as there are lice in the seams of the garment there must be bloodstains on the fingernails (Yoruba, Nigeria).
- If a blind man says lets throw stones, be assured that he has stepped on one (Hausa, Nigeria).
- Until lions have their own historians, tales of the hunt shall always glorify the hunter (Igbo, Nigeria).
- When you are eating with the devil, you must use a long spoon (Igbo, Nigeria).
- The fowl digs out the blade that kills it (Somali).
- Although the snake does not fly it has caught the bird whose home is in the sky (Akan).
- One should never rub bottoms with a porcupine (Akan).
- Fowls will not spare a cockroach that falls in their midst (Akan).
- You do not need a big stick to break a cock's head (Akan).
- Marriage is like a groundnut, you have to crack them to see what is inside (Akan).
- The rain wets the leopard's spots but does not wash them off (Akan).
- If crocodiles eat their own eggs what would they do to the flesh of a frog (Nigeria).
- A man does not wander far from where his corn is roasting (Nigeria).
- Rat no dey born rabbit (Nigeria).
- When man pikin dey piss, him dey hold something for hand. Women wey try-am, go piss for her hand (Palmwine Drinkards, Nigeria).
- Those who get to the river early drink the cleanest water (Kenya).
- Hurry hurry has no blessings (Kenya).

- A person changing his clothing always hides while changing (Kenya).
- A donkey always says thank you with a kick (Kenya).
- Nobody gathers firewood to roast a thin goat (Kenya).
- Having a good discussion is like having riches (Kenya).
- Many births mean many burials (Kenya).
- The important things are left in the locker (Kenya).
- A boy isn't sent to collect the honey (Kenya).
- If you don't wish to have rags for clothes, don't play with a dog (Nigeria).
- No sane person sharpens his machete to cut a banana tree (Nigeria).
- If a monkey is amongst dogs, why won't it start barking? (Nigeria).
- An elephant's tasks are never too heavy for it (Zimbabwe).
- It is the soil that knows that the mouse's baby is ill (Zimbabwe).
- A man who doesn't know his or her family is like a lion wounded while trying to make a kill for lunch (B. Audifferen).
- If you can walk, you can dance; If you can talk, you can sing.
- Greed loses what it has gained.

WORDS TO KNOW

NOTE: When you write the definitions of the following words, make it a point to use at least three of them in conversation over the next day and three of them in your next writing assignment. Many times you'll find it difficult or impossible to use them in everyday speech or writing. What then is the point of defining them? Of learning them? At the very least, in all the following cases where you have unusual vocabulary terms to define, attempt to use them. How does attempting to use vocabulary that feels awkward or different change your view of your common speech and writing patterns? Learning how to use new vocabulary means just that—using the words. Write specifically how, where, when, and why you used the words and discuss with your class.

Benin—
Nigeria—
Uganda—
Akan—

tigritude—
Wole Soyinka—
Yoruba—
Hausa—
Igbo—
pikin—
dey—
wey—
try-am—
Palmwine Drinkards—
Kenya—
Zimbabwe—
B. Audifferen—

QUESTIONS

Make a list of common things that appear and/or occur in a number of the proverbs. Gather a collection of other proverbs from other places, and make the same list. Which specifics do you find in both lists? Where do they differ and why? Create a series of Three-Layered Questions based on this collection of proverbs.

WRITING ACTIVITIES

1. Choose one of your Three-Layered Questions on which to write. Decide what point you want to make about it. Write for five to ten minutes as you normally would, making sure you have a beginning, a middle, and an end to your piece. Use specific details and one outside source to add specifics.
2. Rewrite your piece using the same point, only this time you can only use proverbs to write your piece and elaborate your point. Every sentence must be a proverb in this writing.
3. What was the challenge in the writing? In the thinking involved? Be specific.
4. Share your two writings with your class. What is their response and why?

GRAMMAR AND STYLE QUESTIONS

1. Part of good grammatical usage is the concise and active expression of thoughts and ideas. Looking through this list of proverbs, find concise, active, grammatical expressions, put them into your own words, and see how you can make them still more concise. If you can't, explain why you can't condense the expressions.

2. Now take wordy, general expressions from your own writing that you've done based on this list of proverbs and revise them to make them concise, active expressions that are grammatically correct. How does the brevity of the proverbs help you to make your own writing more effectively brief?

Color Therapy by Deandra

Lisa Jones

Yale and NYU graduate Lisa Jones opens Bulletproof Diva *by saying:*

> *"This is a book of tales.*
> *"It may be the ravings of a madwoman who loved having her hands in other people's hair, and who should have gone to beauty culture school and owned a wig shop like her great-aunt, or moonlighted as a barber like her grandfather, but by happenstance became a writer."*

A friend of and co-author with Spike Lee, Jones lives in Brooklyn and writes for the Village Voice. Her radio and stage plays have been produced nationally.

Introduction Lisa Jones' writing reveals a great deal about her as a person. She uses personal narrative and journalistic techniques as well as academic expositional writing akin to what you would find in a traditional essay. The effect of her combination of techniques is to make you feel part of a conversation taking place in someone's kitchen or porch. While this is entertaining, do you "learn" anything? Explain. Do you "need" to learn anything? Why?

Love, peace, and hair grease, this is Deandra, coming to you live from Minnesota. What do you mean you don't know where Minnesota is? Get out your map, I'm talking Midwest and then some. Malls, snowblowers, jumbo thruways, a Lutheran church on every corner. Don't talk to me about sixty-below wind chill factors and hail the size of deer turds. I will tell you one thing. Hell is *not* about fire.

You know my best friend, Miss Columnist? She's here for nine months to explore the kinder, gentler America, where they don't run folks out of the neighborhood with baseball bats, they just burn a cross on your lawn—your private property—and call it free speech.

Girlfriend asked me to do the column this month, being that she's wrapped up in a severe case of culture shock. It started on the plane with the announcement of connecting flights to Dubuque (where they burn lots of crosses) and Milwaukee (where they eat lots of blacks). Never mind she was on her way to that happening, politically progressive town, Minneapolis, home of the Save the Earth movement and the purple Prince. What if she wandered into some Aryan Nation booby trap? What if Nazi yuppies chanting WELFARE SCUM! ate her for lunch? Poor diva hasn't left the house in two weeks and I'm nothing but an errand girl: Buy me Tampax, buy me blue corn chips, buy me *Essence* magazine.

Now girlfriend is picking up creepy vibes from the wheat field—theme Contact paper in the kitchen, the liver-colored tile in the john, the gerbil-beige carpet in the living room. The color scheme, she's convinced, is sending her subliminal white-supremacist messages. She yells, why didn't I pack her Nelson Mandela and Frida Kahlo T-shirts? She threatens to hang herself with the shower curtain if she doesn't see someone wearing faux kente cloth in the next forty-eight hours. Get to the couch, I tell girlfriend, it's time for color therapy by Deandra.

We begin slowly. I have her read aloud passages from Jean E. Patton's *Color to Color: The Black Woman's Guide to a Rainbow of Fashion and Beauty,* published this year. *Color to Color* is "Afrocentric color analysis" that brings racial uplift work to the closet and makeup counter. Patton claims Charleszine Wood Spears and Ella Mae Washington as godmamas in the struggle. Spears and Washington were African-American home economists who, as early as the 1940s, self-published manuals on selecting colors for skin-tone enhancement. Like "bad hair," Patton preaches, there is no such animal as "bad color." Purge your psyche of old race tales about hussy red and other "loud" hues that call attention to lusciously endowed Negro bodies. Don't take refuge from the hard eye of status quo aesthetics in muddy colors that "recede" you into the background.

Too hip for the "four seasons" approach, Patton arranges black folks in four "palettes" drawn from the diaspora and ancestral cradle. (Miss Columnist, you take the "spice" palette, which makes your celebrity models Tina Turner and Malcolm X.) Skin color variations are christened with references to sensual fabrics and high-caloric foods. And that enduring affliction of being "color struck," the preference for or hatred of complexions dark or light? Patton gives it joyous, new meaning just in time for Kwanzaa. Revel in the rainbow, *struck by color,* praise the Lord! Ssshh! says girlfriend, can't you hear the wallpaper whisper, "white power"?

I try the historical approach. We discuss culture and color research. The "color revolution" of the 1960s (psychedelics, anything-
goes brights, the sophistication of monotone black or white) wasn't
spontaneous generation but the by-product of nothing less than
global political upheaval—the surge of youth culture, feminism,
African independence. Before this, the Euro-American tableau had
shunned colors associated with darker-skinned peoples (the African
indigos, the hot Spanish reds), with a few departures, except as costumes. The enduring symbolism of evil, menacing "black" and innocent, clean "white" has its roots in nineteenth-century Europe's scientific racism. The "blackness" of Africans was seen as a
disturbance of nature. (Were babies born black, French anthropolo-
gists who traveled to West Africa in the early nineteenth century
wanted to know, or did they turn that color from too much sun or
being kept in smoky huts?)

Color theorists in the seventies were quick to conclude that
using "black" as a racial identifier would only hinder the social acceptance of people of African descent. Patton jumps on this in *Color
to Color*, asking, what makes black-as-negative so fixed when the
"values" of color change? Black, featured boldly in many flags of
Africa and revered there as a symbol of power, health, and strength,
has been in transition on Euro-American turf since the color revolution. By the eighties, Real Men Wore Black: It was out of mourning,
it was "daytime." And though in clothing and design "all-black" is
getting kinda tired, what's it being replaced by? High-energy color.
Diaspora color! Girlfriend's still distracted. She throws every white
towel, every curtain, every sheet into the middle of the room and
yells, WESTERN, CHRISTIAN VALUES; EUROPEAN HERITAGE!

I walk girlfriend back to a chair and dump a pile of magazines
and CDs on her lap. Look, I tell her. As they dominate the pop eye,
isn't it arresting, inspiring, titillating to see young African Americans
shake up colors—their iconography, their appeal? How these musicians, actors, and models saturate the cultural canvas with a prism
of skin tones and the way they wear and present colors—Queen Lati-
fah in warm pumpkin crowns, Arsenio in cobalt-blue suits, Living
Colour, the band, throwing paint like Pollock, its Brit spelling shouting out to diaspora blacks: We are living, we are everywhere, we look
good in fuchsia.

Girlfriend throws the magazines on the floor. She misses
Brooklyn. She misses sisters in tangerine lipstick, stoops in Park
Slope painted red, black, and green, nose rings, Isaac's purple high
tops, faux kente shoulder bags, baby jumpers, evening wear, and
place mats.

I give her a new box of Crayola crayons. Listen to this: In the eighty-eight-year history of Crayola, only two colors have ever had their names changed. One was "flesh," which became "peach" in 1962, "a result of the civil rights movement," says the official company fact sheet. (The color "indian red," lowercase to keep it consistent with other crayon names, still remains in the line.) Crayola has been spurred on by American teachers to test-market a "Skin Tones of the World" collection. You'll love the sticker on the pack: "A multicultural assortment . . . plus black and white for blending." Go ahead, I tell girlfriend, draw Brooklyn. She pouts.

Come on, you need a walk. We battle snow in search of cappuccino. We pass buses, billboards. Hey, isn't this a trip, we're in a state with a tiny, 6 percent population "of color," but all the outdoor ads we've seen feature black people: The Virginia Slims Afro-chic model in electric-blue kufi, Oprah in a different color low-cut sweater for each day her show airs, Joey Browner of the Minnesota Vikings in an ad for Zubaz workout wear uses a globe for a footrest. What does it mean? I'll tell you what it means, girlfriend snarls, they don't lynch Negroes here, they just put our faces on pancake mix. Obviously, I tell her, this color therapy stuff isn't doing you any good, maybe you're just PMSing. She sucks teeth: You have twenty-four hours to find faux kente.

In the coffee shop we meet a young man who says things like "my beautiful Nubian princess" and has, thank God, his very own faux-kente kufi. Walking home, Miss Columnist buys the latest *Ebony Man* with chocolate cover boy Wesley Snipes in, all at once, magenta pants, a goldenrod-and-hot-pink vest, and persimmon blazer. She tacks it above her computer.

I think she's gonna make it after all.

WORDS TO KNOW

NOTE: When you write the definitions of the following words, make it a point to use at least three of them in conversation over the next day and three of them in your next writing assignment. Many times you'll find it difficult or impossible to use them in everyday speech or writing. What then is the point of defining them? Of learning them? At the very least, in all the following cases where you have unusual vocabulary terms to define, attempt to use them. How does attempting to use vocabulary that feels awkward or different change your view of your common speech and writing patterns? Learning how to use new vocabulary means just that—using the words. Write specifically how, where, when, and why you used the words and discuss with your class.

contact paper—
Nelson Mandela—
Frida Kahlo—
faux kente—
Jean E. Patton—
Charleszine Wood Spears—
Ella Mae Washington—
palettes—
Kwanzaa—
iconography—
Jackson Pollack—
Zubaz—
kufi—
persimmon—

QUESTIONS

Describe the voice you heard as you read this piece. Describe the colors you saw, heard, and felt. Be as detailed as you can in your description and pick out specific words, phrases, and passages in the reading that gave you your impression. Create a series of Three-Layered Questions related to this reading on which you would like to write.

WRITING ACTIVITIES

1. Choose one of your questions and write at least a page. Set it aside for at least a day after you have done so.
2. Revise the piece you wrote using only specific nouns, colors, objects, and active verbs. Do not use any pronouns, prepositions or prepositional phrases, or passive verbs. Consult your style handbook if you are confused or unsure of what these terms mean.
3. What do you see to be the difference in the two pieces in terms not only of which gets your point across, but which interests your class audience?

4. Review the vocabulary words you've learned thus far in this anthology. Notice how the words in each reading are reflective of that particular reading. Try rewriting your piece so that key words you use are, in fact, reflective of that particular piece of writing and the point you are trying to get across to your audience.

GRAMMAR AND STYLE QUESTIONS

1. Look at the uses of narrative punctuation from a journalist reading and a story-telling reading. How would you describe Jones' reading in comparison or contrast? How are certain kinds of punctuation (i.e. commas, quotation marks) used to create context? Use specific reading examples as well as specific grammar rules and details in your answer.
2. Compare and contrast a reading originally published on the Internet with this reading by Jones. Analyze these examples. What are some of the stylistic differences between the two readings? Use specific examples from the readings as well as specific rules of grammar in your answer.

The Symbol 'Taco Bell' or was Leonardo da Vinci Right Brain Dominant?

Allen Ross

How do we learn? How do we get messages? How many symbols bombard you in a day? How many of them do you recognize? How many of them have become unconscious?

Introduction Allen Ross's writing questions, analyzes, and examines data from pop culture icons to language. The effect of his examinations is to get you to think about what you see and how much you rely on what you think you see in order to make certain determinations. He also uses categorization and definition to show you when you're thinking on an unconscious level versus on a conscious one. Why might this distinction be important?

I would like to demonstrate a little exercise I learned in a Pacific Institute workshop on how the brain functions with the use of symbols. Read the sentence below and count the number of "f's." Give yourself 20 seconds.

FINISHED FILES ARE THE RESULT OF YEARS OF SCIENTIFIC STUDY COMBINED WITH THE EXPERIENCE OF MANY YEARS.

Normally, when someone finishes reading this sentence, they have counted three "f's." A few individuals can see four, five, or even six "f's." There are six "f's" in this sentence. They are located in "finished," "files," and "scientific," and the three "of's." Now go back and read through the sentence again to see if you can find the six "f's."

To explain what might be going on in this scenario: when I said to look for the symbol "f," right away in our minds we thought of the sound of "f" as in "finished," "files," "scientific." But in "of," the sound is not an "f;" it is a "v" sound. You look right at it and still can't see it because you're looking for the sound of "f." The first time I did this exercise, I could see only three "f's." When the instructor in one of my classes told us there were six "f's," I got angry with him, thinking he was playing a trick on us.

Later, when I was studying Jungian psychology, I found that when a person can admit his weakness, no matter what it is, that process is called individuation. If a person can admit they're a left-brain thinker and out of balance, that is known as the process of individuation. Jung said that the conscious coming to terms with the inner self generally starts with the ego being wounded and with the suffering that goes along with that pain.

Another example of individuation is when I had to come to terms with myself about being an alcoholic. I could not admit it for years, but once I conceded that I was an alcoholic, that was a wounding of my ego and I had to suffer the consequences. Individuation is the first step to transcendent function. Dr. Jung said that transcendent function is being whole or being in balance. If we can admit that the English language is a left-brain language and is out of balance, that's the process of individuation. There's nothing wrong with that.

Dr. William Boast stated that a more balanced approach to teaching reading was through the use of McGuffey's readers because the emphasis was on teaching sounds to groups of letters rather than to individual letters. As an example, the word "reader" is divided into two parts by McGuffey—as "read-er." The McGuffey's readers divided the word "eclectic" into three parts—"ec-lec-tic."

The Chinese language has an ideogramic structure. That means they use a symbol for a word or a whole thought. In a diagram taken from *Tao: The Watercourse Way* by Alan W. Watts and Chung Liang-Huang, the symbols on one side of the page are original symbols in Chinese; those on the other side are the English equivalents; the symbols in the middle of the page show the evolutionary development of the Chinese symbols. There is a symbol for "sheep" in the left-hand column. When you see this symbol, the first thing that comes to mind is "sheep," the animal. In the same column is the symbol "mountain." Immediately, a physical mountain comes to mind.

The English equivalents in the right-hand column look quite different. For example, the word "mountain" has eight symbols. The way the word is being taught is that each symbol has its own sound. When the child looks at the word, he sounds it out: MO "mow," UN - "mow-un," TA - "mow-un-ta," IN - "mow-un-ta-in,"—"mountain." By the time you figure out how to say the word mountain, you forgot what a mountain was! In an ideogramic language, when you see the symbol for mountain, you instantly know it's a mountain.

Today as I drive down the highway and look around, I notice all types of ideogramic symbols in our modern culture. When you see the symbol "Taco Bell," you know right away it's a place to eat Mexican food. The McDonald's arches let you know it's a place where you get the Big Mac. Sales people have been using ideogramic symbols to help sell their products for years and years. The media—TV, computers, videos—also use symbols to get their message across.

One of the most common ideogramic symbols is road signs. The symbol for stop, the red hexagon, is almost universal. When you see the symbol, you know it means to stop, whether you can read the words or not.

Author Alan Watts advocated the teaching of Chinese in secondary schools, not only because we must learn how to communicate with the Chinese, but also because of all high cultures in the world, theirs is most different from ours (American) in its ways of thinking. He stated that every culture is based on assumptions so taken for granted that they are barely conscious. It is only when we study these highly different cultures and languages that we become fully aware of them. I pondered what he was trying to say and wondered if his message was, "Do we need to take a look at other people in their culture and develop respect for them?"

Once again, I'd like to share a personal example in this area. My first marriage was to a Hopi woman. I didn't really think about it, but I assumed that Indians are Indians and that we ought to be able to get along. Yet Pat and I ended up fighting like cats and dogs. I remember my confusion at what was happening to me in not being able to put a finger on what I should do in these difficult situations. I decided to study the Hopis to get a better idea of how they thought. What I learned first was that the Hopis are matriarchal. The woman is the head of the clan. She owns the home, she owns the fields, and she owns the sheep.

I grew up with the Oglalas, who were patriarchs. A hunting culture, the man was the head of the societies. The more I studied my former wife's culture and her people, the more I learned about myself. I believe this is what Alan Watts was trying to say when he advocated learning Chinese. In the process of learning another culture, you learn just as much about yourself and how you are a part of your culture. I recognized this as another way of working with the process of individuation and as a step toward transcendent function.

Watts went on to say that standard European languages like English and French have sentences structured so that the verb must be set in motion by the noun, thereby presenting metaphysical problems as meaningless. He said that you cannot solve metaphysical problems by using standard European languages. In order to solve a metaphysical problem, one needs to meditate on that problem and allow the symbols of the unconscious to penetrate consciousness. Dr. Jung said that modern man needs to learn the language of the unconscious.

Japanese prepositional phrases are the opposite of English phrases. The sentence, "The book on the desk" becomes "desk upon book" in saying it the way a Japanese person would. In Japanese sentence structure, verbs come at the ends of sentences. Thinking about this, I recognized a similarity between the structures of Japanese and the Dakota/Lakota languages. A simple Lakota sentence is, "Tatanka wahanpi kagayo." Translated into English, it says, "Buffalo stew make." The verb comes last, at the end of the sentence. Verbs in the Dakota/Lakota language structures come at the end of the sentence. In the structure of English, the sentence would read, "Make the buffalo stew." English is backwards!

Many linguistics scholars have been impressed with the dominance of the verb in American Indian sentences and by the fact that the verb is more oriented to the object than to the subject. This leads one to assume that the American Indian is more interested in the result than in the cause. It appears that people who are oriented toward the cause of an event would be more left-brain-dominant, and those interested in results would have more of a right-brain-dominance.

Was Leonardo da Vinci right-brain dominant? He was five hundred years ahead of his time in his accomplishments and inventions. He was a painter, a sculptor, a mathematician, and an astronomer. He designed aircraft, parachutes, and self-propelled wheeled vehicles. In reviewing a page from his notebook, I discovered that he wrote his sentences from right to left—backwards in mirror writing. In order to read his notebook, the average person had to hold it up to a mirror.

I wanted to experiment with da Vinci's writing habits. I wrote the simple sentence, "Make the buffalo stew." backwards in mirror writing. When I held it up to a mirror, I discovered it said, "Stew buffalo the make." That's exactly how the Dakota/Lakota language is structured: starting with the subject, adding the descriptive word and placing the verb last. Earlier I pointed out that American Indian language structure allowed the right side of the brain to function. My questions then became, "Did Leonardo da Vinci's mind function in such a way? Did he utilize this doorway to the collective unconscious? Is this the reason he was five hundred years ahead of his time?" I feel the majority of people are "book" people. I'm a book person. All I know is what I read in the library. But it appears that Leonardo da Vinci's creativity came to him from the collective unconscious.

Further research into the Dakota/Lakota language structures, in *Oglala Religion* by William K. Powers, identified that separate lexical categories are not employed to differentiate between time and space. Time and space are inseparable. All temporal statements in the Dakota/Lakota languages are simultaneously spatial. Example: A simple sentence in Lakota is, "Letan Pine Ridge towhan hwo." The literal English interpretation is, "When is Pine Ridge from here?" But in the English language, the same sentence is usually stated, "How far is it to Pine Ridge?", indicating left-brain dominance. Thus, in the Lakota language, the spatial or right-brain orientation is dominant.

Marilyn Ferguson said in *The Aquarian Conspiracy* that European languages trap us in a model of understanding that is piecemeal. They pay no attention to relationships by their subject/predicate structure, thus molding our thought patterns by making us think in terms of simple cause and effect. She further stated that, ". . . for this reason it is hard for us to talk about or even think about quantum physics, the fourth dimension, or any other notion without clear-cut beginning and ending, up and down, then and now."

Modern science has discovered that there is something in the cosmos that is not in accord with the concepts that modern man has formed. Charlton Laird's book *Language in America* recorded that linguist Benjamin Whorf suggested that the Hopi language, if it will not help scientists find a new language they need, may at least help them see what is wrong with the old one. My interpretation of this is that Native American languages allow more right-brain expression, whereas European languages encourage almost solely left-brain expression.

A Hopi prophecy told about two brothers—a white one and a red one. The white brother went to the other side of the planet and will return one day. When he comes back, the two brothers will sit down together and learn each other's language. After that, their two lifeways will entwine and become one.

When I heard this prophecy, what first occurred to me was the information about the left and right hemispheres of the brain. To me, the white brother would be left-brain dominant, and the red brother would be right-brain dominant because of their differing language structures. After we learn each other's ways, we will become whole-brain thinkers. Marilyn Ferguson commented that the joining of the two hemispheres creates something new. Whole-brain knowing is more than the sum of its parts and different from either, she said.

Balance, or the Red Road philosophy, is a key to whole-brain knowing. Blakeslee felt that in using the functions of the right side of the brain, one would be able to make contact with the collective unconscious. Carl Jung believed that any time knowledge or information was wanted, it was contained within the collective unconscious portion of the mind.

A man who had a natural ability to make contact with the collective unconscious was Edgar Cayce. He was a spiritual healer. People who had incurable diseases went to him for help. He would enter into a self-meditative state, making contact with the collective unconscious. Then he would "lyeska" the information from that part of the mind, offering diagnoses and natural remedies for the healing of the sick person. Under normal conditions, Cayce had no knowledge of medicinal cures.

I was astounded that the method Edgar Cayce used to receive information was almost identical to those used by traditional D/Lakotas and other Native American holy people.

Additional similarities, besides those dealing with healing techniques, exist. For instance, both the information from the collective unconscious of Edgar Cayce and that from the myths of Native Americans declare that Native Americans have always been in North America. In researching Native American origin stories, I did not find one story stating that American Indians came across the Bering Straits.

Carl Jung remarked that myths from all cultures contain substance and that they originate in the collective unconscious. One of the Native American oral histories states that the people originated in North America. The information coming from the collective unconscious of Edgar Cayce said that the red man appeared in North America ten million years ago.

Recently, a skull was found off the coastal cliffs of San Diego. The scientists called this skull Del Mar Man. When a carbon-14 dating test was done, the skull could not be dated because it was too old. Now there is a new way of measuring the age of bones called acid racemization. The age is determined by measuring the age of the amino acids in the bone. This method was used on the skull of Del Mar Man. The results showed that the skull was almost 50,000 years old! When I read this, I questioned, "How in the world did he get over here? That's 20,000 years before the Bering Straits even opened up." Maybe the origin myths of the Native Americans are true after all!

Sitting Bull, who tried to get the non-Indians to accept his culture, stated shortly before his death that if a man loses something and goes back to look carefully for it, he will find it. This is what I feel the American Indians are doing today in reclaiming the validity of their own culture. It's all a part of the renaissance in American Indian philosophy and thought.

WORDS TO KNOW

NOTE: When you write the definitions of the following words, make it a point to use at least three of them in conversation over the next day and three of them in your next writing assignment. Many times you'll find it difficult or impossible to use them in everyday speech or writing. What then is the point of defining them? Of learning them? At the very least, in all the following cases where you have unusual vocabulary terms to define, attempt to use them. How does attempting to use vocabulary that feels awkward or different change your view of your common speech and writing patterns? Learning how to use new vocabulary means just that—using the words. Write specifically how, where, when, and why you used the words and discuss with your class.

Pacific Institute—
Jungian psychology—
Jung—
individuation—
transcendent—
McGuffey—
eclectic—
ideogramic—
Alan Watts—
linguistics—

collective unconscious —
lexical —
Edgar Cayce —
carbon-14 dating test —
acid racemization —
renaissance —

QUESTIONS

What is Allen Ross writing about in this reading? How successfully does he blend statistics with specific examples with different cultural contexts? Create a series of Three-Layered Questions and Text/You/ Other Questions based on this reading and two additional outside source. Make one of your source choices an interview and the other two print sources: one very recent (published within the last year or two) and one older than five years. Look at how the information and the age of the information in these sources will affect how you answer the question you choose to answer.

WRITING ACTIVITIES

1. Everyone in your class should bring in what they feel to be their most interesting question on a piece of paper. All the questions should be placed in a container, shuffled, and each person draws the question on which he/she will write.
2. Answer the question you chose. Did you feel you had a lot to write about from this question? Why or why not?
3. Now revise your questions, either the one you first wrote, or the one you ended up drawing, using a specific from one of the following contexts: culture, science, art, or language. Review the reading to see how specific Ross is when he uses any of these three subjects. You must be at least as specific as he is.
4. Write a new piece based on the new writing. How do the two compare and contrast? Discuss your findings with your class.

GRAMMAR AND STYLE QUESTIONS

1. Compare and contrast Ross's reading with one of your previous readings from the Internet. Analyze these examples. How are they different

stylistically? Use specific examples from the readings as well as specific rules of grammar in your answer.

2. Take three wordy, general expressions from your own writing that you've done based on these readings and revise them to make them concise, active grammatical expressions.

Until I Got Here—America Boring

Andrei Codrescu

In his introduction to The Dog, *Codrescu says, "Warnings of soul loss were once a constant feature of empathic journalism. Before the crash-landing of Communist ideology, even economics was fraught with strands of (fragile) morality. In the West, psychology held hands with religious ideas often enough to make it seem that a higher purpose attended us, even if it was only a shred of social sensitivity. Those things are gone now. The market is "free," which is to say, savage. Psychology has divorced higher purpose and married Prozac. Religion has become the province of fundamentalists, people whose rock-hard faith is only matched by their bonehead politics. And, in the social arena, we are urged by the Gingrich Party to abandon all face-to-face intercourse and link up by laptop. Which means, death to the cities, they are damned anyway." Sound familiar? What do you think?*

Introduction Andrei Codrescu's writing was originally written to be read aloud over the radio, to be listened to by his audience. What do you see to be the difference between writing you're meant to read with eyes and writing you're meant to speak and/or hear with your ears? Can you pinpoint specific words that make the difference? What about tone of voice? The effect of Codrescu's writing in this manner is to capture those additional oral details that the body fills in to accompany the words. What do you lose when you write something? How do you add to the writing to make up for the loss?

Do you know how boring this country was before I got here? I'm not saying that I made it personally less boring, only that my arrival and the assault on boredom were synchronous. In 1966 in Detroit, Michigan, for instance, if one had a craving for anything except mashed potatoes and roast beef, there were precious few places to go: Greektown, which had Greek food, Hamtramck, which had Polish food, and the Ho Ho Inn, a Cantonese Chinese restaurant where everything tasted like raspberry jam and mustard (which also coated the menu).

Even New York in those days, wasn't the ethnic smorgasbord it is today. Chinese did mean mostly Cantonese, and the ethnic neighborhoods did dish out blintzes and Cuban sandwiches, but for the most part mashed potatoes and gravy ruled. Most of America rested on a bedrock of bland and that was how most people were, too. Everybody was nice and white, for the most part, and geography wasn't anybody's forte. Nobody'd heard of Romania, where I had come from, but they were willing to give it the benefit of the doubt. If I hankered for spice in Detroit I had to go to Twelfth Street, in the ghetto, to get ribs and listen to music in "blind pigs," illegal joints that stayed open past midnight. Gay people met in bars with parrots on the sign and everybody with the least bit of difference in them was afraid of the FBI.

Happily, this state of affairs changed rather suddenly when there was an invasion of color and sound in 1966 and the mental and physical gates of America swung open briefly, letting in some happiness and a whole lot of exotics from Latin America, to be followed, in the coming years by spicier and more vividly hued ones from Asia and Africa. I only mention this because at this moment the same gates seem to be in danger of being shut by bigots in California and everywhere else. Simple-minded souls who want to go back to the safety of their 1950s doo-wop mashed potatoes are fixing to take away our hot sauce. Don't let them, folks. Trust me: boredom is hell.

WORDS TO KNOW

NOTE: When you write the definitions of the following words, make it a point to use at least three of them in conversation over the next day and three of them in your next writing assignment. Many times you'll find it difficult or impossible to use them in everyday speech or writing. What then is the point of defining them? Of learning them? At the very least, in all the following cases where you have unusual vocabulary terms to define, attempt to use them. How does attempting to use vocabulary that feels awkward or different change your view of your common speech and writing patterns? Learning how to use new vocabulary means just that—using the words. Write specifically how, where, when, and why you used the words and discuss with your class.

> synchronous—
> blintzes—
> forte—
> blind pigs—

QUESTIONS

Codrescu has written a rant. How would you define *rant,* given his example here? This particular rant comes from a collection of essays from National Public Radio and elsewhere. How would this piece sound on the radio versus reading it silently in print? What's the difference? Create a series of Three-Layered and Text/You/Other Questions based on this reading.

WRITING ACTIVITIES

1. Choose one of your questions on which to write. Decide your point and write us much as you can, up to two pages.
2. Now revise your same writing as a piece to be read aloud. What does the eye need to see in reading versus the ear need to hear when being read to?
3. Exchange your writings, both to be read on the page and to be read aloud, with your classmates. Limit the length of your oral writing to something that can be comfortably read in under two minutes.
4. What freedoms do you find in the visual writing versus the oral writing, and why? Be specific in your analysis.

Or, try the following:

1. Write one to two pages on the question you've chosen.
2. This time, write on the same question, but choose an entirely different tone of voice, point, agenda, and purpose in your writing. Write your tone of voice, point, agenda, and purpose on a separate piece of paper.
3. Choose a different question and repeat the same two activities as above.
4. Share your results aloud with your class without telling them what your new persona and agenda is, and without telling them which writing is neutral and which has a specific tone and agenda.

GRAMMAR AND STYLE QUESTIONS

1. Look at "exotic" punctuation (e.g., dashes, parentheses, exclamation points) as well as any "exotic" phrasing within this reading, and discuss what effect the author's use of these kinds of punctuation has on the reader. What does the use of grammar tell you about the written word as opposed to the spoken word? (Remember, this reading was originally a piece written for the radio.)

2. An important element of good usage is the concise and active expression of thoughts and ideas. Looking through this reading as well as two or three other readings, find concise, active, grammatical expressions, put them into your own words, and see how you can make them still more concise.

MEDIA RARE, MEDIOCRE, OR WELL-DONE?

Proverb Prints of Kawanabe Kyosai

Kawanabee Kyosai (1831–1889) was undoubtedly the most power-ful painter in the early Meiji era. He drew and painted many works, most of which were printed and became very popular among the common people in Japan. In his "Kyosai Hyakuzu," a series of Nishiki-e prints, he describes Japanese proverbs in a humorous manner. As you look at the paintings below and read the brief say-ing that both inspired and accompanies each, think about what would make his art appealing to the "common man." How do his pictures paint a thousand words? Or even a few words? Do the paintings go with the proverbs? The proverbs with the paintings? Why or why not?

Kawanabe Kyosai (1831–1889) was quite a unique artist, and un-doubtedly, the most powerful painter in early Meiji era. He drew and painted many, many works, most of which were printed and became very popular among the common people in Japan. In his "Kyosai Hyakuzu," a series of Nishiki-e prints, he described Japanese proverbs in a humorous manner.

"Even a dog, if it walks around, will clash with a stick."

"To crush the head of a flea with an axe."

"Transactions in Hell also depend upon money."

"Bugs swarm the food of hungry ghosts."

"A mended lid to a cracked pan."
"Matches are made peculiarly and
marvelously by chance."

"Kyosai Hyakuzu" [Copyright © 1996
Kawanabe Kyosai Memorial Art Mu-
seum]

"All human affairs are like Saio's
horse. (Inscrutable are the ways of
Heaven.)"
"The mouth is the door of evil."

"Kyosai Hyakuzu" [Copyright © 1996
Kawanabe Kyosai Memorial Art Mu-
seum]

WORDS TO KNOW

NOTE: When you write the definitions of the following words, make it a point to use at least three of them in conversation over the next day and three of them in your next writing assignment. Many times you'll find it difficult or impossible to use them in everyday speech or writing. What then is the point of defining them? Of learning them? At the very least, in all the following cases where you have unusual vocabulary terms to define, attempt to use them. How does attempting to use vocabulary that feels awkward or different change your view of your common speech and writing patterns? Learning how to use new vocabulary means just that—using the words. Write specifically how, where, when, and why you used the words and discuss with your class.

> Kawanabe Kyosai—
> Meiji—
> Nishiki-e—
> Kyosai Hyakuzu—
> Saio's horse—

QUESTIONS

Create a series of Text/You/Other or Three-Layered Questions for this mixed-media reading. As you do, think about how you can incorporate another reading or writing project that you've read or written earlier in this anthology into your new questions, and, potentially, into your new writings.

WRITING ACTIVITIES

1. Choose one of your new questions and write a one page response to that question.
2. Analyze in writing first where your response came from. What made you say what you did? Share your responses with your writing class.
3. Revise your response into a one-page essay with a beginning, a middle, and an ending. Remember to include a one-sentence main idea or thesis, so that your essay has a point, both for you and your reader.

4. Did you find it more difficult to do a writing project on a mixed-media reading? Why? Why not? Have you done a writing project on a mixed-media reading yet in this anthology? Which one?

5. How difficult was it to write about a reading which contained more image than words? Why? Which do you prefer, and why?

GRAMMAR AND STYLE QUESTIONS

1. Examine the use of punctuation in three different readings, including this one. How is punctuation and/or a lack thereof used to emphasize the authors' tone and/or purpose?

2. Select a text reading and a reading originally published on the Internet (you may use this reading as your Internet reading). Analyze these examples. What are some stylistic differences? Are there differences in word choice and word order? Use specific examples from the readings as well as specific rules of grammar in your answer.

Teaching As an Amusing Activity

Neil Postman

Neil Postman's insights and sardonic wit have made and kept him a strong media psychiatrist and psychologist. You've got to admit that a guy who would figure out that Sesame Street, The Electric Company, *and, now, such knockoff shows as* Big Bag and Comfy Couch *are laughing the traditional classroom out of existence has got to be pretty cool. More current, and even stranger, more original shows such as the much-extolled and equally criticized* Teletubbies *take the real (not traditional classroom) process of learning still further, into the realm of fun. And, Postman assures us, "Whereas in a classroom, fun is never more than a means to an end, on television it is the end in itself." What a radical concept.*

Introduction Neil Postman uses a traditional essay writing style combining research, analysis, and specific examples to support his point, but he also makes strong use of sarcasm and humor—tones of voice which are integral to getting his words across to his audience. What effect does this use of humor have on you? Where do you find specific signs of humor?

There could not have been a safer bet when it began in 1969 than that "Sesame Street" would be embraced by children, parents and educators. Children loved it because they were raised on television commercials, which they intuitively knew were the most carefully crafted entertainments on television. To those who had not yet been to school, even to those who had just started, the idea of being *taught* by a series of commercials did not seem peculiar. And that television should entertain them was taken as a matter of course.

Parents embraced "Sesame Street" for several reasons, among them that it assuaged their guilt over the fact that they could not or would not restrict their children's access to television. "Sesame

Street" appeared to justify allowing a four- or five-year-old to sit transfixed in front of a television screen for unnatural periods of time. Parents were eager to hope that television could teach their children something other than which breakfast cereal has the most crackle. At the same time, "Sesame Street" relieved them of the responsibility of teaching their pre-school children how to read—no small matter in a culture where children are apt to be considered a nuisance. They could also plainly see that in spite of its faults, "Sesame Street" was entirely consonant with the prevailing spirit of America. Its use of cute puppets, celebrities, catchy tunes, and rapid-fire editing was certain to give pleasure to the children and would therefore serve as adequate preparation for their entry into a fun-loving culture.

As for educators, they generally approved of "Sesame Street," too. Contrary to common opinion, they are apt to find new methods congenial, especially if they are told that education can be accomplished more effectively by means of the new techniques. (That is why such ideas as "teacher-proof" textbooks, standardized tests, and, now, micro-computers have been welcomed into the classroom.) "Sesame Street" appeared to be an imaginative aid in solving the growing problem of teaching Americans how to read, while, at the same time, encouraging children to love school.

We now know that "Sesame Street" encourages children to love school only if school is like "Sesame Street." Which is to say, we now know that "Sesame Street" undermines what the traditional idea of schooling represents. Whereas a classroom is a place of social interaction, the space in front of a television set is a private preserve. Whereas in a classroom, one may ask a teacher questions, one can ask nothing of a television screen. Whereas school is centered on the development of language, television demands attention to images. Whereas attending school is a legal requirement, watching television is an act of choice. Whereas in school, one fails to attend to the teacher at the risk of punishment, no penalties exist for failing to attend to the television screen. Whereas to behave oneself in school means to observe rules of public decorum, television watching requires no such observances, has no concept of public decorum. Whereas in a classroom, fun is never more than a means to an end, on television it is the end in itself.

Yet "Sesame Street" and its progeny, "The Electric Company," are not to be blamed for laughing the traditional classroom out of existence. If the classroom now begins to seem a stale and flat environment for learning, the inventors of television itself are to blame, not the Children's Television Workshop. We can hardly expect those who want to make good television shows to concern themselves with what the classroom is for. They are concerned with what television is for. This does not mean that "Sesame Street" is not educational. It is, in fact, nothing but educational—in the sense that every television show is educational. Just as reading a book—any kind of book—promotes a particular orientation toward learning, watching a television show does the same. "The Little House on the Prairie," "Cheers" and "The Tonight Show" are as effective as "Sesame Street" in promoting what might be called the television style of learning. And this style of learning is, by its nature, hostile to what has been called book-learning or its handmaiden, school-learning. If we are to blame "Sesame Street" for anything, it is for the pretense that it is any ally of the classroom. That, after all, has been its chief claim on foundation and public money. As a television show, and a good one, "Sesame Street" does not encourage children to love school or anything about school. It encourages them to love television.

Moreover, it is important to add that whether or not "Sesame Street" teaches children their letters and numbers is entirely irrelevant. We may take as our guide here John Dewey's observation that the content of a lesson is the least important thing about learning. As he wrote in *Experience and Education:* "Perhaps the greatest of all pedagogical fallacies is the notion that a person learns only what he is studying at the time. Collateral learning in the way of formation of enduring attitudes . . . may be and often is more important than the spelling lesson or lesson in geography or history. . . . For these attitudes are fundamentally what count in the future."[1]* In other words, the most important thing that one learns is always something about *how* one learns. As Dewey wrote in another place, we learn what we do. Television educates by teaching children to do what television-viewing requires of them. And that is as precisely remote from what a classroom requires of them as reading a book is from watching a stage show.

Although one would not know it from consulting various recent proposals on how to mend the educational system, this point—that reading books and watching television differ entirely in what they imply about learning—is the primary educational issue in America today. America is, in fact, the leading case in point of what may be thought of as the third great crisis in Western education. The first occurred in the fifth century B.C., when Athens underwent a change from an oral culture to an alphabet-writing culture. To understand what this meant, we must read Plato. The second occurred in the sixteenth

*All footnotes in this essay can be referenced in the original text which is listed in full on the Credits page.

century, when Europe underwent a radical transformation as a result of the printing press. To understand what is meant, we must read John Locke. The third is happening now, in America, as a result of the electronic revolution, particularly the invention of television. To understand what this means, we must read Marshall McLuhan.

We face the rapid dissolution of the assumptions of an education organized around the slow-moving printed word, and the equally rapid emergence of a new education based on the speed-of-light electronic image. The classroom is, at the moment, still tied to the printed word, although that connection is rapidly weakening. Meanwhile, television forges ahead, making no concessions to its great technological predecessor, creating new conceptions of knowledge and how it is acquired. One is entirely justified in saying that the major educational enterprise now being undertaken in the United States is not happening in its classrooms but in the home, in front of the television set, and under the jurisdiction not of school administrators and teachers but of network executives and entertainers. I don't mean to imply that the situation is a result of a conspiracy or even that those who control television want this responsibility. I mean only to say that, like the alphabet or the printing press, television has by its power to control the time, attention and cognitive habits of our youth gained the power to control their education.

This is why I think it accurate to call television a curriculum. As I understand the word, a curriculum is a specially constructed information system whose purpose is to influence, teach, train or cultivate the mind and character of youth. Television, of course, does exactly that, and does it relentlessly. In so doing, it competes successfully with the school curriculum. By which I mean, it damn near obliterates it.

Having devoted an earlier book, *Teaching as a Conserving Activity*, to a detailed examination of the antagonistic nature of the two curriculums—television and school—I will not burden the reader or myself with a repetition of that analysis. But I would like to recall two points that I feel did not express forcefully enough in that book and that happen to be central to this one. I refer, first, to the fact that television's principal contribution to educational philosophy is the idea that teaching and entertainment are inseparable. This entirely original conception is to be found nowhere in educational discourses, from Confucius to Plato to Cicero to Locke to John Dewey. In searching the literature of education, you will find it said by some that children will learn best when they are interested in what they are learning. You will find it said—Plato and Dewey emphasized this—that reason is best cultivated when it is rooted in robust emotional ground. You will even find some who say that learning is best facilitated by a loving and benign teacher. But no one has ever said or implied that significant learning is effectively, durably and truthfully achieved when education is entertainment. Education philosophers have assumed that becoming acculturated is difficult because it necessarily involves the imposition of restraints. They have argued that there must be a sequence to learning, that perseverance and a certain measure of perspiration are indispensable, that individual pleasures must frequently be submerged in the interests of group cohesion, and that learning to be critical and to think conceptually and rigorously do not come easily to the young but are hard-fought victories. Indeed, Cicero remarked that the purpose of education is to free the student from the tyranny of the present, which cannot be pleasurable for those, like the young, who are struggling hard to do the opposite—that is, accommodate themselves to the present.

Television offers a delicious and, as I have said, original alternative to all of this. We might say that there are three commandments that form the philosophy of the education which television offers. The influence of these commandments is observable in every type of television programming—from "Sesame Street" to the documentaries of "Nova" and "National Geographic" to "Fantasy Island" to MTV. The commandments are as follows:

Thou shalt have no prerequisites

Every television program must be a complete package in itself. No previous knowledge is to be required. There must not be even a hint that learning is hierarchical, that is an edifice constructed on a foundation. The learner must be allowed to enter at any point without prejudice. This is why you shall never hear or see a television program begin with the caution that if the viewer has not seen the previous programs, this one will be meaningless. Television is a nongraded curriculum and excludes no viewer for any reason, at any time. In other words, in doing away with the idea of sequence and continuity in education, television undermines the idea that sequence and continuity have anything to do with thought itself.

Thou shalt induce no perplexity

In television teaching, perplexity is a superhighway to low ratings. A perplexed learner is a learner who will turn to another station. This means that there must be nothing that has to be remembered, studied, applied, or, worst of all, endured. It is assumed that any information, story or idea can be made immediately accessible, since the contentment, not the growth, of the learner is paramount.

Thou shalt avoid exposition like the ten plagues visited upon Egypt
Of all the enemies of television-teaching, including continuity and
perplexity, none is more formidable than exposition. Arguments, hypotheses, discussions, reasons, refutations or any of the traditional
instruments of reasoned discourse turn television into radio or,
worse, third-rate printed matter. Thus, television-teaching always
takes the form of story-telling, conducted through dynamic images
and supported by music. This is as characteristic of "Star Trek" as it
is of "Cosmos," of "Diff'rent Strokes" as of "Sesame Street," of commercials as of "Nova." Nothing will be taught on television that cannot be both visualized and placed in a theatrical context.

The name we may properly give to an education without prerequisites, perplexity and exposition is entertainment. And when one
considers that save for sleeping there is no activity that occupies
more of an American youth's time than television-viewing, we cannot
avoid the conclusion that a massive reorientation toward learning is
now taking place. Which leads to the second point I wish to emphasize: The consequences of this reorientation are to be observed not
only in the decline of the potency of the classroom but, paradoxi-
cally, in the refashioning of the classroom into a place where both
teaching and learning are intended to be vastly amusing activities.

I have already referred to the experiment in Philadelphia in
which the classroom is reconstituted as a rock concert. But this is
only the silliest example of an attempt to define education as a mode
of entertainment. Teachers, from primary grades through college,
are increasing the visual stimulation of their lessons; are reducing
the amount of exposition their students must cope with; are relying
less on reading and writing assignments; and are reluctantly con-
cluding that the principal means by which student interest may be
engaged is entertainment. With no difficulty I could fill the remaining pages of this chapter with examples of teachers' efforts—in some
instances, unconscious—to make their classrooms into second-rate
television shows. But I will rest my case with "The Voyage of the
Mimi," which may be taken as a synthesis, if not an apotheosis, of
the New Education. "The Voyage of the Mimi" is the name of an ex-
pensive science and mathematics project that has brought together
some of the most prestigious institutions in the field of education—
the United States Department of Education, the Bank Street College
of Education, the Public Broadcasting System, and the publishing
firm Holt, Rinehart and Winston. The project was made possible by a
$3.65 million grant from the Department of Education, which is al-
ways on alert to put its money where the future is. And the future is

"The Voyage of the Mimi." To describe the project succinctly, I quote from four paragraphs in *The New York Times* of August 7, 1984:

> Organized around a twenty-six unit television series that depicts the adventures of a floating whale-research laboratory, [the project] combines television viewing with lavishly illustrated books and computer games that simulate the way scientists and navigators work. . . .
>
> "The Voyage of the Mimi" is built around fifteen-minute television programs that depict the adventures of four young people who accompany two scientists and a crusty sea captain on a voyage to monitor the behavior of humpback whales off the coast of Maine. The crew of the converted tuna trawler navigates the ship, tracks down the whales and struggles to survive on an uninhabited island after a storm damages the ship's hull. . . .
>
> Each dramatic episode is then followed by a fifteen-minute documentary on related themes. One such documentary involved a visit by one of the teen-age actors to Ted Taylor, a nuclear physicist in Greenport, L.I., who has devised a way of purifying sea water by freezing it.
>
> The television programs, which teachers are free to record off the air and use at their convenience, are supplemented by a series of books and computer exercises that pick up four academic themes that emerge naturally from the story line: map and navigational skills, whales and their environment, ecological systems and computer literacy.

The television programs have been broadcast over PBS; the books and computer software have been provided by Holt, Rinehart and Winston; the educational expertise by the faculty of the Bank Street College. Thus, "The Voyage of the Mimi" is not to be taken lightly. As Frank Withrow of the Department of Education remarked, "We consider it the flagship of what we are doing. It is a model that others will begin to follow." Everyone involved in the project is enthusiastic, and extraordinary claims of its benefits come trippingly from their tongues. Janice Trebbi Richards of Holt, Rinehart and Winston asserts, "Research shows that learning increases when information is presented in a dramatic setting, and television can do this better than any other medium." Officials of the Department of Education claim that the appeal of integrating three media—television, print, and computers—lies in their potential for cultivating higher-order thinking skills. And Mr. Withrow is quoted as saying that projects like "The Voyage of the Mimi" could mean great financial savings, that in the long run "it is cheaper than anything else we do." Mr. Withrow also suggested that there are many ways of financing such projects. "With 'Sesame Street,'" he said, "it took five or six years, but eventually you can start bringing in the money with T-shirts and cookie jars."

We may start thinking about what "The Voyage of the Mimi" signifies by recalling that the idea is far from an original. What is here referred to as "integrating three media" or a "multi-media presentation" was once called audio-visual aids," used by teachers for years, usually for the modest purpose of enhancing student interest in the curriculum. Moreover, several years ago, the Office of Education (as the Department was then called) supplied funds to WNET for a similarly designed project called "Watch Your Mouth," a series of television dramatizations in which young people inclined to misuse the English language fumbled their way through a variety of social problems. Linguists and educators prepared lessons for teachers to use in conjunction with each program. The dramatizations were compelling—although not nearly as good as "Welcome Back, Kotter," which had the unassailable advantage of John Travolta's charisma— but there exists no evidence that students who were required to view "Watch Your Mouth" increased their competence in the use of the English language. Indeed, since there is no shortage of mangled English on everyday commercial television, one wondered at the time why the United States government would have paid anyone to go to the trouble of producing additional ineptitudes as a source of classroom study. A videotape of any of David Susskind's programs would provide an English teacher with enough linguistic aberrations to fill a semester's worth of analysis.

Nonetheless, the Department of Education has forged ahead, apparently in the belief that ample evidence—to quote Ms. Richards again—"shows that learning increases when information is presented in a dramatic setting, and that television can do this better than any other medium." The most charitable response to this claim is that it is misleading. George Comstock and his associates have reviewed 2,800 studies on the general topic of television's influence on behavior, including cognitive processing, and are unable to point to persuasive evidence that "learning increases when information is presented in a dramatic setting."[2] Indeed, in studies conducted by Cohen and Salomon; Meringoff; Jacoby, Hoyer and Sheluga; Stauffer, Frost and Rybolt; Stern; Wilson; Neuman; Katz, Adoni and Parness; and Gunter, quite the opposite conclusion is justified.[3] Jacoby et al. found, for example, that only 3.5 percent of viewers were able to answer successfully twelve true/false questions concerning two thirty-second seg-ments of commercial television programs and advertisements. Stauf-fer et al. found in studying students' responses to a news program transmitted via television, radio and print, that print significantly in-creased correct responses to questions regarding the names of people and numbers contained in the material. Stern reported that 51 per-cent of viewers could not recall a single item of news a few minutes after viewing a news program on television. Wilson found that the av-erage television viewer could retain only 20 percent of the information contained in a fictional televised news story. Katz et al. found that 21 percent of television viewers could not recall any news items within one hour of broadcast. On the basis of his and other studies, Salomon has concluded that "the meanings secured from television are more likely to be segmented, concrete, and less inferential, and those se-cured from reading have a higher likelihood of being better tied to one's stored knowledge and thus are more likely to be inferential."[4] In other words, so far as many reputable studies are concerned, television viewing does not significantly increase learning, is inferior to and less likely than print to cultivate high-order, inferential thinking.

But one must not make too much of the rhetoric of grantsman-ship. We are all inclined to transform our hopes into tenuous claims when an important project is at stake. Besides, I have no doubt that Ms. Richards can direct us to several studies that lend support to her enthusiasm. The point is that if you want money for the redun-dant purpose of getting children to watch even more television than they already do—and dramatizations at that—you have to escalate the rhetoric to Herculean proportions.

What is of great significance about "The Voyage of the Mimi" is that the content selected was obviously chosen because it is emi-nently *televisible.* Why are these students studying the behavior of humpback whales? How critical is it that the "academic themes" of navigational and map-reading skills be learned? Navigational skills have never been considered an "academic theme" and in fact seem singularly inappropriate for most students in big cities. Why has it been decided that "whales and their environment" is a subject of such compelling interest that an entire year's work should be given to it?

I would suggest that "The Voyage of the Mimi" was conceived by someone's asking the question, What is television good for?, not, What is education good for? Television is good for dramatizations, shipwrecks, seafaring adventures, crusty old sea captains, and physicists being interviewed by actor-celebrities. And that, of course, is what we have got in "The Voyage of the Mimi." The fact that this adventure sit-com is accompanied by lavishly illustrated books and computer games only underscores that the television presentation controls the curriculum. The books whose pictures the students will scan and the computer games the students will play are dictated by the content of the television shows, not the other way around. Books, it would appear, have now become an audio-visual aid; the principal carrier of the content of education is the television show, and its principal claim for a preeminent place in the curriculum is that it is entertaining. Of course, a television production can be used to stimulate interest in lessons, or even as the focal point of a lesson. But what is happening here is that the content of the school curriculum is being determined by the character of television, and even worse, that character is apparently not included as part of what is studied. One would have thought that the school room is the proper place for students to inquire into the ways in which media of all kinds—including television—shape people's attitudes and perceptions. Since our students will have watched approximately sixteen thousand hours of television by high school's end, questions should have arisen, even in the minds of officials at the Department of Education, about who will teach our students how to look at television, and when not to, and with what critical equipment when they do. "The Voyage of the Mimi" project bypasses these questions; indeed, hopes that the students will immerse themselves in the dramatizations in the same frame of mind used when watching "St. Elsewhere" or "Hill Street Blues." (One may also assume that what is called "computer literacy" does not involve raising questions about the cognitive biases and social effects of the computer, which, I would venture, are the most important questions to address about new technologies.)

"The Voyage of the Mimi," in other words, spent $3.65 million for the purpose of using media in exactly the manner that media merchants want them to be used—mindlessly and invisibly, as if media themselves have no epistemological or political agenda. And, in the end, what will the students have learned? They will, to be sure, have learned something about whales, perhaps about navigation and map-reading, most of which they could have learned just as well by other means. Mainly, they will have learned that learning is a form of entertainment or, more precisely, that anything worth learning can take the form of an entertainment, and ought to. And they will not rebel if their English teacher asks them to learn the eight parts of speech through the medium of rock music. Or if their social studies teacher sings to them the facts about the War of 1812. Or if their physics comes to them on cookies and T-shirts. Indeed, they will expect it and thus will be well prepared to receive their politics, their religion, their news and their commerce in the same delightful way.

WORDS TO KNOW

NOTE: When you write the definitions for the following words, make it a point to use at least three of them in conversation over the next day and three of them in your next writing assignment. Many times you'll find it difficult or impossible to use them in everyday speech or writing. What then is the point of defining them? Of learning them? At the very least, in all the following cases where you have unusual vocabulary terms to define, attempt to use them. How does attempting to use vocabulary that feels awkward or different change your view of your common speech and writing patterns? Learning how to use new vocabulary means just that—using the words. Write specifically how, where, when, and why you used the words and discuss with your class.

assuaged—
consonant—
congenial—
standardized—
micro-computers—
decorum—
progeny—
ally—
pedagogical—
fallacies—
collateral—
dissolution—
jurisdiction—
cognitive—
antagonistic—
obliterates—
acculturated—
restraints—
prerequisites—

hierarchical —
perplexity —
perplexed —
hypotheses —
refutations —
refashioning —
reconstituted —
synthesis —
apotheosis —
succinctly —
trippingly —
conjunction —
unassailable —
ineptitudes —
linguistic —
aberrations —

QUESTIONS

Using critical thinking and analysis that Postman uses in his essay, create a group of questions, both Text/You/Other and Three-Layered, on which you would like to write. Did you find yourself agreeing or disagreeing with what he says? What part and why? How much of your view has to do with how you feel about television?

WRITING ACTIVITIES

1. After you've chosen one of your questions on which you'd like to write your essay, choose several objects to accompany your essay, again as integral examples to your essay.
2. Either as you write your essay or after you've written it, think about what form you would like to include your objects in your essay — that is, as print-outs or paper copies, as three-dimensional objects that readers would have to look at as they read your piece, or in some other manner of your choosing that will directly impact on the strength and point of your writing project/essay.
3. Did you feel constrained or freed by this requirement? Why?
4. Try the same writing assignment again, but this time revise it to incorporate one of your earlier questions and/or writing projects from a previous section of this anthology.

5. Try the same writing assignment again, but this time revise it to incorporate one of your earlier questions and/or writing projects from a previous section of this anthology as well as one of the earlier questions and/or writing projects of one of your classmates.
6. Try the above again, but this time, collaborate on the writing project with that fellow classmate.
7. Share your final product with your other classmates. Ask them for specific types of feedback before you present the project. Did they pay attention to your project? To your request for specific feedback? Why or why not?

GRAMMAR AND STYLE QUESTIONS

1. An important element of good usage is the concise and active expression of thoughts and ideas. Looking through three specific readings from this book, including this one by Postman, find concise, active, grammatical expressions, put them into your own words, and see how you can make them still more concise.
2. Now take wordy, general expressions from your own writing that you've done based on these three readings, and revise them to make them concise, active grammatical expressions.
3. One of the best ways to learn grammar, in addition to learning the names and rules of grammatical elements, is to read other people's writing and determine how and why they write well. Take a grammatically imperfect piece of your own work, read or reread two or three readings from this reader, and rewrite your piece afterwards. Is it grammatically better? Why or why not? What was the impact of seeing how other people put together words?

Notes from Nicotine Hell: Quitting Smoking May Be Hazardous to Your Health

Susan Shapiro

How many times have you ever tried to quit something? Did you find the experience a nightmare? Laughable? Both? Why?

Introduction As you enjoy this next reading, look at how journalist and reporter Susan Shapiro combines a diary style of writing (another form of narrative), reporting (giving the facts of what has taken place during a given time), and sarcastic humor to capture a certain absurdity about our need for habits.

Day 1

Wake up and put on nicotine patch to once and for all quit pack-a-day habit. Write a list of reasons: live 15 years longer, have healthy children, be socially acceptable. Tear up list and make better one: look younger, have fewer wrinkles, get more dates, spite enemies. Decide to go out and buy carrots, celery, gum, orange juice, fruit, sugar-free lollipops, and rice cakes. Eat them all by 11 A.M. Try to work. Instead take all-day nap. Have a drink later with old boyfriend Peter, who says, "Kissing a smoker is like licking a dirty ashtray," then drinks seven beers and a cognac and comes on to me. Actually consider it, but can't face sex without a cigarette later. At 2 A.M. go out and purchase three packages of fat-free Entenmann's brownies.

Day 2

Wake up sick from brownies and cold caught walking 14 blocks to get them. Put on patch. Buy Sudafed. Take two. Feel better. Feel delirious. Take a nap. Try to work but can't concentrate on anything but wanting to smoke. One hour on exercise bike: Oprah's "Mothers Who Want Their Kids Taken Away" puts problem into perspective. Read that schizophrenics and manic-depressives in mental hospitals commit suicide when their cigarettes are taken away. Ask brother, the doctor, for 65 more patches. Take another Sudafed. Is there a Sudafed group in the city?

Day 3
Put on patch. Have breakfast with friend Vern, who says that after he quit smoking, his concentration didn't come back for two years. Take 100 deep breaths. Breathing is overrated. Take a walk and count how many stores on the block sell cigarettes. Get more patches in mail from brother, along with pictures of cancerous tumors. Try to work. See a movie with Peter in which all actors smoke. Eat two buckets of popcorn. Peter suggests that I try Nicorettes because his cousin Janet quit in three days on them. I remind him that I tried Nicorettes once and threw up, then smoked two packs to get the taste out of my mouth. Don't invite him in. Read that nicotine's harder to quit than heroin. Take another Sudafed.

Day 4
Put on patch. Think of smoking. Brother calls to say don't even think of smoking with patch on, someone's fingers fell off. Lunch with Andrea, who coughed every time I took out a cigarette for 15 years but now says, "I can't hang out with you when you're like this, you're too intense." Bump into old colleague Dave, who quit smoking and gained 29 pounds in four months but thinks it was the smart choice. Consider heroin. Try to work but realize it's impossible to be a freelance writer, a nonsmoker, and thin in the same year. Sudafed losing its bite, check into Comtrex. Negotiate self-destructive behaviors: decide that taking sleeping pill, smoking a joint, getting drunk, or having sex with Peter one more time is better than a Marlboro or Oreos, though not all on the same night.

Day 5
Put on patch. Feel depressed and edgy, sweating. Hands shaking while I read the paper, where tobacco company executives say nicotine isn't addictive. Buy a pacifier, pretending it's a cool rap toy, wondering why anyone expects morality from people who plaster penis-faced camels all over the country. Think of ten 70-year-old smokers still alive. Dinner with novelist friend Kathy, who chain-smokes in my face while saying she thinks it's great that I'm quit-

ting. On the way home, try to buy a 25-cent loosie—loose cigarette—at a local bodega but guy thinks I'm cigarette police. Take it as an omen. Try to think of one famous writer who doesn't drink or smoke.

Day 6
Put on patch. Do high-impact aerobics for three hours. Walk out of health club wanting cigarette. Stare at people smoking and wonder why they look so beautiful and happy. Think of money I'm saving from not smoking. Spend $46 on seven boxes of fat-free cookies, 27 cinnamon sticks, and three Lean Cuisines. Snap rubber band around wrist 100 times. On stationary bike, watch Saturday Night Live, which quotes tobacco company execs saying that the victims of the 400,000 annual smoking-related deaths aren't really dead. Neighbor complains bike makes too much noise. Do serenity exercises. Picture sitting on a tropical beach, where I'm happily smoking.

Day 7
Put on patch. Have brunch with Peter, who says, while drinking six margaritas, that I've gained weight and need to learn more self-control. Make note to quit Peter. Read article about Bosnia and the only thing I notice is that soldier in picture is smoking. Eat more celery, fruit, salad. Polish off Oreos. Feel sick and bloated, dying for cigarette. Take off patch. Run outside. Bum cigarette from homeless person. Puff slowly. Feel happy for the first time in six days. Stop coughing, calm down. Finish two articles. Go back outside, offer same guy two bucks for two more cigarettes. Smoke them quickly. Feel nauseated, dizzy. Bump into Vern and Andrea, who say, "We were just coming by to say how proud we are that you haven't smoked in a week! Congratulations!" Feel guilty, defeated. Drink bottle of wine by myself. Fall asleep on couch with clothes on.

Day 1
Wake up and put on nicotine patch once and for all . . .

WORDS TO KNOW

NOTE: When you write the definitions of the following words, make it a point to use at least three of them in conversation over the next day and three of them in your next writing assignment. Many times you'll find it difficult or impossible to use them in everyday speech or writing. What then is the point of defining them? Of learning them? At the very least, in all the following cases where you have unusual vocabulary terms to define, attempt to use them. How does attempting to use vocabulary that feels awkward or different change your view of your common speech and writing patterns? Learning how to use new vocabulary means just that—using the words. Write specifically how, where, when, and why you used the words and discuss with your class.

Entenmann's—

Sudafed—

schizophrenics—

manic-depressives—

Nicorettes—

loosie—

bodega—

serenity—

QUESTIONS

Create a series of questions (both Text/You/Other and Three-Layered) to accompany this reading. As you create your questions, consider what other previous readings, what other previous writing projects you can include as part of your new set of questions. Think, too, about how you can include possible outside readings on smoking that take a very different approach and tone to the subject. Which do you like best, and why?

WRITING ACTIVITIES

1. Choose one of your new questions on which to write.
2. Before you begin writing, plot out a process strategy as Shapiro has— that is, writing paragraphs organized by time, by steps in the process, by humorous or bizarre headings. Write down separately why you've selected the process strategy that you have. What will it do for your new project?
3. Write your response to your question, making sure that it has a point, that it has a focus.
4. This time, choose a particular publication to which you would send

your writing. For a starting idea, look at the *Funny Times* issue from October 1996 in which Shapiro had her piece published. What are the requirements? Who will be reading what you write? (Remember your piece has to fit with the scope of the entire publication.) Choose a specific publication, make a list of requirements and describe the audience of the publication where you will direct your piece. You can choose either a hard-copy publication (a newspaper, magazine) or an electronic publication on the Internet, but you must choose a specific publication that is already in existence.

5. Make the necessary revisions for that publication.

6. Share the two versions with your classmates. Which do they respond to more positively and why? Write your own reasons as well as the reasons they give you.

7. Send your writing to that publication in the requested format (either hard-copy or electronic version).

GRAMMAR AND STYLE QUESTIONS

1. Using Shapiro's piece as well as one other piece from any of the readings you've done so far, look at the uses of punctuation from a journalistic reading and a storytelling reading. How is punctuation used stylistically? Use specific examples from these readings as well as specific rules of grammar and details in your answer.

2. One of the most difficult tasks for any new writer is to express time and timelines consistently and to match actions to those times and timelines. Take a paragraph from Shapiro's reading that has a strong sense of either past, present, or future tense, and rewrite it using a different verb tense (i.e., if it was written in the present tense, rewrite it in the past tense, and so forth). What is the effect of such a change? Were you consistent in your new selection of verb tense in your revision? And, if you had difficulty with consistency, without referring back to the text, restore the original tense and see how closely the paragraph matches how the author originally wrote it.

Warlukurlangu: What Happened at the Place of Fire

Uni Nampijinpa

"Warlukurlangu: What Happened at the Place of Fire" is told by Uni Nampijinpa, one of the Warlpíri people of Central Australia. Translators Peggy Rockman Napaljarri and Lee Cataldi write, "It is well known that for Australian Aboriginal people religious beliefs are inseparable from the land to which the different language groups, families, and individuals belong. Thus the narratives . . . which describe the travels of ancestral figures from place to place also describe actions which caused the natural features of the land, particularly water, rock formations, and trees, to come into being. The ancestral figures are often also food, either vegetable or meat. The narrative is simultaneously an account of the creation of the places in the story, an account of the mythical but human behaviour of the ancestral figures, and a mnemonic map of the country with its important, life-giving features for the purpose of instructing a younger listener. These elements make up Warlpíri Jukurrpa, commonly translated as the Dreaming. The Jukurrpa or 'Dreaming' is Warlpíri culture and law. It is the time of the creation of the world which continues to exist as an eternal present embodied in songs, stories, dances, and places. It is always there, although many people may forget or abandon it. While the Jukurrpa or Dreaming is a universal, each person and place has their own particular dreamings."

Introduction What is unusual about this next work, which you might be tempted to call a standard piece of fiction, is that it is in fact history, real history and historical narrative for the Warlpíri—quite different than the way Westerners interpret tales. Would you know this just by reading the piece? Which events seem realistic? Fantastic? Why? On what do you base your determination? The original language has been included so that you can see what the tale looks like in its native tongue.

Warlukurlanguwardingki Jampijinpa purlka manu kajanyanujarra Jangalajarra. Wapaja, maju-majulpala watijarra, maju-majulpala watijarra wapaja kajanyanujarra. Jajinyanulpapalangu pardarnu yuntangka purlku. Wirlinyilpapala yanu. Kuyulpapalarla yinja-yanu, yinja-yanulpapalarla kuyu, Lungkardaku yirdijiji.

Warlukurlangurla maju-maju.

"Nyinakarla waja pulya nyampurlajuku muurlpa," kalapala ngarrirninja-yanu Jangalajarrarluju Jampijinpa purlkapardu milpa-parnta. Pampa kala nyinaja.

Kalapalangu karrinja-pardinjarla nyangu. Parrarl-parrarl-nyangu kala milpangku. "Wurnturulku kapala yanirra ngajunyan-gujarraju kajajarraju. Kukurna mani waja kurlarda ngajunyangu. Kapirna wirlinyi waja jalanguju yani ngajulku."

Wirlinyirlirla kala panturnunjunu. Milya-pinjawangu kalapala kajanyanujarra nyinaja, lawa. Kulanganta pampakuju kalapalarla nyinaja.

Kalapala kulpajarni. Ngulakungarntijala kala yangka kuyuwiyi nyanungurlu purraja. Kala kanunjumparralku yirrarnu kuyuwanay-ijala, yangka linjiwana. Mungalyurruwarnu pirrarniwarnuwana kala kanunjumparra yirrarnu, wati yangka yinyajarrakujaku watijar-rakujaku Jangalajarrakujaku. Ngulajangkaju, kalapalangu wapirdi-nyangu wurnturukurra. Yanurnu kalapala kuyukurlu yijalyikirli wirlinyijangka. Kala pampajarrijalku. Kutungkarnijiki kala nyinaja pampalku nganta.

Kalapalarla manngu-nyanja-yanu, kalapala yangka wirlinyi-jangkarlu,

"Wiyarrpa, marda ka pampa nyina purlkayijala ngurrangka ngurrju marda."

"Yuwayi, ngurrju ka nyina!"

Kala nganayilkijangka pampa-jarrija nganta–nyanjarla ku-tungkalku–watijarrakujaku, yinya kuja kalapala watijarra yanurnu, Jangalajarra, kajanyanujarra nyanungunyangujarra. Kalapalarla wara-parnpija.

"Ngajunyangugujarranyanupala, ayi?"

"Yuwu, wirlinyijangka waja nyurrurlujarra yanurnu."

"Kuyukurlu, mayi waja?"

They had great difficulty in walking, those two men, they walked in great pain, the two sons. The father, the old man, waited for them at the windbreak where it was warm. The two went out hunting. The went about giving him meat, they went about giving meat to the one called Bluetongue [Lizard].

At Warlukurlangu, in great pain.

"Stay here in this place quietly and look after yourself," the two Jangala used to say to Jampijinpa, to the blind old man. He was blind.

Having stood up, however, he used to watch them go. He glanced around to see where they were, with his eyes. "They are going a long way off, my two sons. Now I am free to get my own spear. I will go hunting now, for myself."

He used to go hunting and spear game. His two sons knew nothing about this, nothing. They thought he was blind.

Eventually they would come back. He was ready for this, having already cooked his own meat. He used to bury it along with the dried meat left over from the morning or the day before, so that the two men, the two Jangala, did not know about it. Then he would watch them as they approached. Returning from hunting, they came towards him carrying pieces of meat. He pretended to be blind. When they were close he sat like a blind man.

As they returned from hunting, the two sons would think about their father.

"Poor thing. I hope all is well with the old blind man at the camp."

"Yes, he is well."

Well, after, you know, having watched the two men coming towards him, the two Jangala, his two sons, he appeared to be blind. But he knew where they were.

"My two sons, ayi?"

"Yes, here we are back from hunting."

"With meat I hope?"

"Yes, here is the meat."

He had already hidden his own meat.

Then, "Will you eat this meat, old man?"

"Yes, just give me a little." He seemed to only eat a little. "Could you put some meat for me up on top so that while I am sitting here at home I can have something to eat, here at home?"

"Yuwayi, kuyu waja nyampurra."

Nyurrujukujala kala nyanungurlu wuruly-yirrarnu kuyuju.

Ngulajangkaju, "Kuyunpa ngarni purlka nyampu waja?"

"Yuwa, witajupala yungka!" Kala ngarnu wita nganta. "Kuyuju-pala yurdingka yirraka waja yuwalirla yungujupala nguna, yunguju nguna waja yantarliji yingarna ngarni yantarlirli."

"Yuwa purlka, nyampurla karlijarrangku kuyu yirrarni waja, karnangku!" kala kukurnunyanu wangkaja.

Ngulajangkaju, ngulajangkaju, ngulajangkaju, ngunaja kalalu ngurrangkalku. Kalalu ngunaja sleep-lki ngurrangkalku. Warlu kalapalarla yarrpirninja-parnkaja yitipijarra kajanyanujarrarlu nya-nungunyangujarrarlu watijarrarlu yuntardijarrarlu Jangalajarrarlu Warlukurlanguwardingkijarrarlu, yalumpurla kujapala palka-jarrija, ngulajarrarlu.

Yakarra-pardija kalalu mungalyurru, Kalalu yangka kuyu war-lungka kardu-yungu maninjarla mungalyurrurlu. Nyampurlaju kalu mangarriji, flour-lkujala ngarni, nyampurlaju kardiyarlaju. Kala kardiyawangurlawiyiji kalalu ngarnu jukurrparluju nyurruwiyiji mangarri puurdapinki, yumurnunjupinki, janmardapinki. Marlu kalalu kuyu ngarnu, luwajirripinki.

Kalapalarla ngarrirninja-yanu, "Purlka nyinayarra. Nyampunya mardakarra waja."

"Yirrakajupala warlurlangujupala waja. Marlurnparla jamulu-yarrpika yungurna nyinami waja; kuyu yirna linji waja ngarni pur-dangirlirli, kuyu wajarna ngarni purdangirlirli linji. Kajinpala kuyukurlu yani waja papankurlangu." Kalapalangu ngarrurnu ka-janyanujarra nyanungunyangujarra kujapala yalumpurla palka-jarrija Warlukurlangurla.

Kalapala yanu wirlinyi. Kalapala wapaja yinyakula karlarra Jarlarripinkikirra. Jarlarri-yirrarnu kalapala. Kalapala warrulparni kulpaja. Warlukurlangukurra yangka, yalumpu kulkurrukurra, kuja kapalangu rduyu-karri warlu jukurrpawarnu. Ngulangka kala Lungkardaju nyinaja.

Kalapalangu yarda yirri-puraja. Milpa kala yakarra, milpa kala tiirl-pardija milpa purdangirli. Kala yakarra-pardija. Karrinja-pardija kala.

"Kari wurnturulku kapala yanirra ngajunyangujarraju

"Yes, old man. We are putting the meat here for you. I have put it right here for you," the younger brother used to say to him.

Then they all lay down in the camp and went to sleep. The two Jangala, the two sons, the two beautiful young men, the two from Warlukurlangu, the two who had been born there, those two ran and made fires on each side of the camp.

In the morning they awoke. In the morning after getting the meat, they warmed it on the fire. These days they eat bread and flour, in the days of the white man. But before the white man, in the time of the Jukurrpa [Dreaming], in the old days, they used to eat all kinds of big and small yams, and things like wild onions. They used to eat the meat of kangaroos and all kinds of goannas.

They left him saying, "Stay here, old man. Here, take this for yourself."

"Put some firewood here for me as well, and build me a shade so I can sit here, and later I can eat some of the dried meat. Later you, my two sons, will come back with fresh meat." This is what he used to say to his two sons who had been born there at War-lukurlangu.

They walked away from there towards the country near Jarlarri. At Jarlarri they used to start hunting. They would then circle back round towards Warlukurlangu, towards the centre, towards where the fire from the jukurrpa burns for them.

He used to watch where they went, with his awakened eyes. He used to open his eyes, after they had gone, he opened his eyes. Then he used to stand up.

"Ah well, they are going a long way, my two sons."

Then he would pick up his spear and spear-thrower. He too would set off to find meat. He would go and spear it. He used to cook it in great haste. Then he would cover it all up near the meat from before that the others had already left. He used to cook his own meat until it was dry. Then he used to bury it. Then with his eyes he would look around for the others.

"Well, there are my two sons approaching. They are coming this way loaded down with meat."

Then, "Old man, are you well?"

"Are you bringing meat?"

"Yes, meat."

kajanyanujarrju!" Kala kurlarda manu, pikirri kala manu. Kala yarnkaja kuyukurrayijala. Kala panturnunjunu. Kala purraja yaruju-yarujurlu. Kala muku jurrurr-yungu kuyungka yangka nyurruwarnu kujapala kamparruwarnurlu yirrarnu Kala linjikarda purraja nyanungunyanguju. Kala yirrarnu kanunjumparra. Ngulajangkaju kalapalangu wapalpa nyangu milpangkuwiyi,

"Kari yinyapala rdipijarni waja ngajunyangujarraju kajajarraju. Kuyukurlu kapala yanirni waja, wawurla-wawurla-yanirni yangka."

Ngulajangkaju, "Purlka, ngurrjunya kanpa nyina?"

"Yuwayi, ngurrju karna nyina. Kuyukurlu mayinkili rdipija?"

"Yuwa, kuyu waja!"

Kala, kalapalangu nyurruwiyi nyangu. Ngayi kala wangkaja. Ngulajangkaju, kalapalarla kuyu yungu.

"Kuyunpa ngarni!" Ngirntirlangu kalapalarla yungu kuyu marlu nyampupiya. Kala ngarnu. Pakarninjarla kalapalarla yungu, milpakurlukujala. Well, pampa-jarrija kala. Ngulajangkaju, ngunajalku kalalu. Warlulku kalapalarla yarrpu-yarrpurnu. Ngunaja kalalu. Kala ngunaja jajinyanu, kajanyanukari, kajanyanuyijala. Jampijinpa kala ngunaja kulkurrujarraju, Lungkarda yirdiji. Kalapala Jangalajarra ngunaja nyanungu-nyangujarra.

Ngulajangkaju yanu, mungalyurru, yanupala watijarra yangkajarraju. Yanupala. Well kala wati nyampuju yanu purlkapardu. Kala wurnturu yangka nyinaja-aa.

"Walykakurra karna yani waja. Yinya walykangka waja karna nyina, yarlungka waja.

"Ya, nyinaya waja!"

"Walykangka karnangkupala jurnta nyina waja nyampujuku," kala wangkaja purlkaparduju. "Yuwaw!"

Kala marlu nyanungurluju kala purda-nyangu, kurdu yangka, kuja kala yangka kirrkirr-manu yinyarla, Kirrkirrmanurla yirdingkaju, nyanungunyangu maralypirla, mayi? Marlu kala witaju purda-nyanguwiyi. Kala kujarlu yangka purda-nyangu. "Kari palkajuku waja ka wangka."

Kulpajarni kala ngunanjakulku.

Ngulajangkaju, ngunajalkulpalu. Yanulkulpapala watijarra wirlinyi. Ngulajangkaju, lawa-lawapala parnkaja kujarra, yangka yungupala nyurruwiyi mukupungu Warlukurlangurla kutuju.

Although he had already seen them, he used to speak to them in this way. Then they would give him meat.

"Please eat this meat."

They would give him the tail of the kangaroo to eat. He ate it. After hunting the animal, they used to give him meat although he could see. However, in camp he used to pretend to be blind. Then they would lie down to sleep. The two of them built him a fire. Then one would lie down. They would lie down, the father, one son, the other son. Jampijinpa whose name was Bluetongue slept in the middle. The two Jangala would sleep beside him.

Then in the morning the two men would leave. They went. Then the old man would leave. Sometimes he sat down some distance away.

"I'll just go over there to where it is cool. I will sit there where it is cool, in the open. There, sit down! I'll sit here in the cool away from you two," the old man used to say to himself. "Yes, indeed!"

Here he used to listen to his own kangaroo, a baby one which used to whimper in that place, the place called Kirrkirrmanu, which was very sacred to him. He always used to listen to the little kangaroo, before. He used to listen to it, saying to himself, "It is still here, the one that talks."

Then he would go back to the camp and lie down.

Then they slept. The two young men went out hunting. They ran in that direction, away from the camp, but found nothing, that is, in the area where before they had caught everything, near Warlukurlangu. So they continued along the south side towards the place called Kirrkirrmanu. It was in that place that an animal used to call out, that particular kangaroo. He used to listen to the little animal.

What did the old man do with it in that place? Did he turn it into a person? I do not know.

Well, the two of them speared and killed it, the one that was particularly sacred to him. They speared and killed it. They cooked it. They killed the little animal. Kirrkirrmanu is the place where the child kangaroo first hops around on its four legs, like that. It was a young kangaroo like that that the two sons, the two Jangala, killed. And then, to tell the truth, they cooked it. They took it back to their camp, back there to Warlukurlangu, nearby. Where they had their camp, that is where they took it.

Kurlirra side-lki kalapala yanu nganayikirra yirdikirraju Kirrkir-rmanukurra. Kuyu yalumpuju kuju kalapalangu kirrkirrmanu, nganayi nyanungu marlu. Kala purda-nyangu kurdu.

Well, nyarrpa-mantarla marda watingkiji yinyarluju purlka-ngku? Yapa-jarriyarla marda? Karijaju.

Well, jurntapalarla panturnu kajilpa nyinaja nyanungunyangu yaliji maralypinyayirni. Jurntapalarla panturnu. Purrajalkulpapala. Kurdupala pakarnu kurdukurlu. Warrulpa yangka Kirrkirrmanu kujaka kurdurlangu warru yirrirlji-kanyi, ngulapiya. Ngulapiyanya-palarla jurnta-panturnu Jangalajarrarluju kajanyanujarrarlu. Yi-jardupala purraja. Kangupala ngurrakurra yangka yinya nganay-ikirra Warlukurlangukurra, kutukurra. Kujalpapala ngurrangka nyinaja, ngulakurrapala kangu.

Yungupalarla kuyu yirlara. Kulanganta yapakari, kulanganta yapakari wurnturujangka, kala nyanungunyangu yinyaju kuyu maralypirla, kujalpapalangu nyanungujarra nyanungukulparla nyi-najalku, yilparla kuyu. Kuyulpala nyinaja yapa marda, karija–mara-lypirla.

Ngulajankaju, mayajarrakurralkurla yanu,

"Ngurrjunyayirnirli kuja. Nyiya nyampuju ngurrjungku wajaju kaaly-pungu kuyungku? Nyarrpara marlurlu?" Manngu-nyan-gulkulpa, "Nyarrparawardingkiwiyiji nyampuju kuja kuyu maya-kurra yanu? Yangka kaaly-pungu ngurrjunyayirnirli." Ngurrjun-yayirni purda-nyangu kuyu. Nyampujarrakurrarla yanu, mayajar-rakurra yanu. "Ngurrju-manu yangka, nyampu ngurrjunyayirni waja mirnimpaju. Nyarrparajangka kuyu kujajupala kajanyanujar-rarlu kangurnu waja?" Yirlarapalarla yungu wita.

Yanu. Wuraji-wuraji-jarrija. Wanta yukaja and munga-munga-jarrijalku. Yarlukurralku yanu. Nyinajalpa purlkaparduju. Ngula-jangkaju, purda-nyangulparla. "Kari, lawajuku." Ngunajalpa yangka kuja. Well, kuja kala ngunaja-yi, "Nyarrpara kujaka wangka? Nyarrpara? Nyarrpa-manupala nyampujarrarlujuku waja-pala paka-rnunjunu. Pungupala nyampujarrarlujuku? Yangkajuku kujaju waja ngurrjunyayirni mayakurra yanu, nyampujuku marda?"

Ngulajangkaju, wurra-jarrija. Ngunajalkulpalu. Ngulajangkaju wirlinyikirralkupala yanu. Wirlinyilkipala yanu watijarraju. Wirlinyi-pala yanu. Mungakarirlakulpa yarda ngunaja. Kari

They gave him the meat, from the muscle. He thought it was meat from a different animal from much further away, but it was his own sacred animal, from there where the sacred animal which belonged to him alone had presented itself to the two men. It was meat from that animal.

Then he wanted to eat more.

"Very good! What is this meat which tastes so good to me? Where did this kangaroo come from?" He considered the matter. "From what particular place did this meat come from which makes me want to eat more? It tastes really wonderful." He found that the meat tasted very good. He went to the two of them and asked for more. "That was well done. That I found delicious. Where did my two sons get that meat?" They gave him a piece from a muscle, a small one.

He went. It became late afternoon. The sun set and it became dark. He went out into the open. The old man sat down. Then he listened for it. "Still nothing." He lay down there, he lay down in that place. "Where is the one who talks? Where? What have those two done with it? Have those two killed it? Have they hunted it? Was it that which was so good to eat that I wanted more, was it that meat?"

Then some time later, they all lay down to sleep. The two went hunting again. That night he lay down at the same place again. Still nothing, nothing at all. He listened for the call of the little kangaroo that used to call out for its mother, but he heard nothing.

Then he lay down on his own, alone. He returned to that open space. Still nothing. He began to grow very angry with the two men, his two sons. They went hunting. Still he could not find that animal. He looked into his own feelings. He began to feel hatred towards those two, his own two.

So he cut a stick. He began to concentrate his thoughts in the manner of a sorcerer, to harm them. He sent a fire to wait for them, like one you might light with a firestick, when they returned from hunting.

"Ayi, ayi."

They came along, coming back from hunting, from a long distance.

"Hey, perhaps that fire has burnt the old man, poor thing, the old man!"

The old man had concentrated his thoughts to harm those two. He had sent a sorcerer's fire by concentrating his thoughts precisely to lawajuku, lawajuku. Wanjani karla kirrkirr-manu, yangka marluju yirdija kala kirrkirr-manu, marlu wita-witaju ngati nyanunguku. Lawajuku.

Ngulajangkaju jintakulku ngunajarni, jintakulku. Yarda yanu yarlukurra. Ngulajangka yanu. Lawajuku. Jungajuku waja miyalurlulkupalangu nyangu wati nyampujarraju kajanyanujarraju nyanungunyangujarra. Yanupala wirlinyi. Ngulajangkaju, walkulku nyangu yangkaju kuyu. Miyalulkunyanu nyangu. Maju-jarrijalku miyalu—yangka nyanungunyangurlu.

"Nyampujarra nyampujuku waja."

Watiyalku pajurnu. Jangkardulkupalangu manngu-nyangu juyurdukurlurlu. Warlulkupalangu jirriny-pungu nyampupiya ngiji, jangunyu wirlinyijangkaku.

"Ayi! Ayi!"

Yaninja-yaninjarlalkupala yanu wurnturungurluju.

"Purlka marda ka kampa warlungku wiyarrpa, purlka marda!"

Purlkangkunyapalangu jangkardu juyurdu-manu. Nganayikipalangu manngu-nyangu jangkardu juyurdulku warlu. Nyurruwarnupaturlu kujalpalujana jangkardu manngu-nyangu yangka juyurdukurlurlu. Ngulajangkaju, purlka-purlkarluju kalu yangka nganayi mardarni juyurdu—yunparninjakurlangu.

Kuturnupala jarrija. Nyampu, "Purlka ka rduyu-karri! Purlka marda kampaja warlungku purdangirli pampa."

Kala lawa. Nyanungujarrakulaku yinyaju yungkurnu. Kuturnupala jarrija, kuturnupala jarrija. Warlumanji jankajarralku. Wapirdipalangu wajili-pungu warlungku. Wajili-pungupalangu. Palu-pungulpapala, palu-pungulpapala, palu-pungulpapala Lawajukulpapala palu-pungu parrkangku nyampurrapiyarlu. Ngula lawajuku. Juyurdu yalumpuju. Puyurrparlu pungulpapalangu. Palupungulpapala, palu-pungulpapala, palu-pungulpapala yalumpuwardingkirli yantarlirli, palu-pungulpapala, palu-pungulpapala, palu-pungulpapala.

Kurlirralkupala pardijarra tarnngalkujuku. Ngurra, ngurrangkalpa wantija. Nyanungu palijalku. Kulanganta yijardu warluju. Ngulajangka yakarralpapala pardija watijarra, Jangalajarra. Nyanungulpa warlu yakarra-pardi-jarrijalku. Yarnkajalpalu wurnalku. Kurlulumpayi-ii yarnkajalpalu. Palu-pinja-yanulpapala, harm them. It is for purposes like these that old have the powerful incantation that is used in singing.

They came closer. One of them said, "The old man is burning! Maybe the blind old man has been burnt by the fire."

But no. The fire had been lit for them. They came closer and closer. The trees were burning all around. The fire chased after them, coming nearer and nearer. It pursued them. They kept putting it out all around them, again and again. They kept extinguishing it with branches but to no avail. It continued to burn. It was a fire fuelled by sorcery. They could not breathe because of the smoke. The two who had been born in that place, in their own home, kept on putting it out and putting it out but it burnt on and on.

They travelled away for a long time to the south. When they camped overnight, it died away. They assumed it was a real fire. Then the two Jangala woke. The fire became active at the same time. They left on the journey. They travelled a long way to the south. As they walked they kept on putting the fire out, again and again. As when we look at the top part of a big fire, where it pushes itself right up to the clouds, well, it was a fire like that. As the old man had imagined it, so he watched it rise right up, like the top of a fire.

Then they lay down again. The fire died down and stopped. They set out towards the east. They awoke and the two of them travelled a long way. The sorcerer's fire woke at the same time, always present, always present. The fire chased them away from here, always further off it chased them, and they became more and more badly burnt. As they put it out, it consumed their feet. It ate at their feet, their knees, their heads until their skin was covered in burns.

At this point in the journey, the story belongs to the Pitjatjantjara [people in the neighboring country].

Then the fire sent them back. It brought them back. "This fire has burnt us from head to foot. It has burnt us all over. What shall we do? Shall we turn back towards home? Shall we go up into the sky? Shall we go under the earth?" they asked themselves. This is what they said, their skin covered in burns from the fire.

So they returned to this place, to the same place. They travelled and traveled, back to this place. As they walked along they still had to keep putting out the fire that burnt them. It continued to follow them,

palu-pinja-yanulpapala, palu-pinja-yanulpapala, palu-pinja-yanulpapala, palu-pinja-yanulpapala, palu-pinja-yanulpapala, palu-pinja-
yanulpapala, palu-pinja-yanulpapala. Yangka kujakarlipa lirranji
warlu nyanyi, lirranji yangku mangkurdurlangu kujaka yirrarni
warlungka, kujaka wirjarlu warlu ngula yangkaju fire, ngulangka.
Kankarlumparralku yirrarnu lirranjilki milya-pinjarlalku nyampurluju.

Ngulajangkaju, still ngunajalpalu yarda. Warlulpa lawa-jarrija,
walku-jarrijalpa yalumpuju. Kakarraralpapala pardija. Wurnturul-
kulpapala, yakarralpapala pardija nyanungulpapala. Warlu yakarra-
pardijayijala palkaju, palkayijala, juyurdujangarra. Wajili-pungulpa-
palangu warlungkuju kujarrarlalku, maju-maju wajili-pungul-
papalangu kujarrarlalku, wurnturulku. Wurnturulkupalangu wajili-
pungu. Palu-pungulpapala warluju. Palu-pinjarla nyampujarrajul-
papalangu ngarnu. Ngarnulpapalangu nyampujarraju mirdijijarra,
jurru nyampujarra winyirl-winyirlpalku. Ngarnulpapalangu.

Ngulajangkaju, wurnturulku yinya yimikari kujakalu wangka–
Pija-pija kujakalu wangka.

Ngulangkapalangu warlungkuju kulpari-kujurnu, kulpari-
manupalangu. "Karinganta warlungkungalingki waja nyampurluju
jurrupikni waja maju-manu. Mukungalingki kampaja! Nyarrparli
jarri? Warrulparli kulpa ngurrakurra waja? Nyarrpa-jarrirli? Yalkiri-
wana japarli yani? Kanunjumparrajaparli yani?" manngu-nyangul-
papala. Wangkajalpapala nyampujarraju winyirl-winyirlpalku warlu-
jangkaju.

Kulparirnipala yanu jurrkukurra ngurrakurra, nyampukurra.
Yanurnupala, yanurnupala, yanurnupala, yanurnupala, yanurnupala, yanurnupala. Palu-pinjarlalpapala wapaja, kuja. Yangkapi-
yarlujala kujapalangu kujapurdarlu puraja, ngulapiyarlujala. Yanurnupala, yanurnupala. Lirranjiwanapala yanurnu. Ngulangku-
pala jiwin-pungu, jiwin-pungu, jiwin-pungu. Yanurnupala. Pakaju-
manuwanapala yanurnu. Mata-jarrijapala ngulangkajuku.

Yalumpu ka karri watikirlangulku. Nganayilki maralypilki ka
karri. Mardukuja-yaninjawangu, lawa, watimipakurra.

Ngulajukurna ngarrurnu.

Recorded at Yuendumu, May 25, 1990

always with them, always burning in the same way. They came back. They came back past Lirranji. They staggered along in agony, trying not to brush against places where they had been burnt. They returned. The came past Pakajumanu.

There they stopped, exhausted. That place belongs to men. That is a sacred place. Women do not go there, only men.

That is all I have to tell.

TRANSLATORS' NOTE

This account of the Warlukurlangu (fire dreaming) story by Uni Nampijinpa is distinguished by its psychological realism, the detailed attention given to the characters and their feelings. The traditional story, very ancient, has great dramatic potential, describing as it does the persecution by the father, a figure of great magical power, of his two sons after they have broken a taboo of which they were not aware, ironically in order to satisfy him, and the subsequent painful deaths of the two young men.

In this version, the father, always deceitful, seems to take a delight in deceiving, and also in inflicting pain. The sons, always innocent, are also beautiful, young, open-hearted and generous. Thus, the way the boys die, driven for ever greater distances by a sorcerer's fire that seems to die out at night but each morning inexorably returns and, as exhaustion overtakes them, inflicts worse and worse burns, is beautifully and movingly described.

The activities of the father and the two sons in the area around Warlukurlangu and Kirrkirrmanu, and the flight of the two sons away from Warlukurlangu to the south and their return, map the locations of the important places in what one might describe as one of the Warlpiri heartlands. Thus, the story is a major Warlpiri jukurrpa, frequently performed as a dance, and also recorded in a number of large and important paintings.

WORDS TO KNOW

NOTE: When you write the definitions of the following words, make it a point to use at least three of them in conversation over the next day and three of them in your next writing assignment. Many times you'll find it difficult or impossible to use them in everyday speech or writing.

What then is the point of defining them? Of learning them? At the very least, in all the following cases where you have unusual vocabulary terms to define, attempt to use them. How does attempting to use vocabulary that feels awkward or different change the way you view your common speech and writing patterns? Learning how to use new vocabulary means just that—using the words. Write specifically how, where, when, and why you used the words and discuss with your class

windbreak—
Warlukurlangu—
Jangala—
Jampijinpa—
ayi—
Jukurrpa—
goannas—
Jarlarri—
Kirrkirrmanu—
Pitjatjantjara—
Lirranji—
Pakajumanu—

QUESTIONS

Before you create your collection of questions, remember that this type of narrative is very different from other types of readings in this anthology. The Aborigines tell stories; they don't write them. Writing them has come to be as a result of their encounters with Western culture. And, each story has a special map, a special painting that goes with it to show the audience where the story is in the universe. When you look at the painting that goes with this story, you should understand that the painting is the visualization of this story, an integral part of the story.

WRITING ACTIVITIES

1. Spend a half-hour researching Aborigine Dreaming and Dreamtime Stories. What do you learn that enlightens your understanding/appreciation for Warukurlangu? Jot down what you find to be interesting quotes (minimum a phrase, maximum a sentence) and follow each

quote with one or two sentences discussing why you noted it.

2. Choose one of your questions and write at least a page. Select and include one of your quotes in that page.

3. Set aside that writing for a day or so, and then expand the writing so that you have written two pages. Again, select one of your quotes to include on the second page. When you write the quote, put quotation marks around the entire phrase or sentence. Refer to your writing handbook to guide you as to which method of citing quotes is appropriate. Most often, you will be asked to use either the MLA or APA method of citing. Discuss with your instructor which method he or she wishes you to use.

4. You will note that this Aborigine story includes the original Warlpírí. What difference did that make to your reading of the story, if any? Discuss.

5. Include bits of a language other than standard English in your writing project. Select a new question to write on, if you wish, and include another established foreign language, a code you use with your friends, jargon, or some other non-mainstream terms which you feel will add detail, give strength to your writing.

6. Revise the writing to simply use standard English words in place of your foreign language, personal code, and/or jargon words.

7. Share your two writings with your classmates. Which did they respond to more strongly and why? What do "exotic" word choices add to the writing and why?

8. Do you feel your writing was balanced in its word choices? That is, did all the words flow well together, or were there places where words stood out in an inappropriate manner?

GRAMMAR AND STYLE QUESTIONS

1. An important element of good usage is the concise and active expression of thoughts and ideas. Looking through the Warpírí reading, find concise, active, grammatical expressions, put them into your own words, and see how you can make them still more concise.

2. Now take wordy, general expressions from your own writing that you've done based on this reading, and revise them to make them concise, active grammatical expressions.

The Origin of Rudolph
the Red-Nosed Reindeer

The Snopes Urban Legends Reference Pages is devoted to offering verification and/or verification of falsification of the origins of particular folklore and legends. The lead-in to the Snopes Urban Legends Reference Pages for Christmas reads "No celebration, religious or secular, dominates western society as thoroughly as Christmas. For nearly two months of the year we find ourselves awash in all the trappings of the season: Christmas cards, Christmas music, Christmas trees, Christmas lights—even Christmas postage stamps! Nativity scenes depicting the birth of Jesus dot the landscape, and images of Santa Claus are inescapable during the two-month long advertising blitz, mounted by purveyors of merchandise. A celebration so venerated, so long-lasting, and so ubiquitous—rich with traditions of both religious and secular origins—could scarcely avoid creating a rich legacy of folklore and legends." What follows is an index of colored bullets which identify each true story, false claim, item of undetermined veracity, and legend that is unverifiable.

Introduction This reading, which, the last time I read it on the Internet, played the theme song from Rudolph the Red-Nosed Reindeer as I read, includes historical information on the origin of Rudolph and a list of resources which not only support the writer's debunking of the Rudolph myth that we've all come to believe in, but allow you to do your own research and confirm what is posted on this site. Pictures and bullet points break up the flow of language in a way that reinforces the pop-culture nature of the subject and also adds humor and a "light" tone to the writing. But they also clearly point out what is fact and what is fiction—the purpose of the site's existence.

RUDOLPH

Claim
The character Rudolph the Red-Nosed Reindeer was created for the Montgomery Ward group of department stores.

Status
True

Synopsis
Rudolph the Red-Nosed Reindeer was created in 1939 by a copy-writer named Robert L. May, who came up with a poem about a mis-fit reindeer at the request of his employer, Montgomery Ward, for a Christmas story they could use as a store promotion.

Origins
The most of us, the character of Rudolph the Red-Nosed Reindeer—immortalized in song and a popular TV special—has always been an essential part of our Christmas folklore. But Rudolph is a decidedly twentieth-century invention whose creation can be traced to a specific time and person.

Rudolph came to life in 1939 when the Chicago-based Montgomery Ward company (operators of a chain of department stores) asked one of their copywriters, 34-year-old Robert L. May, to come up with a Christmas story they could give away to shoppers as a promotional gimmick. (The Montgomery Ward stores had been buy-ing and giving away coloring books for Christmas every year, and May's department head saw creating a giveaway booklet of their own as a way to save money.) May, who had a penchant for writing chil-dren's stories and limericks, was tapped to create the booklet.

May, drawing in part on the tale of The Ugly Duckling and his own background (he was often taunted as a child for being shy, small, and slight), settled on the idea of an underdog ostracized by the reindeer community because of his physical abnormality: a glow-ing red nose. Looking for an alliterative name, May considered and rejected Rollo (too cheerful and carefree a name for the story of a misfit) and Reginald (too British) before deciding on Rudolph. He then proceeded to write Rudolph's story in verse, as a series of rhyming couplets, testing it out on his 4-year-old daughter Barbara as he went along. Although Barbara was thrilled with Rudolph's story, May's boss was worried that a story featuring a red nose—an image associated with drinking and drunkards—was unsuitable for a Christmas tale. May responded by taking Denver Gillen, a friend from Montgomery Ward's art department, to the Lincoln Park Zoo to sketch some deer, Gillen's illustrations of a red-nosed reindeer over-came the hesitancy of May's bosses, and the Rudolph story was ap-proved. Montgomery Ward distributed 2.4 million copies of the Rudolph booklet in 1939, and although wartime paper shortages curtailed printing for the next several years, a total of 6 million copies had been given by the end of 1946.

The post-war demand for licensing the Rudolph character was tremendous, but since May had created the story as an employee of Montgomery Ward, they held the copyright and he received no royalties. Deeply in debt from medical bills resulting from his wife's terminal illness (she died about the time May created Rudolph), May persuaded Montgomery Ward's corporate president, Sewell Avery, to turn the copyright over to him in January 1947. With the rights to his creation in hand, May was set to become a wealthy man. "Rudolph the Red-Nosed Reindeer" was printed commercially in 1947 and shown in theaters as a nine-minute cartoon the following year. The Rudolph phenomenon really took off, however, when May talked his brother-in-law, songwriter Johnny Marks, into developing lyrics and a melody for a Rudolph song. Marks' musical version of "Rudolph the Red-Nosed Reindeer," recorded by Gene Autry in 1949, sold two million copies that year and went on to become one of the best-selling songs of all time, second only to "White Christmas." A TV special about Rudolph narrated by Burl Ives was produced in 1964 and remains a perennially popular holiday favorite in the USA.

May quit his copywriting job in 1951 and spent seven years managing his creation before returning to Montgomery Ward, where he worked until his retirement in 1971. By the time May died in 1976, his reindeer creation had indeed made him a rich man.

It might be fitting to close this page by pointing out that, although the story of Rudolph in primarily known to us through the lyrics of Johnny Marks' song, the story May wrote is substantially different in a number of ways. Rudolph was not one of Santa's reindeer (or the offspring of one of Santa's reindeer), and he did not live at the North Pole. Rudolph lived in an "ordinary" reindeer village elsewhere, and although he was taunted and laughed at for having a shiny red nose, he was not regarded by his parents as a shameful embarrassment. Rudolph was brought up in a loving household, and he was a responsible reindeer with a good self-image and sense of worth. Moreover, Rudolph did not rise to fame when Santa picked him out from the reindeer herd because of his shiny nose. Santa discovered the red-nosed reindeer quite by accident, when he noticed the glow emanating from Rudolph's room while delivering presents to Rudolph's house. Worried that the thickening fog—already the cause of several accidents and delays—will keep him from completing his Christmas Eve rounds, Santa taps Rudolph to lead his team, observing upon their return that "By YOU last night's journey was actually bossed./Without you, I'm certain we'd all have been lost!"

SOURCES

Archibald, John J. "Rudolph's Tale Left Him Cold." *St. Louis Post-Dispatch.* 6 December 1989 (p. 3E).

Frankel, Stanley A. "The Story Behind Rudolph the Red-Nosed Reindeer." *Good Housekeeping.* December 1989 (p. 126).

Lillard, Margaret. "Rudolph Lit Up Creator's Career." *Los Angeles Times.* 17 December 1989 (p. A7).

Lollar, Kevin. "Reginald the Red-Nosed Reindeer?" Gannet News Service. 21 December 1989.

Murphy, Cullen. "Rudolph Redux." *The Atlantic.* August 1990 (p. 18).

Ogintz, Eileen. "The Man Who Created Rudolph . . ." *Chicago Tribune.* 13 December 1990 (Tempo, p.1).

The Time-Life Book of Christmas. New York: Prentice Hall, 1987. ISBN 0-13-133679-7 (p. 101).

WORDS TO KNOW

NOTE: When you write the definitions of the following words, make it a point to use at least three of them in conversation over the next day and three of them in your next writing assignment. Many times you'll find it difficult or impossible to use them in everyday speech or writing. What then is the point of defining them? Of learning them? At the very least, in all the following cases where you have unusual vocabulary terms to define, attempt to use them. How does attempting to use vocabulary that feels awkward or different change your view of your common speech and writing patterns? Learning how to use new vocabulary means just that—using the words. Write specifically how, where, when, and why you used the words and discuss with your class

purveyors—
venerated—
ubiquitous—
unverifiable—
copywriter—
gimmick—
penchant—
ostracized—
alliterative—

couplets—
hesitancy—
royalties—
Johnny Marks—
Gene Autry—
Burl Ives—
perennially—

QUESTIONS

Create a series of questions—Text/You/Other and Three-Layered—for this reading on which you would be interested in developing a writing project. How do the stories, such as this one, of American culture compare/contrast to the stories of the Aborigine culture? What makes the story true? What makes it false? (This may seem like an easy question to answer, but it's harder than you think. Consider your answer carefully.)

WRITING ACTIVITIES

1. Trace the history of another urban myth. The Snopes web site is a good source to use to research other myths, but you should also investigate the sources given on the web site. Choose a myth which you have always been interested in and/or heard somewhere, from a friend perhaps, or that you believed.
2. Select one of your questions on which to write one to two pages and create your own story about something as part of the major point of that writing.
3. Don't let on to your audience, your readers, that what you're writing about isn't true, or don't let on to your audience, your readers, that what you're writing about may or may not be true.
4. Create several versions and hand them out to your classmates and see if they can determine which is the truth. What do they use to make their determination?

GRAMMAR AND STYLE QUESTIONS

1. One of the best ways to learn grammar, in addition to learning the names and rules of grammatical elements, is to read other people's

writing and determine how and why they write well. Take a grammatically imperfect piece of your own work, read two or three readings from this book, (including this piece from the Snopes web site as one of the selected readings), and rewrite your piece afterwards. Is it grammatically better? Why or why not? What was the impact of seeing how other people put together words?

2. Using a standard grammar reference (e.g., Strunk and White's *Elements of Style*), find three exceptions in this reading to the rules that such a standard reference has created, and discuss why the author broke those rules. Which impacted the author's choices more, the point that the author wanted to get across or the audience whom he wanted to reach, and why? Show support for your answer using specific examples from both the reading and your handbook of rules of grammar.

Of the Sorrow Songs

W. E. B. Du Bois

Born in 1868, Du Bois became one of the great pioneer sociologists. He was also the first African American to earn a Ph.D. from Harvard, as Randall Kenan points out in his foreword to The Souls of Black Folk. *In the Forethought of* The Souls of Black Folk, *Du Bois writes, "Herein lie buried many things which if read with patience may show the strange meaning of being black here at the dawning of the Twentieth Century. This meaning is not without interest to you, Gentle Reader; for the problem of the Twentieth Century is the problem of the color line."*

Introduction One of the most interesting and unusual aspects of Du Bois's style is that he begins each chapter with not just stanzas from the Sorrow Songs, but with a bar of the actual music itself, written in musical notation. Despite his having written this piece long before you were born, do you find the music helps you relate to the overly formal (contrasted to your everyday speech) language? In what way? The effect is to allow you to accept or see something you might not otherwise accept or see because words alone allow you to block yourself from it, whereas music works on an unconscious level and slips in the message, whether you want to hear it or not. Think about modern-day examples which have the same effect on you.

> I walk through the churchyard
>   to lay this body down;
> I know moon-rise, I know star-rise;
> I walk in the moonlight, I walk in the starlight;
> I'll lie in the grave and stretch out my arms,
> I'll go to judgment in the evening of the day,
> And my soul and thy soul shall meet that day,
>   When I lay this body down.
>
> NEGRO SONG.

They that walked in darkness sang songs in the olden days—Sorrow Songs—for they were weary at heart. And so before each thought that I have written in this book I have set a phrase, a haunting echo of these weird old songs in which the soul of the black slave spoke to men. Ever since I was a child these songs have stirred me strangely. They came out of the South unknown to me, one by one, and yet at once I knew them as of me and of mine. Then in after years when I came to Nashville I saw the great temple builded of these songs towering over the pale city. To me Jubilee Hall seemed ever made of the songs themselves, and its bricks were red with the blood and dust of toil. Out of them rose for me morning, noon, and night, bursts of wonderful melody, full of the voices of my brothers and sisters, full of the voices of the past.

Little of beauty has America given the world save the rude grandeur God himself stamped on her bosom; the human spirit in this new world has expressed itself in vigor and ingenuity rather than in beauty. And so by fateful chance the Negro folk-song—the rhythmic cry of the slave—stands to-day not simply as the sole American music, but as the most beautiful expression of human experience born this side of the seas. It has been neglected, it has been, and is, half despised, and above all it has been persistently mistaken and misunderstood; but notwithstanding, it still remains as the singular spiritual heritage of the nation and the greatest gift of the Negro people.

Away back in the thirties the melody of these slave songs stirred the nation, but the songs were soon half forgotten. Some, like "Near the lake where drooped the willow," passed into current airs and their source was forgotten; others were caricatured on the "minstrel" stage and their memory died away. Then in war-time came the singular Port Royal experiment after the capture of Hilton Head, and perhaps for the first time the North met the Southern slave face to face and heart to heart with no third witness. The Sea Islands of the Carolinas, where they met, were filled with a black folk of primitive type, touched and moulded less by the world about them than any others outside the Black Belt. Their appearance was uncouth, their language funny, but their hearts were human and their singing stirred men with a mighty power. Thomas Wentworth Higginson hastened to tell of these songs, and Miss McKim and others urged upon the world their rare beauty. But the world listened only half credulously until the Fisk Jubilee Singers sang the slave songs so deeply into the world's heart that it can never wholly forget them again.

There was once a blacksmith's son born at Cadiz, New York, who in the changes of time taught school in Ohio and helped defend Cincinnati from Kirby Smith. Then he fought at Chancellorsville and Gettysburg and finally served in the Freedman's Bureau at Nashville. Here he formed a Sunday-school class of black children in 1866, and sang with them and taught them to sing. And then they taught him to sing, and when once the glory of the Jubilee songs passed into the soul of George L. White, he knew his life-work was to let those Negroes sing to the world as they had sung to him. So in 1871 the pilgrimage of the Fisk Jubilee Singers began. North to Cincinnati they rode,—four half-clothed black boys and five girl-women,—led by a man with a cause and a purpose. They stopped at Wilberforce, the oldest of Negro schools, where a black bishop blessed them. Then they went, fighting cold and starvation, shut out of hotels, and cheerfully sneered at, ever northward; and ever the magic of their song kept thrilling hearts, until a burst of applause in the Congregational Council at Oberlin revealed them to the world. They came to New York and Henry Ward Beecher dared to welcome them, even though the metropolitan dailies sneered at his "Nigger Minstrels." So their songs conquered till they sang across the land and across the sea, before Queen and Kaiser, in Scotland and Ireland, Holland and Switzerland. Seven years they sang, and brought back a hundred and fifty thousand dollars to found Fisk University.

Since their day they have been imitated—sometimes well, by the singers of Hampton and Atlanta, sometimes ill, by straggling quartettes. Caricature has sought again to spoil the quaint beauty of the music, and has filled the air with many debased melodies which vulgar ears scarce know from the real. But the true Negro folk-song still lives in the hearts of those who have heard them truly sung and in the hearts of the Negro people.

What are these songs, and what do they mean? I know little of music and can say nothing in technical phrase, but I know something of men, and knowing them, I know that these songs are the articulate message of the slave to the world. They tell us in these eager days that life was joyous to the black slave, careless and happy. I can easily believe this of some, of many. But not all the past South, though it rose from the dead, can gainsay the heart-touching witness of these songs. They are the music of an unhappy people, of the children of disappointment; they tell of death and suffering and unvoiced longing toward a truer world, of misty wanderings and hidden ways.

The songs are indeed the siftings of centuries; the music is far more ancient than the words, and in it we can trace here and there signs of development. My grandfather's grandmother was seized by an evil Dutch trader two centuries ago; and coming to the valleys of the Hudson and Housatonic, black, little, and lithe, she shivered and shrank in the harsh north winds, looked longingly at the hills, and often crooned a heathen melody to the child between her knees, thus:

Do ba-na co-ba, ge-ne me, ge-ne me!

Do ba-na co-ba, ge-ne me, ge-ne me!

Ben d' nu-li, nu-li, nu-li, nu-li, ben d' le.

The child sang it to his children and they to their children's children, and so two hundred years it has travelled down to us and we sing it to our children, knowing as little as our fathers what its words may mean, but knowing well the meaning of its music.

This was primitive African music; it may be seen in larger form in the strange chant which heralds "The Coming of John":

"You may bury me in the East,
You may bury me in the West,
But I'll hear the trumpet sound in that morning,"

—the voice of exile.

Ten master songs, more or less, one may pluck from this forest of melody—songs of undoubted Negro origin and wide popular currency, and songs peculiarly characteristic of the slave. One of these I have just mentioned. Another whose strains begin this book is "Nobody knows the trouble I've seen." When, struck with a sudden poverty, the United States refused to fulfill its promises of land to the freedmen, a brigadier-general went down to the Sea Islands to carry the news. An old woman on the outskirts of the throng began singing this song; all the mass joined with her, swaying. And the soldier wept.

The third song is the cradle-song of death which all men know,—"Swing low, sweet chariot,"—whose bars begin the life story of "Alexander Crummell." Then there is the song of many waters, "Roll, Jordan, roll," a mighty chorus with minor cadences. There were many songs of the fugitive like that which opens "The Wings of Atalanta," and the more familiar "Been a-listening." The seventh is the song of the End and the Beginning—"My Lord, what a mourning! when the stars begin to fall"; a strain of this is placed before "The Dawn of Freedom." The song of groping—"My way's cloudy"—begins "The Meaning of Progress"; the ninth is the song of this chapter— "Wrestlin' Jacob, the day is a breaking,"—a pæan of hopeful strife. The last master song is the song of songs—"Steal away,"—sprung from "The Faith of the Fathers."

There are many others of the Negro folk-songs as striking and characteristic as these, as, for instance, the three strains in the third, eighth, and ninth chapters; and others I am sure could easily make a selection on more scientific principles. There are, too, songs that seem to be a step removed from the more primitive types: there is the maze-like medley, "Bright sparkles," one phrase of which heads "The Black Belt"; the Easter carol, "Dust, dust and ashes"; the dirge, "My mother's took her flight and gone home"; and that burst of melody hovering over "The Passing of the First-Born"—"I hope my mother will be there in that beautiful world on high."

These represent a third step in the development of the slave song, of which "You may bury me in the East" is the first, and songs like "March on" (chapter six) and "Steal away" are the second. The first is African music, the second Afro-American, while the third is a blending of Negro music with the music heard in the foster land. The result is still distinctively Negro and the method of blending original, but the elements are both Negro and Caucasian. One might go further and find a fourth step in this development, where the songs of white America have been distinctively influenced by the slave songs or have incorporated whole phrases of Negro melody, as "Swanee River" and "Old Black Joe." Side by side, too, with the growth has gone the debasements and imitations—the Negro "minstrel" songs, many of the "gospel" hymns, and some of the contemporary "coon" songs,—a mass of music in which the novice may easily lose himself and never find the real Negro melodies.

In these songs, I have said, the slave spoke to the world. Such a message is naturally veiled and half articulate. Words and music have lost each other and new and cant phrases of a dimly under-stood theology have displaced the older sentiment. Once in a while we catch a strange word of an unknown tongue, as the "Mighty Myo," which figures as a river of death; more often slight words or mere doggerel are joined to music of singular sweetness. Purely secular songs are few in number, partly because many of them were turned into hymns by a change of words, partly because the frolics were seldom heard by the stranger, and the music less often caught. Of nearly all the songs, however, the music is distinctly sorrowful. The ten master songs I have mentioned tell in word and music of trouble and exile, of strife and hiding; they grope toward some unseen power and sigh for rest in the End.

The words that are left to us are not without interest, and, cleared of evident dross, they conceal much of real poetry and meaning beneath conventional theology and unmeaning rhapsody. Like all primitive folk, the slave stood near to Nature's heart. Life was a "rough and rolling sea" like the brown Atlantic of the Sea Islands; the "Wilderness" was the home of God, and the "lonesome valley" led to the way of life. "Winter'll soon be over," was the picture of life and death to a tropical imagination. The sudden wild thunder-storms of the South awed and impressed the Negroes,—at times the rumbling seemed to them "mournful," at times imperious:

> "My Lord calls me,
> He calls me by the thunder,
> The trumpet sounds it in my soul."

The monotonous toil and exposure is painted in many words. One sees the ploughmen in the hot, moist furrows, singing:

> "Dere's no rain to wet you,
> Dere's no sun to burn you,
> Oh, push along, believer,
> I want to go home."

The bowed and bent old man cries, with thrice-repeated wail:

> "O Lord, keep me from sinking down,"

and he rebukes the devil of doubt who can whisper:

> "Jesus is dead and God's gone away."

Yet the soul-hunger is there, the restlessness of the savage, the wail of the wanderer, and the plaint is put in one little phrase:

My soul wants something that's new, that's new

Over the inner thoughts of the slaves and their relations one with another the shadow of fear ever hung, so that we get but glimpses here and there, and also with them, eloquent omissions and silences. Mother and child are sung, but seldom father; fugitive and weary wanderer call for pity and affection, but there is little of wooing and wedding; the rocks and the mountains are well known, but home is unknown. Strange blending of love and helplessness sighs through the refrain:

> "Yonder's my ole mudder,
> Been waggin' at de hill so long;
> 'Bout time she cross over,
> Git home bime-by."

Elsewhere comes the cry of the "motherless" and the "Farewell, farewell, my only child."

Love-songs are scarce and fall into two categories—the frivolous and light, and the sad. Of deep successful love there is ominous silence, and in one of the oldest of these songs there is a depth of history and meaning:

A black woman said of the song, "It can't be sung without a full heart and a troubled sperrit." The same voice sings here that sings in the German folk-song:

> "Jetz Geh i' an's brunele, trink' aber net."

Of death the Negro showed little fear, but talked of it familiarly and even fondly as simply a crossing of the waters, perhaps—who knows?—back to his ancient forests again. Later days transfigured his fatalism, and amid the dust and dirt the toiler sang:

> "Dust, dust and ashes, fly over my grave,
> But the Lord shall bear my spirit home."

The things evidently borrowed from the surrounding world undergo characteristic change when they enter the mouth of the slave. Especially is this true of Bible phrases. "Weep, O captive daughter of Zion," is quaintly turned into "Zion, weep-a-low," and the wheels of Ezekiel are turned every way in the mystic dreaming of the slave, till he says:

> "There's a little wheel a-turnin' in-a-my heart."

As in olden time, the words of these hymns were improvised by some leading minstrel of the religious band. The circumstances of the gathering, however, the rhythm of the songs, and the limitations of allowable thought, confined the poetry for the most part to single or double lines, and they seldom were expanded to quatrains or longer tales, although there are some few examples of sustained efforts, chiefly paraphrases of the Bible. Three short series of verses have always attracted me,—the one that heads this chapter, of one line of which Thomas Wentworth Higginson has fittingly said, "Never, it seems to me, since man first lived and suffered was his infinite longing for peace uttered more plaintively." The second and third are descriptions of the Last Judgment,—the one a late improvisation, with some traces of outside influence:

> "Oh, the stars in the elements are falling,
> And the moon drips away into blood,
> And the ransomed of the Lord are returning unto God,
> Blessed be the name of the Lord."

And the other earlier and homelier picture from the low coast lands:

> "Michael, haul the boat ashore,
> Then you'll hear the horn they blow,
> Then you'll hear the trumpet sound,
> Trumpet sound the world around,
> Trumpet sound for rich and poor,
> Trumpet sound the Jubilee,
> Trumpet sound for you and me."

Through all the sorrow of the Sorrow Songs there breathes a hope—a faith in the ultimate justice of things. The minor cadences of despair change often to triumph and calm confidence. Sometimes it is faith in life, sometimes a faith in death, sometimes assurance of boundless justice in some fair world beyond. But whichever it is, the meaning is always clear: that sometime, somewhere, men will judge men by their souls and not by their skins. Is such a hope justified? Do the Sorrow Songs sing true?

The silently growing assumption of this age is that the probation of races is past, and that the backward races of to-day are of proven inefficiency and not worth the saving. Such an assumption is the arrogance of peoples irreverent toward Time and ignorant of the deeds of men. A thousand years ago such an assumption, easily possible, would have made it difficult for the Teuton to prove his right to life. Two thousand years ago such dogmatism, readily welcome, would have scouted the idea of blond races ever leading civilization. So woefully unorganized is sociological knowledge that the meaning of progress, the meaning of "swift" and "slow" in human doing, and the limits of human perfectability, are veiled, unanswered sphinxes on the shores of science. Why should Æschylus have sung two thousand years before Shakespeare was born? Why has civilization flourished in Europe, and flickered, flamed, and died in Africa? So long as the world stands meekly dumb before such questions, shall this nation proclaim its ignorance and unhallowed prejudices by denying freedom of opportunity to those who brought the Sorrow Songs to the Seats of the Mighty?

Your country? How came it yours? Before the Pilgrims landed we were here. Here we have brought our three gifts and mingled them with yours: a gift of story and song—soft, stirring melody in an ill-harmonized and unmelodious land; the gift of sweat and brawn to beat back the wilderness, conquer the soil, and lay the foundations of this vast economic empire two hundred years earlier than your weak hands could have done it; the third, a gift of the Spirit. Around us the history of the land has centred for thrice a hundred years; out of the nation's heart we have called all that was best to throttle and subdue all that was worst; fire and blood, prayer and sacrifice, have billowed over this people, and they have found peace only in the altars of the God of Right. Nor has our gift of the Spirit been merely passive. Actively we have woven ourselves with the very warp and woof of this nation,—we fought their battles, shared their sorrow, mingled our blood with theirs, and generation after generation have pleaded with a headstrong, careless people to despise not Justice, Mercy, and Truth, lest the nation be smitten with a curse. Our song, our toil, our cheer, and warning have been given to this nation in blood-brotherhood. Are not these gifts worth the giving? Is not this work and striving? Would America have been America without her Negro people?

Even so is the hope that sang in the songs of my fathers well sung. If somewhere in this whirl and chaos of things there dwells Eternal Good, pitiful yet masterful, then anon in His good time America shall rend the Veil and the prisoned shall go free. Free, free as the sunshine trickling down the morning into these high windows of mine, free as yonder fresh young voices welling up to me from the caverns of brick and mortar below—swelling with song, instinct with life, tremulous treble and darkening bass. My children, my little children, are singing to the sunshine, and thus they sing:

And the traveller girds himself, and sets his face toward the Morning, and goes his way.

WORDS TO KNOW

NOTE: When you write the definitions of the following words, make it a point to use at least three of them in conversation over the next day and three of them in your next writing assignment. Many times you'll find it difficult or impossible to use them in everyday speech or writing. What then is the point of defining them? Of learning them? At the very least, in all the following cases where you have unusual vocabulary terms to define, attempt to use them. How does attempting to use vocabulary that feels awkward or different change your view of your common speech and writing patterns? Learning how to use new vocabulary means just that—using the words. Write specifically how, where, when, and why you used the words and discuss with your class.

Jubilee Hall—

ingenuity—

caricatured—

minstrel—

uncouth—

Thomas Wentworth Higginson—

Miss McKim—

Fisk Jubilee Singers—

Freedman's Bureau—

Henry Ward Beecher—

brigadier—

doggerel—

dross—

cadences—

woof—

QUESTIONS

Create a series of questions, both Text/You/Other and Three-Layered, based on this reading. As you've done previously, see how you can revise questions from earlier readings to incorporate this new reading, in addition to creating new questions. Du Bois has included yet another form of media in his "Of The Sorrow Songs." Have you seen music used in this way before? How does it add to the text? How does it help to create the reading? Do you agree with his statement about these songs representing "the sole of American music"?

WRITING ACTIVITIES

1. Before or as you write your questions, select a piece of music to incorporate into your piece, using Du Bois' piece as a model to follow. Don't feel like you have to use your music in the exact same way that he did; instead, use his style to suggest a style and organization to you. Think about how you used images as both central and additional sources in earlier writing projects and play with how you could use music in similar ways.

2. Du Bois really makes use of the music itself, not just the lyrics. Which do you see to be more important and why?

3. Write two different versions of your piece, one that relies on the audience having heard the music before or hearing it as they read what you've written, and one that doesn't. What do you see to be the differences between these two writing projects?

4. When you present your writing to your classmates, make sure that you either have a recorded version of the music you can play to them (you might even be prepared to sing it if no recording is available to you). How do they respond to the two different written approaches to the same initial question?

GRAMMAR AND STYLE QUESTIONS

1. Compare and contrast Du Bois's reading with another selected author's reading from this book. How do they use forms of grammar and elements of style to get their points across? How does their use of grammar to get their points across differ? What are the common features of both? Use specific rules of grammar and details in your answer.

2. Using these same two authors, how does each author use unconventional layouts and/or sources and examples in their readings to help readers visualize their words? How do these examples affect their adherence to standard rules of grammar? Use specific examples from the readings in your answer.

A Sorcerer's Bottle: The Visual Art of Magic in Haiti

Elizabeth McAlister

When you think about it, Christianity and its practices have been held up as the standard by which all other religions have been deemed civilized or primitive, good or evil, right or wrong. In a very real sense Vodou, of most of the major non-Christian world religions, has suffered the worst at the punishing hand of the Christian "Right." Haitian vodou has held together a whole country of people in a way which makes its spirituality a waking and sleeping part of life—always. Vodou isn't something one tries on for effect—contrary to what Hollywood would have us believe. Think about where you learned what you know (or don't know) about Vodou. Do you trust those sources? Why? Why not?

Introduction Elizabeth McAlister's piece is a good one to compare and contrast with the piece you read earlier in this reader about the Indian deity idol. Again, you have very intensive description and a particular chronological order (and reason for that order) in which she describes the object. She also ponders over her description; she doesn't simply describe the object as though she'd rather be looking at something else or as though she were writing her piece for an English class assignment. Where are the signs of her taking her time and "savoring" her description so that as readers, we can also "savor" it? Do you see signs of this relishing of details in your own writing? Why or why not? What examples could you use or revise from your own writing to demonstrate its effect?

I stepped into a dry dusty alleyway lined with brightly painted houses in a poor neighborhood in Port-au-Prince one summer to pay my respects to the mother of a Haitian friend I know in New York.

Sanpwèl bottle containing zonbi (spirits of the dead). Glass, fabric, string, mirror, scissors, magnets. Approx. height, 30.5 cm. Courtesy of Elizabeth McAlister.

Kissing and exclaiming my way through the various homes of his family, I was weak from the unspeakable heat and the loud pounding of *Compas* music coming from outdoor speakers. At one disoriented moment I found myself shaking hands with a solid man who had small, baby-like teeth, and a huge grin. "If you're really an *ethnologue* you should visit him. He's a *bòkò*," someone said.

A bòkò is a Haitian expert in supernatural matters. He is a bit of a man out for himself, a freelancer, unlike the *oungan* or *manbo* who establish religious family networks. A bòkò is an entrepreneur, and has a reputation as a man who will "work with both hands," that is, for healing *and* revenge. Traditional anthropology would call him a sorcerer.

The next day I made my way to his house—one of many in a labyrinth of colored concrete boxes with tin roofs along a sewage ravine in Monatuf, a downtown Port-au-Prince slum. The bòkò, named St. Jean, invited me in, smiling to show his tobacco-stained baby teeth and speaking in a very staccato Creole. We stuck to a "nice day, nice house" sort of conversation while he treated me to swigs of *kleren* cane liquor laced, he said, with anti-poison remedy. I couldn't help but stare at his altar, which took up most of the room. There sat an object as beautiful to my eye as it was strange: a bottle wrapped in cloth of red, white and black, with mirrors fastened around its midriff like headlights. Scissors, frozen in an open position and lashed to its neck, made big exes. "Nice bottle," I said. "Thank you," he said. "Do you want me to make you one?"

The bottle was thus commissioned; I thought of it as my first piece of art. Or was it? Right before he gave it to me, the bòkò turned it into a work of magic, a *wanga*.[1] He performed a ritual on it that I didn't fully comprehend. Even after I brought the bottle home, it remained an enigma. How can a person from one culture fully understand an object from another culture? I decided to work to find out what this wanga was, how it worked, why it was so visually arresting. As I gazed at the bottle, I found it gazing back at me. It began speaking loudly in visual language, teaching me about the interrelatedness of secrecy and knowledge in Haitian magic arts, and about the poetics of will and desire, and slavery and death. Together, the bottle and I taught each other about the deep-rootedness of central African religions in Haiti, and about where it is that history lies in a land where people don't read and write. My conversations with the bottle became a journey, and this essay its story.

*The footnotes can be found in the original text listed in full on the Credits page of this book.

The bottle is an artistic creation, but it is also a wanga, or *travay maji*, a "magic work." How was I to find out what it means, *how* it works? Recent work in material culture studies gave me an avenue of investigation: any human-made object, even one whose meaning is obvious, is a site for multiple layers of meanings, uses, symbolisms, and connotations. Any object is a possible key to the culture that designed it.

Whatever the meaning of this bottle for its maker, in my possession it immediately began to function within a "capitalist system of objects," as an acquired, collected possession, displayed on my coffee table for people to admire.[2] It was only later when I realized the seriousness of the bottle that I removed it out of sight of visitors to my home. The bottle was a constructed, visually coded object, of great aesthetic sophistication, and so on one hand it was art. Yet it was a "fetish" made by a "sorcerer" and so it was also ethnographic. It might occupy a place in what James Clifford calls the "institutionalized systemic opposition between art and culture," into which objects collected from non-Western places inevitably fall. "Generally speaking the system confronts any collected exotic object with a stark alternative between a second home in an ethnographic or an aesthetic milieu," says Clifford.[3] As I began to understand this Haitian piece I came to see how its proper home, if it is to have a public home, can only truly appreciate its aesthetic style together with its cultural history.

Almost everyone who saw the bottle on my coffee table commented on it. "You know, that thing never stops," remarked one friend absently as she spoke about something else. Indeed, the bottle moves and swirls in its own way. This observation is the sort that material culture studies can build on. Begin with the axiom that any made object embodies the assumptions or beliefs of the maker's culture. Then, start an analysis using one's own senses. The object will provide its own evidence for research and interpretation. Back home in my living room, I scrutinized the bottle for clues.[4]

"That thing never stops." It is a bottle, but a most spectacular bottle. It is actually a Barbancourt rum bottle, as one can see by reading the label as it shows through its cloth covering. (Barbancourt is a Haitian rum-maker.) But the label and the shape are the only evidence that it is a bottle. There is no longer any rum inside it. What is inside is not potable; it is filled with a heavily scented liquid. The liquid smells overwhelmingly of perfume, and it has sediment in it, which one can see encrusted along the inside of the bottle's neck. The liquid gives the bottle a weighty quality, a bottom-heaviness which is quite pronounced when I hold it. When I open the cap three pins lie across the inside of the bottleneck, held there by magnets on the outside. Pins join, pins prick, pins hold. They seem to stand in relation to the rest of the bottle simply as pieces of metal—in terms of their most essential characteristic; their metal-ness.

The bottle has a top-heaviness, because of the three magnets that encircle the outside of the bottle's neck. They are industrial magnets, perhaps, round and three-quarters of an inch thick, the color of stainless-steel. They protrude from the thin neck of the bottle, making a collar or necklace. A woman's yellow earring perches on one of the magnets, giving the bottle a jaunty look. Magnets are elemental forces; a magnetic field surrounds the planet itself. Compasses steer travelers by way of magnetism, lining up the arrow with the northernmost point of the earth. Magnetism creates the earth's life-force at its foundations. In this bottle, magnets creates a dynamism so that the pins inside stick to the bottleneck. They make up an enclosed polarity, a discrete ecosystem.

The entire bottle save for the unadorned Barbancourt cap is covered in black, white and red cloth in three vertical sections. These are all strong colors with symbolic associations in every culture. Except for the magnets the whole bottle is constructed in terms of a theme of wrapping. This suggests an element of secrecy, for whatever is inside the bottle is hidden.

Two pairs of small opened scissors stand lashed on either side of the bottle neck with red thread. A basic tool in many cultures, scissors cut paper, cloth, cardboard and string. Like pins they are sharp and can be dangerous. Scissors are also anthropomorphic, with four "limbs." These scissors stand lashed in an open position across from one another on opposite sides, giving the bottle an illusion of formal symmetry. However the symmetry is broken, subtly, because there are only three rather than four colored panels of cloth, and also because of the positioning of the four mirrors that sit tied to the bottle directly under but slightly to the side of the scissors. It is this asymmetry alongside symmetry that causes the eye to spiral around the bottle, making it look as though "it never stops."

Four mirrors below the scissors are round, and about one and a half inches across, with a green plastic frames. They have been lashed to the bottle with red thread, in such a way as to make both a horizontal and a vertical line through each mirror. The mirrors are slightly dusty. Between the thread and the dust one can't see very much of a whole reflection in them. The mirrors seem to be *refracting* more than *reflecting*. Shiny light-catchers: they both attract the eye and reflect light.

Perfume, pins, magnets, scissors, mirrors: all of this bottle's features are elemental and simple. Interestingly, each feature has opposing characteristics that lead to a practical impasse: perfume with something sharp in it, huge magnets holding only three small pins, sharp scissors frozen in a useless, open position, mirrors that you can't see yourself in, wrapped with thread that obscures them. What do perfume, pins, magnets, scissors, and mirrors mean in Haitian symbolic codes? What do they mean in relation to each other?

Below the mirrors nothing more protrudes from the bottle, which simply continues down to its cloth-wrapped bottom. The midpoint of the bottle seems to be at the same line as the horizontal thread that spreads across each mirror. This line cuts the object in half horizontally, then, while the scissors, which are symmetrically opposed to one another, cut it vertically. But these two aspects of symmetry are set in opposition at different points along the colored cloth wrapping, putting the viewer off balance. The lines of scissors and mirrors lead the eye around and around the bottle in a colorful spiral of red, white, and black.

Red, white, and black, it turns out, are the primary colors of the Petwo rite, the *nanchon* or "nation" within Afro-Haitian religion that likes its drums played by hand with slaps and pops that crack like whip lashes. Petwo is the rite whose spirits are invoked, in fact, by cracking whips, by lighting gunfire, by pouring cane liquor kleren libations instead of rum. Petwo lwa like fire, they are "hot," and their magic can work fast and be dangerous. Maya Deren wrote that while the Rada nanchon descended from various West African cultures, Petwo spirits were "creole," born in Haiti out of slavery and rebellion.[5] This is articulated over and over by elders, and there is an historical link between Petwo and resistance.[6] Writing in the Fifties before recent research, Deren had no way of knowing that many Petwo spirits, colors, magical practices and ritual gestures are elements found in the Kongo kingdom that yielded so many of its people to the Atlantic slave trade.[8] Some words in Petwo song prayers are in KiKongo. "Petwo and Kongo, it's the same path," the spirits will tell you.[9]

To identify linguistic and symbolic elements in Afro-Haitian religion that derive from Kongo cultures is not to suggest that Kongo languages and religious systems are flourishing in Haiti, centuries after the slave trade. It is to point out that these cultural elements, which have since been creolized and re-configured, have an identifiable historical source. Knowing this may lead us to suggestions about meanings, logics, and aesthetic principles fueling subsequent cultural expression. Identifying something of the sources is always only the beginning. We must then hold meanings and aesthetics up against the reality of changing political and economic processes. Afro-Haitian religion is a creolized New World system with multiple sources throughout Africa and also Europe and the indigenous peoples of Haiti. It continues to be influenced by militarism, U.S. popular culture, and trans-migrants from the Haitian diaspora.

As with any cluster of symbols that moves through time, Kongo-Haitian elements have changed and interacted with the lives of other sign systems. They may feed from other cultural logics— here the Fon, or the Yoruba, or French-style Catholicism, or postcolonial capitalism, or the codes of the Duvalier regime. The Haitian flag under Duvalier, for example, was black and red (with white in the inset)—changed by the dictator himself from the blue and red in a display of Haitian negritude. And black, red, and white are also the primary colors in Central African religions and cultures.[10]

Of this color triad, Fu-Kiau Bunseki-Lumanisa, the Zairean scholar, himself a MuKongo, writes that "the life of man in this country turns around these three colors, and they constitute the principle base of knowledge."[11] The colors, used in religious rituals, healings, and magical work, express the range of possibilities within the cosmic and social order. In Kongo ritual work, the three colors are combined and contrasted by the *nganga* (doctor-priest) according to the situation at hand. (His Haitian male counterpart, the *oungan*, is also called *gangan*.)

The colors black, white, and red are dressing this bottle to indicate that it is a Petwo *wanga*. This broadcasts its "hot" nature, its willingness to "do work" *(fe travay)*. But what of the rest of the bottle's "costume"? What of the four mirrors lashed to the bottle's midsection, bisected by red string.

Mirrors in Haitian thought can stand in poetically for conceptions of the afterlife, the passage between life and death. They signify water, and water, in turn, is of sacred importance. *An ba dlo* literally means, in Kreyòl, "underneath the water," and it stands for the land where the *lwa* live, and where human souls go for a year and a day after they die. One prayer song makes these three connections explicit:

Anonse, O zanj nan dlo,
Bak, O sou mirwa,
L'a wè l' a wè . . .

Announcing, oh angels in the water,
Boat, oh on the mirror,
He'll see (or) she'll see . . .

Death is a new beginning; it represents a passage into the spirit realm. The initiated soul will go to "an ba dlo," a spiritual dwelling full of spirits and other souls. It is conceived as being a land underneath the water itself, but not necessarily underwater. Sometimes it is *lòt bo* or "the other side." Sometimes it is called *nan Ginen*, the mythological, spiritual Africa that lies across purifying, ancestral waters.

Likewise, in traditional Kongo cosmology, the lands of the living and the dead are separated by a horizontal line referred to as *nlangu*, "separated by water."[12] The universe is a circle, and the upper sphere is the earth, where we, the living dwell. The bottom sphere, under the water, is the land called Mpemba, that belongs to the dead, and is signified by the color white. The sun, as it makes its journey through the sky, visits the living and the dead at opposite times, so that noon for the living is midnight for the spirits of the dead. Likewise, dawn for the living is dusk for the dead. These four points in the sun's travels, in two opposing worlds, stand in for the human life cycle itself, *ziingu kia muuntu*, or "life of man." The sun at dawn signals birth, the sun at noon the peak of youth. The sun's setting at dusk represents the declining years, and the sun at our midnight travels, of course, to where people do: the white *mpemba*, land of the dead.[13]

These four points are a generative scheme for a great deal of Kongo art and philosophy, both in Africa and in the Afro-Americas, as Robert Farris Thompson has demonstrated.[14] In any Vodou ritual the four corners are saluted at each new phase of the ceremony. Candles are held to the four directions when lit, and liquids shown to the four corners before libations are poured. There is a two-fold idea that the spirits of the four directions must be saluted, and also that the energies of the four directions be consolidated in order to draw them onto a specific point or *pwen*, either in a *vèvè* drawing, or in a magical work, *wanga*. With this in mind, this bottle's four mirrors fixed at opposing points can be seen as yet another reference to the life cycle in Kongo-Haitian cosmology. By using four mirrors, the bòkò creates his own site of spiritual "heat" and a place of action and "work," and at the very same time he elegantly references the landscape of the Kongo-Haitian life cycle: the world of the living and the world *an ba dlo*, under the water.

Reading in the literature on black, white, and red in Kongo culture, it seems that the colors are, in a sense, a way to think. Loosely stated, the color white stands for reason, truth, health, good luck, intelligence, and clear sight; also for Mpemba, the land of the dead. Black, in turn, symbolizes guilt, wrong, envy, social disorder, intentions of killing, and rebellion.[15] The color red signifies sexual desire, vulnerability, magical power, and mediation. The colors are also "thought" into the cosmological theories of the BaKongo: the circle of the sun's path surrounds two mountains in two spheres, one of which is black (for the living) and the other, below, is white, for the dead. So if the white is associated with the ancestors, with purity, truth, and clear sight, then the world of the living, in turn, is imperfect, ignorant, a site for evil and secrecy. The water separating them is the great barrier between the worlds; is life-giving, mediating, and associated with the color red, sunrises and sunsets. Red, then, is implicated in passages, ambivalences, in-between stages of a social or religious nature. This tri-color classifying system is integrated with Kongo cosmology to express the most fundamental of the culture's philosophies.[16]

Kongo body language gives us a possible meaning for the scissors that stand lashed to the bottleneck. Thompson writes that "Where hands are brought in, the palms are placed in either shoulder, the arms are crossed before the heart . . . this is *tuluwa ku luumba*, literally "placing oneself within the enclosure."[17] The scissors seem to be limbs indeed; arms crossed under the bottleneck. Now we can understand why the bottle looks like a person, arms crossed. The bottle as a whole is protected by this gesture of defense, in a visual pun using everyday objects.

The bottle's "dress" is a signifying system: it is wearing Petwo colors, which I have suggested derive from Kongo religious thought. It speaks metaphorically about the watery passage from life to death, and about the four cardinal directions. The scissors signal negation, protection, and self-control. Not a simple piece of art, the wanga is, in Haitian vernacular, a *gwo koze*, or a "big talk." It delivers an enormous message in "visual vocabulary."[18] As such it is an abbreviation of centuries-old Kongo cultural knowledge, reincorporated into a larger Afro-Haitian religious tradition.[19]

If this is a Petwo wanga, descended from Kongo spirit practices, then one would expect the BaKongo people to have had a similar magic—and they do. In the Kongo context, containers with instructive visual codes, puns, and specific work to do are called *minkisi* (singular, *nkisi*). Labeled "charm" and "fetish" by Europeans, an *nkisi* was essentially a container of spirit, constructed and controlled by humans.[20] Usually drawn from the spirits of the dead, the nkisi was there to act, or activate, a particular desire of its maker, the *nganga-nkisi*. More often than not, minkisi were used in healings, and could also be used for good luck, good hunting, and the like. Like the bottle, minkisi were colored red, white and black, in combination depending on their use.[21]

If the bottle is a Haitian version of an nkisi, which it certainly must be, then I actually witnessed its consecration when I went to pick up what I thought was my "commissioned art piece." I was admiring the bottle when St. Jean presented it to me. "Would you like me to put good luck in?" he pushed. It seemed like an intriguing idea.

I sat across from St. Jean the bòkò's altar, on his bed, and he sat in an enormous barber's chair. He rummaged around for a cassette tape and snapped it into his Panasonic tape player. Out came the chants of a song recorded at a Sanpwèl society, of which, he said, he was a member. He sang along to the tape while playing an accompanying rattle and bell, and waved a red satin cloth dramatically. Wyatt MacGaffey has remarked of Kongo minkisi that they are show business, a spectacle featuring music and singing and drama and taking anywhere from days to months to consecrate—that is, to infuse with spirit. Being alone with the sorcerer himself in this Haitian slum setting made for a very-much scaled down drama. Still, the cassette gave us a reference to a grander, more elaborate tableau.[22]

I, meanwhile, whipped out my tiny notebook and pen and wrote down everything the bòkò did:

- *St. Jean had the little boy buy three needles, asked [my intended's] name. Took the needles with a magnet and put on the top of a long green rock.*[23]
- *Then poured some pink powder into the bottle.*
- *Then took from under where I'm sitting two human skulls and a— human neckbone—and set them on the floor—!!!*
- *Poured rum over them.*
- *Set them on fire . . . Blue flame.*
- *Shaved some bone off the skulls with a knife.*
- *Put the shavings in a bowl with the rock on top.*
- *Burned an American dollar on a knife and mixed with the skull shavings.*
- *Poured into bottle.*
- *Poured in some mixture of liquor and leaves.*
- *Perfume.*
- *Another perfume.*
- *All the while playing a tape of singing and cha-chas. Wrapped the bottle in red cloth, waved the cha-chas and bell at it. Set the bottle in a bowl of rocks.*[24]

'But death is all around St. Jean's neighborhood, this slum which adjoins the sewage canal . . . and the simityè, where Duvalier was buried.' Photograph, Daniel Morel, 1994.

To me, an American accustomed to sanitized experiences of death, it was surprising to see someone produce two human skulls from a sack under his bed. But death is all around St. Jean's neighborhood, this slum which adjoins the sewage canal on one side and the *simityè*, the famous cemetery where Duvalier was buried, on another. At the time of this writing, Haiti is in a state of acute political and economic crisis and thousands of people are dying of starvation, military-backed violence, and disease. Death lives under St. Jean's bed—and he uses death to "make business." For me, it was unnerving, and I didn't know what to make of his elaborate "good luck" process. It wasn't until I associated my bottle with minkisi that I realized the reason for the human skulls. Thompson writes:

> The *nkisi* is believed to live with an inner life of its own. The basis of that life was a captured soul. . . . The owner of the charm could direct the spirit in the object to accomplish mystically certain

things for him, either to enhance his luck or to sharpen his business sense.[25]

WORDS TO KNOW

NOTE: When you write the definitions of the following words, make it a point to use at least three of them in conversation over the next day and three of them in your next writing assignment. Many times you'll find it difficult or impossible to use them in everyday speech or writing. What then is the point of defining them? Of learning them? At the very least, in all the following cases where you have unusual vocabulary terms to define, attempt to use them. How does attempting to use vocabulary that feels awkward or different change your view of your common speech and writing patterns? Learning how to use new vocabulary means just that—using the words. Write specifically how, where, when, and why you used the words and discuss with your class

Port-au-Prince—
ethnologue—
bòkò—
freelancer—
oungan—
manbo—
ravine—
Montauf—
staccato—
Creole—
kleren—
midriff—
wanga—
travay maji—
fetish—
ethnographic—
systemic—
milieu—
axiom—

Barbancourt—
sediment—
discrete—
anthropomorphic—
asymmetry—
refracting—
impasse

QUESTIONS

Create a series of questions based on this reading, both Text/You/Other and Three-Layered Questions. Look over your questions. Which seem to you to be the most objective? The most biased or prejudiced? What are your biases, your prejudices in these questions? Write them down because you will need to find a way to use them in your writing projects. Research what some of the materials might mean in the context of both the object and the culture described in this short reading and exchange the information you discover with your classmates. What sources did you consult and why?

WRITING ACTIVITIES

1. Research a topic, issue, object, or practice with which people come in contact with on a daily basis. Select questionable as well as knowledgeable sources concerning this topic, issue, object, or practice. Note in writing how you determine which is a trustworthy source versus a "careless" source.

2. Choose one of your questions on which to write. Revise it to encompass the general boundaries of this set of writing activities.

3. Write an *uninformed* piece or essay on the topic, issue, object, or practice, that, despite the fact that it contains misinformation and/or errors, still fools people into believing that it is knowledgeable and informed. Use quotes or bits from your "careless" sources in your writing. Convince your audience that the piece is correct.

4. Write an *informed* piece or essay on the topic, issue, object, or practice, that, despite the fact that it contains verifiable, correct information, still fools people into thinking it's not to be believed or trusted. Use quotes or bits from your knowledgeable sources in your writing. Again, test your audience's gullibility.

5. Don't tell your classmates which is which and read one of the pieces

aloud. How do they respond? On a different class meeting day, read the other piece. How do they respond? Did you fool them? Why or why not?

GRAMMAR AND STYLE QUESTIONS

1. What is the effect of using vocabulary from a language other than English in this reading? Try using specific non-English vocabulary in a piece of your own writing. How did you decide what words to use? Describe what words you used and how you used them. Have you used those words so that they enhance your piece of writing? Why or why not?

2. An important element of good usage is the concise and active expression of thoughts and ideas. Looking through the McAlister reading, find concise, active, grammatical expressions, put them into your own words, and see how you can make them still more concise.

Fading Nations

Stewart Brand

In his introduction to The Media Lab, *written in March 1988, Stewart Brand writes, "The time to understand a subject whole is when it's changing. Understanding is easier then because everything—even the deep premise structure—is up for grabs. And, with whole understanding, there's a better chance that the changes will be directed toward improvement." Brand founded, edited, and published the* Whole Earth Catalog *and the* Whole Earth Review.

Introduction Stewart Brand has written this piece (whose original purpose is as an essay within a chapter in his nonfiction book on media labs and how they change learning and communication) as an essay with a thesis and examples to support his thesis. The interesting thing he does in structuring the essay is to organize the first half of the essay in the form of a conversation he has had with several other people. In the second half, he moves into a meditation about the implication of the ideas raised by the people he's talking to which leads him to certain other conclusions, linked to still more interactions and observations . . . the effect of which shows you the growing interconnectedness and complexity of a number of issues we often take for granted.

In Anthony Smith's *The Geopolitics of Information* is a remarkable statement:

> The whole history of the nation as a political unit of mankind has been predicated upon territoriality; the technology of printing came into being in the same era as the nation-state and both seem to be reaching the end of their usefulness in the era of the computer; it is physically impossible to impose upon data the same kinds of controls that are imposed upon goods and paper-borne informa-

tion, though the world will inevitably continue to try to do so for some years. . . .

The problem is simply that there is no room in the long run for conflicting information doctrines within a world which is becoming increasingly interconnected.

That observation from 1980 is corroborated by Peter Schwartz' recent studies.

One commercial phenomenon that fascinated the strategic planners at Shell was the world success of the Italian clothing chain Benetton. Schwartz: "They're *staggeringly* successful. Benetton really operates as if there's a kind of world uniform. There's a sort of 'color of the week,' and because of the media, that color sweeps the world very quickly. There must be five or six thousand Benetton shops worldwide. You walk into one and you'll see the same colors and designs you would find in any Benetton shop anywhere in the world on that day. The colors will change by next week. Benetton's computer analysis shows what is selling in terms of type, price, and color of every Benetton item all over the world, every day. They dye 15 percent of their colors every day on the basis of the information they get that day."

I opined, "It sounds like fashion is an electronic entertainment medium that operates on a very tight feedback loop. So does world news. How well does news get around?"

Schwartz: "Now we get into one of the most interesting public policy debate issues—the control of the flow of information, including news. The question is, will there be technical mechanisms by which governments can prevent information from flowing across their borders? Clearly governments outside of the United States, with almost no exceptions, reserve unto themselves the right to determine what their citizens will see. This is true for Britain, I might add."

I wondered, "Is that one shifting at all? Do other countries see the U.S. as just being crazy continually, or do people see a free press as having some corrections built into it?"

Schwartz: "No, I think most of the world still believes it is appropriate for the government to control what people will know. It's really quite amazing—to me at least, having grown up in the United States. Regimes nearly everywhere are—a term which is not well known in the United States—*dirigiste*. French word. Literally, it means state direction. It isn't socialism, it isn't fascism, it's essentially the idea that part of the central role of the state is to direct society—as opposed to take care of a few things and let everybody else take care of themselves, which is the U.S. philosophy. Most every other country in the world is in some sense *dirigiste.*

"The debate is always in these terms: 'If we permit private media, even if people like it, and it competes successfully with our state media, we may be degrading the quality of our public. They will be getting poorer information, less culture, less of the things which they ought to have.' The debate in Britain right now, for example, is: is independent television pulling down the BBC, which is supposed to be the flagship of high quality news and so on? Everybody is saying, 'Oh, BBC news has deteriorated to compete with ITV news, and, gee, maybe we should cut ITV news and not permit them to do certain things so we can preserve the BBC.' That sort of debate goes on in France, in Italy, in Holland. Commercial success does not guarantee further growth."

Ogilvy piped up from the bed, "Say something about transborder data flows."

Schwartz: "That's a huge issue. For example, Shell is not permitted as a company to ship computer data to Brazil. And we're not allowed to take computer data out of Brazil. We cannot establish a communication link between our computer in Britain and a computer in Brazil, because they want to be able to control what we send down that line. The result in various places in the world, as you would expect, is that there's a huge subculture of illegal phone lines and intermediaries running trucks across national borders carrying cans of data tapes."

"What does all this do to politics?" I asked. "Will the governments get more control or less?"

Schwartz: "I think inescapably less. They can push against the river a bit, but it's an incredibly powerful river that's coming at them. They can channel it a bit, but not completely. The kids are going to listen to rock 'n' roll. People are going to watch 'Dallas' no matter what."

Hmm. Maybe we're already seeing the first effects of the restructuring that Schwartz is predicting from world electronic entertainment. You could make a case that there is a worldwide loosening of communication controls going on. In China students have demonstrated for a freer press. In the U.S.S.R. a top dissident like Sakharov was permitted a public hearing (via Voice of America, deliberately unjammed that night). In Italy, France, Spain, West Germany, and Britain, television is being opened up to more private ownership, and advertising is beginning to take off, along with its customary freeing and, in some eyes, degrading of program content.

Even strait-laced Indian television has discovered advertising and the allure of popular soap opera programming. There is talk in Europe of broadcasting shows Europe-wide simultaneously in a number of languages, and interest there has revived in direct satellite TV broadcasting, which ignores national boundaries. In late 1986 the America-based firm of BBDO negotiated the first major deal in global advertising—Gillette paid millions to media baron Rupert Murdoch for TV time in seventeen countries on three continents.

If that trend continues, what effect would it have on generations growing up in a denationalized entertainment environment? Schwartz: "We've spent a lot of time talking about the role of information and computing in education, but by far the dominant curriculum in education today does not take place 8 a.m. to 3 p.m., it's 4 p.m. to midnight, when the kids watch television at home. Actually the teaching time at school is probably only about four hours. They've got seven hours later on of much higher quality (in the sense of access to communications), much more potent information, which completely overwhelms anything they get in the classroom. The second-order consequence is in some sense like what we were talking about with the inversion of trade and finance. Electronic entertainment will be the dominant educational medium that will shape global consciousness."

Global consciousness is not everybody's idea of a good thing. Apart from the draining of national sovereignty inherent in the global cash register, there is the threat of the global jukebox and the global movie projector weakening cultural identities worldwide. Nothing, apart from physical home turf, is as ferociously defended as a group's unique sense of who it is and what constitutes right behavior. But the means of physical defense of territory are well known; the means of electronic communication defense have to be invented while the damage is being done, and all the skilled inventors work for the invaders.

A Spanish ecologist, Ramón Margalef, wrote in 1968 after a lifetime of observing the transactions between ecological subsystems, "It is a basic property of nature, from the point of view of cybernetics, that any exchange between two systems of different information content does not result in a partition or equalizing of the information, but increases the difference. The system with more accumulated information becomes still richer from the exchange." In terms not just economic, the rich get richer and the poor get poorer. That imbalance is exactly what Seymour Papert and Negroponte were trying to redress when they worked at the World Center for Personal

Computation and Human Development in Paris. Their personalizing technology showed promise; the institution failed (it finally closed its doors in 1986).

Different cultures will defend themselves in different ways. Some will join the game, exporting their own music (Jamaica), or finer films (Australia), or cheaper, high volume films (Hong Kong), or snazzier equipment (Japan, Taiwan, South Korea). Some will build high, fierce walls against electronic invasion with tight political controls, and pay the price of isolation. Some will lie low and let it all pass over them. Some will be flattened. The world will continue to be a patchwork of different communication regimes, but the sheer traffic will erode everyone.

In 1985 a vice president at Hewlett-Packard, Charles House, put the following message online to a group of corporate executives with whom he was teleconferencing on the subject of global scarcity and abundance:

> We were in Guaymas, Mexico, several weeks ago, riding through a small poverty-stricken area with a guy from Chicago. He was busy denigrating the area, "Who could stand to live here, you wouldn't know anything about the world, it is so squalid, etc." I was busy taking pictures of houses perhaps 25 feet square with a 1954 Chevy pickup in the driveway and a satellite dish on the roof. An area of perhaps 1,000 people, with about 50 satellite dishes!
>
> He said, "What do those dishes do, anyway?" I said, well, these people can get 130 TV channels from at least seven nations in five languages, and in addition they can get sub-carrier FM stereo. In other words, they have Quebec, Venezuela, Mexico City, all of America, BBC, and even Japan occasionally; and they get the Chicago Symphony as clearly as you do.
>
> He was stunned. Then he said, "What do they think when they see all that, and they look at this, where they live?" And I was silent, and my wife was silent, and he was silent.
>
> The way things are shaping up, Third World nations are likely to get communications primarily by satellite while the affluent nations are being wired with fiberoptic cable. Audiences of satellites will be more passive recipients of more attenuated signals, because satellites are almost entirely one-way traffic: down. Fiberoptic audiences could be more interactive, in Media Lab terms, with much richer signals. The passive might be made more passive, the active more active, in full view of each other. That could be a recipe for violence. New communications technologies are political dynamite.
>
> As the significance of territoriality fades, and nations fade, what will be the new grain of variety?

WORDS TO KNOW

NOTE: When you write the definitions of the following words, make it a point to use at least three of them in conversation over the next day and three of them in your next writing assignment. Many times you'll find it difficult or impossible to use them in everyday speech or writing. What then is the point of defining them? Of learning them? At the very least, in all the following cases where you have unusual vocabulary terms to define, attempt to use them. How does attempting to use vocabulary that feels awkward or different change your view of your common speech and writing patterns? Learning how to use new vocabulary means just that—using the words. Write specifically how, where, when, and why you used the words and discuss with your class

geopolitics—
predicated—
territoriality—
doctrines—
corroborated—
opined—
regimes—
dirigiste—
transborder—
subculture—
intermediaries—
Sakharov—
strait-laced—
sovereignty—
fiberoptic—

QUESTIONS

As you create your Text/You/Other and Three-Layered Questions based on this reading, think about where you receive the most information in a single day. What source offers you the most information? The best information? The worst information? Why? Are you a passive or an active receiver of that information? Why?

WRITING ACTIVITIES

1. Choose one of your questions and write one to two pages addressing that question.

2. Revise this new writing to leave out a crucial piece of information that the audience would need or want in order to get "the whole story" behind what you've writing, behind your point.

3. Read what you've written to your classmates. Do they even know what information is missing? Do they even care? Why or why not?

4. Revise the informed version to take on an aggressive tone, a preachy tone, a silly tone, or some other tone of your own choosing.

5. Revise the uninformed version to take on a seductive tone, a knowledgeable tone, or some other tone of your own choosing. Remember that you accomplish setting a tone in your writing through your word choices.

6. Read your revisions to your classmates. Which were they taken by and why?

GRAMMAR AND STYLE QUESTIONS

1. Examine the use of punctuation in three different readings, including this reading by Brand. How would you describe the tone of each reading? The purpose of each reading? How is punctuation used to emphasize each author's tone and purpose?

2. Compare and contrast this text reading by Brand to a previous reading originally published on the Internet. Analyze these examples. What are the differences between them stylistically? Use specific examples from the readings as well as specific rules of grammar and details in your answer.

Acid Tatto [sic] Scare:
Why Do People Persist in Believing That Children Are under Threat from Psychedelic Transfers?

Paul Sieveking

Interestingly, during the review process of this anthology, a teacher informed me that, in fact, the Acid Tattoo Scare was real because her students had, in fact, confirmed it for her. Well?

Introduction This article, originally published in print and made available on a sponsored Web site, is written in the manner of a newspaper or magazine article. Additionally however, it works harder to prove its case—particularly in light of its sensationalist subject: drugs. It uses research and refers to over ten different sources. Furthermore, the majority of those references are to other pieces in its own category of writing: newspaper articles. The additional sources are to full-length works that explore the truth and fiction behind urban myths. The cumulative effect works to reassure you as an uninformed reader about what is a danger and what isn't at the same time that the tone of the article slyly chastises you for falling for the original myth.

Last year, a pamphlet called Metropolitan Police Neighbourhood Watch (Issue No. 10, February 1991) dropped through my door in Hampstead. The lead story began: "Information has been received from HQ EAOR of a worrying new drug danger to school children which has emerged on the continent. To date it is confined to Holland and Switzerland [..]

"Gifts, in the form of self-adhesive stickers, designed to be stuck to the skin for decoration, are being offered to children of all ages. The stickers are soaked with LSD and strychnine which causes a quick and unpredictable reaction. The aim is ultimate dependency and therefore new customers. The drug is absorbed through the skin, even if only held in the hand.

"The stickers discovered to date are: Bluestar on white background; small card with ROTE PYRAMIDE (Red Pyramid) printed on it; small tokens named 'Window Pane' with motifs to cut out and tiny coloured grains/seeds to swallow.

If either you or your children see or are offered any of the above, DO NOT TOUCH, prevent contact to the skin and inform local police. If contact has been made and the following occurs the individual must be taken to hospital immediately: hallucinations, vomiting, headaches and/or fluctuating temperature."

As any informed student of contemporary folklore, chemist or drug squad policeman will tell you, there is not, and never has been, a distribution of LSD 'tattoos,' but two decades or more of official denials seem to have no effect. (The reference to 'dependency' shows that the instigators of this hoax know nothing about LSD anyway: the drug is not addictive.) The story is a bit like a vampire; no matter how many times it is cut down it rises again to scare the pants off another generation of ill-informed parents.

This was not the first police bulletin to help spread the story; a Baltimore police precinct bulletin did it in August 1986. One version of the story had a brain-damaged child dying in a Baltimore hospital after handling the blue stars. In Tacoma around the same time, a police query, apparently a response to the rumour, was worded: "Have you seen any drug-laced tattoos?" This was repeated as: "We have seen many drug-laced tattoos!" That's one way these stories build up steam. (See *Curses! Broiled Again!* by Jan Harold Brunvand, W. W. Norton & Co. 1989.)

In March 1991, a similar letter was pinned on a notice board at BICC Cables in Wrexham, North Wales. This one was said to have first circulated in Merseyside. One sentence read: "A young child could happen upon these [tattoos] and have a fatal trip." Wrexham drug squad officer DS John Atkinson said: "These are just stupid chain letters that cause nothing but alarm." *Evening Leader,* (Clwyd and Chester) I Mar 1991.

In July 1991, Detective Inspector Neil Kingman, head of Hampshire drug squad, was busy rubbishing similar leaflets circulating in Portsmouth. The News (Portsmouth) 4 July 1991. A week later, the Yeovil (Somerset) Star (12 July) said a similar letter was being distributed in schools and workplaces in Somerset, with the added detail that the 'tattoos' depicted "brightly coloured cartoon characters

such as Bart Simpson and the Turtles characters." The dire symptoms included "uncontrolled laughter and changes in mood." Yeovil
police spokesman Paul Hardiman said that the letter was panic material, an "elaborate hoax started in Canada some years ago." (Have
you noticed that hoaxes are nearly always 'elaborate'?)

POLICE WARNING LETTER

Obviously, the West Midlands police had never heard of the 'elaborate hoax' because they were busy frightening parents in September
1991 with a tattoo warning letter. Additional tattoo images were
mentioned: Superman, clowns, butterflies and Mickey Mouse. "Each
one is box wrapped in foil" the parents were told. A facsimile of the
letter to Grestone junior School in Birmingham, dated 10 September
1991, is reproduced in *FLS News* (The newsletter of the Folklore Society) No. 14 Jan. 1992.

Despite the earlier denials in March, LSD transfer scare letters
were again circulating in Wrexham in November. This time they
purported to come from the Welsh Office, and the chief environmental officer of Wrexham Maelor Borough Council did the rumour-
trashing. *Evening Leader* 13 Nov 1991.

The fear spread to France in December. A much-photocopied
leaflet, apparently bearing a French police stamp, turned up in of-
fices and schools. The drugs, it stated, were "probably already circulating in Switzerland and will rapidly invade the rest of Europe." A
spokesman for the narcotics department of the French Interior Ministry asserted that the hoax surfaced in Western Europe a few years
ago. *Int. Herald Tribune* 19 Dec 1991.

MICKEY MOUSE ACID

A poster warning parents about LSD transfers was given to a sub
post office in Gunard, Isle of Wight, in March 1992. A spokesman for
South West Surrey Health Authority, whose name was printed at the
foot of the poster, said the posters were bogus. "We have been receiving calls from all over the country where these posters are appear-
ing", he said. *Isle of Wight County Press* 3 April 1992.

The Blue Star acid transfer story was long discredited when it
reappeared in a big way across America in 1986. In Newsweek (24
November 1986), reporters investigated rumours of LSD microdots,
resembling blue stars, in New York, New Jersey, Texas, Georgia,
Kansas and Nebraska, and concluded that some may have existed"

around 1971. By the end of 1987, the scare letters had been circulated coast to coast in the USA and Canada.

The forklorist Jan Harold Burnvand studied the acid transfer legend in 1981, calling it "Mickey Mouse acid" because this character was most often named in the warnings. I remember seeing tiny squares of LSD-impregnated cellulose with a picture of Mickey Mouse back in 1969, but they weren't skin transfers.

A 1980 New Jersey police bulletin did warn: "Children may be susceptible to this type of cartoon stamp believing it a cartoon transfer"; but there is no evidence that actual cartoon 'tattoos' have ever circulated.

LSD call, of course, be ingested through the skin if the amounts are large enough. The police dismantling the Hampton Wick 'acid factory' in the London suburbs a week after the massive 'Operation Julie' bust in March 1977 had been warned by the chemist that a carpet was saturated with LSD after a mishap where enough acid for 150,000 trips had been split. Three policemen took insufficient precautions and soon afterwards headed for outer (inner?) space after handling the carpet and other items. After some hilarity down the pub, they became confused and had themselves arrested and carted off to Kingston Hospital. Leaf Fielding gives a colourful account of the policemen's trip in City Limits (1-7 Nov 1985). A string debunking newspaper articles in the American press a few years seemingly had little effect: "Tattoo Tripped Up (*Chicago Sun-Times* 20 May 1987); "Only a Folk Tale" (*Dubuque Telegraph-Herald* October 1987); "No Cause for Alarm" (*Washington Post* 2 June 1988). No drug enforcement agency has ever seen an LSD transfer; but the "stupid chain letters" carry on to eternity.

WORDS TO KNOW

NOTE: When you write the definitions of the following words, make it a point to use at least three of them in conversation over the next day and three of them in your next writing assignment. Many times you'll find it difficult or impossible to use them in everyday speech or writing. What then is the point of defining them? Of learning them? At the very least, in all the following cases where you have unusual vocabulary terms to define, attempt to use them. How does attempting to use vocabulary that feels awkward or different change your view of your common speech and writing patterns? Learning how to use new vocabulary means just that—using the words. Write specifically how, where, when, and why you used the words and discuss with your class

strychnine—
Rote Pyramide—
fluctuating—
facsimile—
bogus—
impregnated—
cellulose—

QUESTIONS

Create a series of Text/You/Other and Three-Layered Questions. How might you be able to combine some of these new questions based on this reading with questions from earlier readings and writing projects? What was your response to this story about drugs? Have you heard it before? Where? From whom? Did you believe it? Any variations?

WRITING ACTIVITIES

1. Choose one of your questions on which to write. As you start writing in response to this question, gradually insert something made-up; create your own legend, if you will.
2. Modify the question as it suits your purpose. Remember you want to have a point in mind as you create your own myth. Make sure the myth carries credence so that people will think it's the truth as opposed to a legend.
3. The way to make an audience believe what you're writing lies in using truths in an erroneous manner. Look to the Blue Star LSD myth for an example, or the Kentucky Fried Rat incident (was it true, or not?). For more help, search on the Internet for more information on urban myths.
4. Revise your writing so that one version begins false and becomes true and the other version begins true and becomes false.
5. Read each version to your classmates on two separate days.
6. How do your classmates respond? Can they tell the difference? Why or why not? What draws them into believing or not believing?

GRAMMAR AND STYLE QUESTIONS

1. Compare and contrast author Sieveking's reading with another author's reading from this book. Specifically how does each author use grammar? How does each author's use of grammar differ? What are the common features of both? Use specific rules of grammar and details in your answer.

2. One of the best ways to learn grammar, in addition to learning the names and rules of grammatical elements, is to read other people's writing and determine how and why they write well. Take a grammatically imperfect piece of your own work, read two or three readings from this reader (including Sieveking's reading), and rewrite your piece afterwards. Is it grammatically better? Why or why not? What was the impact of seeing how other people put together words?

Summary Description
of the Warnings

Why do people enjoy urban myths? Why do they make them up? Why might social forces that we believe are in the business of always providing us the truth participate in spreading urban myths such as the one about the Blue Star LSD Tattoo? This reading mentions Jan Harold Brunvand's book The Choking Doberman and other "New" Urban Legends. *This book is a classic.*

Introduction This piece, originally published on the Internet, is written in the form of an example that incorporates detailed description with categories. The specifics are bullet-pointed to inflict a cumulative effect of horror and fear on the reader, making the reader aware of his or her own susceptibilities to the suggestion that "what we have been told is true." At the same time, the piece ends with the simple, single, forceful line debunking all the bullet-points that have come before it. It concludes with the line, *"Get the facts,"* which is underlined, indicating that it is a hyperlink that can connect you to other Web resources. This keeps your focus on taking the myth apart, piece by piece.

The "Blue Star" LSD tattoo warning is a classic urban legend—it has been terrorizing parents, fooling journalists, bewildering authorities and delighting urban legend researchers for over 15 years.

It is an example of a "contamination" legend and can be classed with such others, such as the "Spider eggs in Bubble Yum" legend. But it is also part of the growing ranks of "xeroxlore" or "faxlore" like the *"send a dying boy postcards"* plea and the new variant "emailore" often of *a similiar bent.*

Recently, the legend has picked up new virulence and new credibility through the internet, where it has appeared in mailing lists, newsgroups and on web pages.

Popular folklore chronicler Jan Harold Brunvand devoted a chapter of his book *The Choking Doberman and Other "New" Urban Legends* to the "Mickey Mouse Acid" scare.

In a typical outbreak, a school, hospital, or police station will get a copy of a photocopied flyer warning that LSD-laden lick-and-stick tattoo transfers are being given to children in local school-yards. The allegations in the warning typically include:

- A new type of tattoo called "Blue Star" is being sold or given away to school children.
- The stars, which are about the size of pencil erasers, are designed to be removed and ingested.
- This form of LSD-laced tattoo is available all over the country.
- The LSD can be absorbed through the skin by handling the tattoos.
- Other LSD-containing tattoos, resembling postage stamps, also exist, depicting:
  - Superman
  - Butterflies
  - Clowns
  - Bart Simpson
  - Mickey Mouse
  - Disney characters in general
  - Red Pyramids
- Other varieties include "micro dot" in various colors and "Window Pane" (or "Window Pain").
- These drugs are packaged in a red cardboard box wrapped in foil.
- This use of cartoon characters is a new way of selling acid by appealing to young children.
- Dealers or older children give these drugs to younger children either for kicks or to hook new customers.
- These drugs are known to react very quickly and some are laced with strychnine.
- These tattoos could cause a "fatal 'trip'" in children.
- Many children have already died from accidental ingestion of these tattoos.
- Symptoms you might see in children who have encountered these tattoos include hallucinations, severe vomiting, uncontrolled laughter, mood changes, and changes in body temperature.
- This warning has been authorized by the authorities, such as:
  - Beth Israel Medical Center in New York
  - The Cumberland County Sheriff's Department
  - The Police Department
  - The PTA of Willow Tree Day Care Center

- J. O'Donnel of Danbury Hospital's Outpatient Chemical Dependency Treatment Service
- El Hospital de Saint Roch
- La Brigada de Estupefacientes
- Der Waadtländer Polizei
- The Valley Children's Hospital
- Die New Yorker Polizei
- La Brigada Francesa de Estupefacientes
- Mr. Guy Chaillé, Advisor to the President
- The Sputnik Drug Information Zone
- You should contact the police if you see these tattoos.
- You should spread the word of this danger far and wide.

This warning spreads dependably and rapidly, but alas, it is almost 100% bogus. <u>Get the facts.</u>

WORDS TO KNOW

NOTE: When you write the definitions of the following words, make it a point to use at least three of them in conversation over the next day and three of them in your next writing assignment. Many times you'll find it difficult or impossible to use them in everyday speech or writing. What then is the point of defining them? Of learning them? At the very least, in all the following cases where you have unusual vocabulary terms to define, attempt to use them. How does attempting to use vocabulary that feels awkward or different change your view of your common speech and writing patterns? Learning how to use new vocabulary means just that—using the words. Write specifically how, where, when, and why you used the words and discuss with your class

Xeroxlore—
emailore—
virulence—
chronicler—
La Brigada de Estupefacientes—

QUESTIONS

Create a group of Text/You/Other and Three-Layered Questions from this reading. As you do, think about how you can include earlier questions and/or readings, incorporate those earlier questions and readings into your new questions even though they might seem at first not to belong together, not to be related in any obvious way. What do you come up with for potential writing projects?

WRITING ACTIVITIES

1. Choose one of your questions on which to write.
2. This time, select both a genuine object (one that already has a social or cultural context with which people would be familiar), and a made-up object that you've created (if you go with this second option, be sure to bring the actual object in to show your classmates) to focus your writing and the point of your writing.
3. Write two different one to two page papers, one on the genuine object, one on the object fabricated by you. Use a completely serious tone and believable sources to support the point you want to make about each object.
4. Share your pieces and objects with your classmates. Remember, not everyone is familiar with every cultural (genuine) object so you can still test their powers of perception, again by analyzing why they believe in particular things.

GRAMMAR AND STYLE QUESTIONS

1. One of the most difficult tasks for any new writer is to express timelines consistently and to match actions to those times and timelines. Take a paragraph from this reading that has a strong sense of either past, present, or future tense, and rewrite it using a different verb tense (i.e., if it was written in the present tense, rewrite it in the past tense, and so forth). What is the effect of such a change? Were you consistent in your new selection of verb tense in your revision? And, if you had difficulty with consistency, without referring back to the text, restore the original tense and see how closely the paragraph matches how the author originally wrote it.
2. Look at "exotic" punctuation (e.g., dashes, parentheses, exclamation points) within any of this text's readings (including this one), and discuss what effect the authors' use of these kinds of punctuation marks has on the reader. What does this use of grammar tell you about the written word as opposed to the spoken word?

TECHNOLOGY: GENIUS, NIGHTMARE, OR POSSIBILITY?

The Virtual Pet Cemetery

Pet gravestones in cyberspace. As we run out of land and spiritual tolerance, technology (which may or may not have taken away these things in the first place) in the form of the Internet offers us freedom in these matters in abundance. But can it replace a real-time graveyard? What happens to the way we think about death?

Introduction you've all seen at least one gravestone with an epitaph. An *epitaph* is a short tribute to someone who is dead. In this case, the epitaphs are to dead pets from people, adults and children, around the world. Many of the epitaphs are longer as people aren't limited by space and stone in cyberspace—they can and do feel free in fact to make their epitaphs an interesting mix of third-person tribute and first-person conversation with the dead animal. This Internet site's examples combine epitaph with eulogy with memorial with conversation, creating a whole new form of expression. What does this form say to you about the relationship between life and death for the living versus for the dead?

Over the years, the Virtual Pet Cemetery has grown to become the world's best known and most cherished online burial ground. Thousands of visitors from all over the world come to the cemetery every day to read and share the epitaphs.

All of us, at one time or another, have had a pet we loved and lost. If you wish to immortalize your beloved pet in the tombs of cyber-space for eternity, now is you chance.

Touche Turtle—R.I.P.

When I was a small child, I was given a Desert Tortoise as a pet. I loved him dearly and named him Touche Turtle after the famous Hanna-Barbera cartoon character. One day, I was shocked to find that Touche had dug himself into a burrow and had died. I was heartbroken, and was afraid to touch him for a couple of days, but I decided I had better be brave and give him a decent Christian burial. I put him in a cardboard box, dug a deep hole in the back yard and laid him to rest with a few improvised words and a bier of flowers from the garden. As time went by, I adjusted to the loss of my cherished pet, until several years later, when I discovered to my horror that Desert Tortoises hibernate through the Winter. I'm sorry Touche . . . where ever you are! Please forgive me!

Blackie

Here lies Blackie,
Chased a car,
Caught in the muffler,
Dragged through the tar,
Around the corner,
Across the track,
He might not be dead,
But he never came back.

But if he is,
This I pray,
He's running through green fields,
At play.
Chasing frisbees
Eating Rump Roast round,
Up in Heaven,
Not here in the cold, cold ground.

A Labrador Retriever,
One of the best,
He saved a child,
they put medals on his chest.
Beloved by all,
Especially my niece,
WE LOVED YOU BLACKIE,
REST IN PEACE!

MICKEY HUFFSTETTER

Popeye

Been gone for a long time, never forgotten. He was a good ol' boy, born somewhere in the Blue Ridge Mountains. Endured a lot of hard times with us, and the good times, too. The old man got him when he was just a tiny pup and Pop hung tough for damn near 17 years. In the end I reckon he just got tired. Deaf, gimpy with arthritis, shotgun pellets in his ass, shrapnel wounds perhaps from taking down a deer (or a prize cow) or from messing around with the wrong woman. But, Popeye was always one hell of a dog. Eat the ass out of an intruder (or mailmen or cops), all's we had to do was just grab that ruff of fur around his neck and holler "Go!" Climb a 6 foot fence, ford a raving river for a stick or a frisbee. Didn't have much tolerance for other male dogs or cats of any kind. Nope, none a'tall. Had a few war wounds to prove it, too.

Pop used to run away. Not because he didn't love us. Just because . . . Doggie wander-lust and a crazy need for adventure. The old man always ran ads in the paper for him (sure, Pop could read) or just mapped out miles and scrounged around till he found Pop. One time these kids had him tied to a tree, had re-named him Killer and were counting on siccing him on other dogs. Another time, some old redneck had him and was going to breed him with his dog, that's just how good looking Popeye was. I suppose the only time Pop didn't want to come back home was the time he ran off and landed on easy street. Be damned if some rich one wasn't riding Pop around on his yacht, feeding him top sirloin and calling him "Handsome" But the old man whistled and Pop sailed right on up into the bed of that pickup truck. Think he held a grudge about being found that time . . .

Popeye crossed the country at least three times and back, in all sorts of bogus vehicles—slept in motels and under trucks and out in the cold and down by the river. He was always there and he was always just a good old boy. He's buried up in the Oregon Cascades next to a river, in the cool of an old Douglas Fir. He died in California, but the old man didn't feel it was fitting to lay his boy down in the land o' fruit and nuts. So, we made a sad sojourn to lay Pop away fittin'. The old man got drunk and stayed drunk for about a year after Pop died. The old man won't ever be the same. I'm just glad he didn't have Pop stuffed and mounted on wheels so he could always have him nearby. Took a heap of talking, but I finally convinced the old man that Pop was the best of dogs and deserved a safe, comfortable place to rest.

So, Popeye, here's to you, boy. Thanks for being a fine friend and courageous companion.

Stout of heart, Sound of spirit
the very last of all the Carolina Yeller Dogs
Good Boy.
Popeye The Dog

Bear the Magnificent 1988–1990

Bear was a 125 lb Bouvier De Flandres. He was what is termed a "serious" dog.

My wife is only 4'5" and has Cerebral Palsy. We lived in L.A. at the time, and one day while I was at work, a car pulled into our driveway and a young gang member type got out and came up to our front door. It was summer time, and the door was open with only the screen door preventing him from coming in. He claimed he wanted a drink of water, but my wife was afraid and said he could get water from the hose but could not come inside. This angered him and he made an attempt to force open the screen.

The inside of the house was dark, especially compared to the bright sunshine outside, and the unfortunate man did not see the massive Bear-Dog sitting at my wife's side! The minute he touched the front screen, Bear went into action. He let out a growl and lunged *through* the screen and onto the intruder. The guy went into hysterics and dashed to the awaiting car and dove through its open window. Bear was close behind, and with a screech of tires the thirsty visitor departed.

I am sure that my wife would have come to grievous harm had Bear not been there to save her, and for that he has my undying love and eternal gratitude!! It is doubly painfully because when he swallowed the bone that killed him (not given to him by us) we could not save him.

If there is a Heaven for Dogs, then I'm sure he has an honored place there.

REGARDS,
LOU DUNCAN

Henry I Sven 1991–1994

At first I wanted a gerbil. But my friends were able to convince me to get a hamster. Three weeks later we went to the pet store to buy a hamster. I chose one that I liked but accidentally got another one that looked exactly the same. We took the hamster home, and I decided to name him Henry Sven (We were living in Sweden at the time). At first Henry and I played a lot together. One day Henry bit me, and I had to go to the nurse. He was still young at the time so we figured that he didn't know that my finger wasn't food.

We had many adventures together. One day when we had some guests over, a two year old girl decided to pick Henry up. We don't know why but our guess is that when his nails touched her hand it hurt a little and she threw him against the wall. I put him back in his cage, and he stayed in his little house for a few days, but after a while he was good as new.

One day when it was getting close to the time to bring Henry to America, we found Henry in a coma. One or two days later, I woke up at about 6:00 A.M. and found Henry dead in his little nest that he had made a few weeks earlier. After a nice little burial I got used to life without Henry, but I needed another pet. Now I still miss Henry, but in my room is Henry II.

SAM LEVEN, AGE 10.

Lady Louise Ciccone 1994–1996

My St. Bernard was named Lady Louise and she was 2 years old when she died. She was the sweetest animal I ever knew and would do anything to protect you. She was outside in the yard one morning in October of 1996 and she was barking because kids at a bus stop were fighting. One kid knocked down another and Lady Louise jumped over the fence to go over and help the kid. While running she crossed the street and was hit by the school bus. She died instantly.

The reason why you meant so much to me was because in 1992 at the age of 18 I was diagnosed with cervical spine cancer and I lost pretty much all of my friends. Then 2 years into my treatment, things were only getting worse. I was pretty much all alone and had no one to talk to. Then I decided to get a dog. I went into the pet store and saw you and said "that's the one I want." I left that day feeling that I might be able to overcome this disease. I don't know why, but all of a sudden I started to feel stronger.

After 2 years, you were my best friend. When I cried because of the pain from the cancer, and when I got sick because of the chemotherapy, you were there. You would lie next to me and lick the tears away from my face.

I want you to know how much you meant to me and how

much I loved you. I know that you are in a safe and nice place now with all your canine and feline friends. I think about you all the time. I think about all the fun times we had. I wish you were here to greet me when I come home from my treatments but you're not here anymore. It's hard for someone who has been diagnosed with a disease to lose friends, but when they gain a new best friend they feel better and feel they can fight it. You made me think there was hope and you made me strong.

I wish you could be here Lady Louise, because my cancer is now in remission. They think they might be able to do surgery and I might just make it. I'm feeling a little better everyday and I wish you could be here to see me because I look and feel better. And guess what? I finally have a little hair again! You always had more hair than me.

Anyway, Lady Louise, remember the good you did and the hope you gave to an 18 year old cancer stricken person. I am now 22 years old and I'm doing OK. A little better than before. If something should happen to me along the way, Lady Louise, I want you to know that I'm coming to where you are. I will meet you and we will pick up where we left off.

CHUCK

Misty 1979–1988

Misty was a brown mutt. She was very loved. My parents had saved her from being killed by some people who didn't want her any more. My parents had her a couple of years before I was born. She passed away when I was 8 years old.

Misty and I were very attached. I would not be alive today if it wasn't for her. I lay choking in my crib when she awoke my parents. We had our bad times when I was bugging her and she bit me, but I always forgave her. We also had our fun times like when we played Tug Of War with her sock.

We soon found out she was blind when she got lost in the woods. We found her though. She was then diagnosed with Kidney failure. She passed away at the vet's office. I will never forget that dog. I cried for 3 days straight and still get choked up when I think of all the fun we had together. We used to do everything together. I am now 14 years old and miss Misty very dearly.

MELANIE GILLIS
CALGARY, ALBERTA, CANADA

Moretta and her kittens

Moretta and her kittens will live forever in our hearts. We are sure that we will meet again, someday

PAOLO AND MARIA TERESA (ITALY).

Carnate (Italy), January 29, 1996

In Memory of Moretta and her Kittens

Dear Sirs,

I sent you an epitaph yesterday for some cats of mine who died or disappeared. After the delivery of the message I printed some pages of your site and I read them carefully.

I seldom read before some thoughts as touching as those read in the Virtual Pet Cemetery™. And I suddenly cried after reading some of them because I understood the sorrow of the owners of those pets, having experienced the same feeling when I lost some cats of mine: Moretta who died from a mistaken sterilization, two kittens of hers who died under cars, and two others who disappeared.

I can state that my pets surely made me a better person. They have taught me and are continually teaching me a lot of things: for example how it is possible (and right) to live happily with not too much, and how they can fight to defend their dears. They have brought a lot of joy and happiness in the lives of my wife and of myself. I live with ten cats now, but I never bought one, all of them were wandering. One of them (Trullina Pooh Trezampe, Three Legs) has three legs, and in spite of this, she gave birth to a nice kitten who lives with us too. They run together in my garden now. That was a great lesson of optimism and trust in life, too!

But each cat has a special personality of its own. And, for this reason, when a cat dies it can not be replaced in our heart by another one. Our heart is the greatest Cemetery for our pets.

The sensibility of these pets, the gaze we saw in the eyes of some of them when they were dying, taught us the most important thing and made us closer to God. These creatures MUST have a special type of soul and that is why we are sure that we will meet our lost pets, some day.

For this wonderful, tender and educational site we say: thank

you from the deep of our hearts where our pets sleep, waiting
for us.

PAOLO AND MARIA TERESA SASSETTI—ITALY

Ode to Spanky

Oh I remember the telephone cords you used to eat,
The funny way that you walked (so ungraceful and un-feline-like),
That blank stare, so void and yet so characteristic of you,
Would touch upon my heart as you meowed.

Countless dead birds littered the carpet in those days,
Brought forth with a hunter's skill; but so bloody and unclean!
Father used to say that you were fit only to be made into tennis
racquet strings,
But I loved you all the same.

And then came that fateful day when even the most patient heart
was tried:
With so many phone-cords inside you, its a wonder you were still
alive, to see the light of day!
But alas, what could we do?

Emergency surgery and fourteen hundred dollars later,
Our efforts were a testament to our devotion, Spanky.
But once recovered there was but a brief respite,
Before you turned back to your obsessive self-indulgence.

Cured though you had been by the surgeon's shining blade,
We had hoped and we'd prayed for even a more miraculous cure:
That you would cease and desist from your peculiar eating habits,
And save us all some money and grief.

But when once again the doctor proclaimed "It's in there all right,"
The reminder of money past-spent was too much for Dad.
And though we loved you very much,
We could not come to terms with one hard fact:

That the mental disorder that plagued you,
Was once again made manifest,
This time to the tune of over two grand.
Goodbye, Spanky.

T.J.

Father would not have it. He was haunted by images of
wasted money past-spent, as he suffered flashbacks of money
once spent.

Emerson the Parakeet 1995 to 1995

A Poem for Emerson

Emerson, you silly bird . . . you've left us in the lurch!
You only lasted three days before falling off your perch!
At first it was a crushing blow (though now we are much calmer),
And still we have your cage-mates: the feathered "Lake" and
"Palmer."
So Emerson you leave behind this simple legacy:
a deep appreciation for the "Pet Smart" Guarantee!

THE HARBUR FAMILY:
JIM, KAREN, ANDY AND CASEY

Buster Brown 1992–1995

Buster Brown was a little brown mutt. He weighed twenty
pounds and was bow-legged. He chased cars and wouldn't
come in at night. He loved everyone but my grandpa. He slept
in my bed at night, he puked on my pillow at least once every
three months. We will all miss him. Buster Brown was two
and a half. We had him since he was six weeks. We saved his
life. He was being sent to the pound. My mother saved him
from that fate and took him home to us. He got ran over when
we were going to the fair. Ironically, my mother accidently ran
him over. We love him.

HALEY, BILL, LEISA, JASIE, AND LINDY STOKES.

P.S. "To fear death is nothing other than to think oneself wise when
one is not."—Socrates

WORDS TO KNOW

NOTE: When you write the definitions of the following words, make it a
point to use at least three of them in conversation over the next day
and three of them in your next writing assignment. Many times you'll
find it difficult or impossible to use them in everyday speech or writing.
What then is the point of defining them? Of learning them? At the very
least, in all the following cases where you have unusual vocabulary
terms to define, attempt to use them. How does attempting to use vo-

cabulary that feels awkward or different change your view of your common speech and writing patterns? Learning how to use new vocabulary means just that—using the words. Write specifically how, where, when, and why you used the words and discuss with your class

Hanna-Barbera—
gimpy—
shrapnel—
siccing—
sojourn—
Yeller Dog—
Bouvier De Flandres—

QUESTIONS

Make a list of the single-word topics that come out of this reading. Then, using these topics as categories, create and categorize your groups of Text/You/Other and Three-Layered Questions from this reading. As you do, think about how you can include earlier questions and/or readings, incorporate those earlier questions and readings into your new questions even though they might seem at first not to belong together, not to be related in any obvious way. What do you come up with for potential writing projects?

WRITING ACTIVITIES

1. Get together with two other people. Decide on one of the questions (all of you distribute the questions you came up with to each other); all of you will write on this question.
2. Without exchanging any information, individually put together an oral presentation based on this question.
3. Your presentations should include all of the following: an non text source (visual or audio sources are appealing to audiences), a text source, a hand-out that you create that is related to your presentation (something your audience can refer to as they listen to your presentation), and questions for your audience or some other verbal means of directly involving them in your presentation. All three of you (you and your two writing partners) will each give separate presentations on the same question.
4. Write a one to two page paper draft on your question.

5. After you give your presentation, request feedback from your audience and use this feedback to revise your paper draft.
6. Whose presentation was received the most successfully, and why?
7. How did giving the presentation improve your draft? Did you see these two projects as totally separate? Why?
8. If you wrote the paper completely differently from the presentation, revise it to link it more directly with your presentation. How does the oral thinking through of your subject and main idea help you focus your written subject and main idea?

GRAMMAR AND STYLE QUESTIONS

1. Select a text reading to compare and contrast to this reading, consisting of a collection of postings on a Web site. Analyze these examples. What are the differences stylistically? Use specific examples from the readings as well as specific rules of grammar and details in your answer.
2. Using a standard grammar reference (e.g., Strunk and White's *Elements of Style*), find three exceptions (from any of the readings in this reader, including this one) to the rules such a standard reference has created, and discuss why the authors broke those rules. (Remember, there are multiple contributors to the "Virtual Pet Cemetery" reading.)

An Egg a Month from All Over

Margaret St. Clair

Just as death can be "technologized," so can life and more specifically that precious source of shaping our lives: our mothers. I remember as a child getting rare-breed chicken eggs and chicks in the mail to raise in a cardboard box with heat lamps and special cornmeal mash and water out of an upside down cup in a bowl. Never would I have imagined the chicks turning out the way the one in the following story does. Of course, whether you've got "prey" or "predator" stamped on your shell all depends on which side of the cardboard box or incubator you stand. And, if you'd lost your mother as opposed to never knowing you had one in the first place . . .

Introduction Margaret St. Clair's piece is a short story written in the "soft" science fiction genre; that is, a genre that concerns some aspect of science that plays a secondary role in the story to a conflict going on between the main characters. Because of the science fiction element in the story, you will see some made-up words that at first glance will seem strange and undefinable. You can determine their meaning, however, if you look at their context within the story; and, while they may seem absurd to include, think instead about why the writer has included them and what purpose they serve to the writing itself.

When the collector from Consolidated Eggs found the mnxx bird egg on the edge of the cliff, he picked it up unsuspiciously. A molded mnxx bird egg looks almost exactly like the chu lizard eggs the collector was hunting, and this egg bore no visible sign of the treatment it had received at the hands of Jreel just before Krink's hatchet men caught up with him. The collector was paid by the egg; everything that came along was grist to his mill. He put the molded mnxx bird egg in his bag.

George Lidders lived alone in a cabin in the desert outside Phoenix. The cabin had only one room, but at least a third of the available space was taken up by an enormous incubator. George was a charter member of the Egg-of-the-Month Club, and he never refused one of their selections. He loved hatching eggs.

George had come to Phoenix with his mother for her health. He had taken care of her faithfully until her death, and now that she was gone, he missed her terribly. He had never spoken three consecutive words to any woman except her in his life. He fantasies, when he was base enough to have any, were pretty unpleasant. He was forty-six.

On Thursday morning he walked into Phoenix for his mail. As he scuffled over the sand toward the post office substation, he was hoping there would be a package for him from the Egg-of-the-Month Club. He was feeling tired, tired and depressed. He had been sleeping badly, with lots of nightmares. A nice egg package would cheer him up.

The South American mail rocket, cleaving the sky overhead, distracted him momentarily. If he had enough money, would he travel? Mars, Venus, star-side? No, he didn't think so. Travel wasn't really interesting. Eggs . . . Eggs (but the thought was a little frightening), eggs were the only thing he had to go on living for.

The postmistress greeted him unsmilingly. "Package for you, Mr. Lidders. From the egg club. You got to brush for it." She handed him a slip.

George brushed, his hand shaking with excitement. This must be his lucky morning. It might even be a double selection; the package seemed unusually big. His lips began to lift at the corners. With a nod in place of thanks, he took the parcel from the postmistress, and went out, clutching it.

The woman looked after him disapprovingly. "I want you to stay away from that gesell, Fanny," she said to her eleven-year-old daughter, who was reading a postcard in the back of the cubicle. "There's something funny about him and his eggs."

"Oksey-snoksey, mums, if you say so. But lots of people hatch eggs."

The postmistress sniffed. "Not the way he hatches eggs," she said prophetically.

On the way home George tore the wrapper from the box. He couldn't wait any longer. He pulled back the flaps eagerly.

Inside the careful packing there was a large, an unusually large, pale blue-green egg. Its surface stood up in tiny bosses, instead of being smooth as eggs usually were, and the shell gave the impression of being more than ordinarily thick. According to the instructions with the parcel, it was a chu lizard egg from the planet Morx, a little-known satellite of Amorgos. It was to be incubated at a temperature of 76.3 C. with high humidity. It would hatch in about eight days.

George felt the surface of the egg lovingly. If only Mother were here to see it! She had always been interested in his egg hatching; it was the only thing he had ever wanted to do that she had really approved of. And this was an unusually interesting egg.

When he got home he went straight to the incubator. Tenderly he laid the *soi-disant* chu lizard egg in one of the compartments; carefully he adjusted the temperature control. Then he sat down on the black and red afghan on his cot (his mother had crocheted the coverlet for him just before she passed away), and once more read the brochure that had come with the egg.

When he had finished it, he sighed. It was too bad there weren't any eggs in the incubator now, eggs that were on the verge of hatching. Eight days was a long time to wait. But this egg looked wonderfully promising; he didn't know when the club had sent out an egg that attracted him so. And from one point of view it was a good thing he hadn't any hatchings on hand. Hatching, for all its excitement, was a sort of ordeal. It always left him feeling nervously exhausted and weak.

He had lunch, and after lunch, lying under the red and black afghan, he had a little nap. When he woke it was late afternoon. He went over to the incubator and looked in. The egg hadn't changed. He hadn't expected it would.

His nap hadn't cheered or refreshed him. He was almost more tired than he had been when he lay down to sleep. Sighing, he went around to the other side of the incubator and stared at the cage where he kept the things he had hatched out. After a moment he took his eyes away. They weren't interesting, really—lizards and birds and an attractive small snake or two. He wasn't interested in the things that were in eggs after they had hatched out.

In the evening he read a couple of chapters in the *Popular Guide to Egg Hatchery.*

He woke early the next morning, his heart hammering. He'd had another of those nightmares. But—his mind wincingly explored the texture of the dream—but it hadn't been all nightmare. There'd been a definitely pleasurable element in it, and the pleasure had been somehow connected with the egg that had come yesterday. Funny. (Jreel, who had molded the mnxx bird egg from its original cuboid into the present normal ovoid shape, wouldn't have found it funny at all.) It was funny about dreams.

He got grapes from the cupboard and made *café à la crème* on the hotplate. He breakfasted. After breakfast he looked at his new egg.

The temperature and humidity were well up. It was about time for him to give the egg a quarter of a turn, as the hatching instruction booklet suggested. He reached in the compartment, and was surprised to find it full of a dry, brisk, agreeable warmth. It seemed to be coming from the egg.

How odd! He stood rubbing the sprouting whiskers on his upper lip. After a moment he tapped the two gauges. No, the needles weren't stuck; they wobbled normally. He went around to the side of the incubator and checked the connections. Everything was sound and tight, nothing unusual. He must have imagined the dry warmth. Rather apprehensively, he put his hand back in the compartment— he still hadn't turned the egg—and was relieved to find the air in it properly humid. Yes, he must have imagined it.

After lunch he cleaned the cabin and did little chores. Abruptly, when he was half through drying the lunch dishes, the black depression that had threatened him ever since Mother died swallowed him up. It was like a physical blackness; he put down the dish undried and groped his way over to a chair. For a while he sat almost unmoving, his hands laced over his little stomach, while he sank deeper and deeper into despair. Mother was gone; he was forty-six; he had nothing to live for, not a thing . . . He escaped from the depression at last, with a final enormous guilty effort, into one of his more unpleasant fantasies. The imago within the molded mnxx bird egg, still plastic within its limey shell, felt the strain and responded to it with an inaudible grunt.

On the third day of the hatching, the egg began to enlarge. George hung over the incubator, fascinated. He had seen eggs change during incubation before, of course. Sometimes the shells got dry and chalky; sometimes they were hygroscopic and picked up moisture from the air. But he had never seen an egg act like this one. It seemed to be swelling up like an inflating balloon.

He reached in the compartment and touched the egg lightly. The shell, that had been so limey and thick when he first got it, was now warm and yielding and gelatinous. There was something uncanny about it. Involuntarily, George rubbed his fingers on his trouser leg.

He went back to the incubator at half-hour intervals. Every time it seemed to him that the egg was a little bigger than it had been. It was wonderfully interesting; he had never seen such a fascinating egg.

He got out the hatching instructions booklet and studied it. No, there was nothing said about changes in shell surface during incubation, and nothing about the egg's incredible increase in size. And the booklets were usually careful about mentioning such things. The directors of the Egg-of-the-Month Club didn't want their subscribers to overlook anything interesting that would happen during the incubation days. They wanted you to get your money's worth.

There must be some mistake. George, booklet in hand, stared at the incubator doubtfully. Perhaps the egg had been sent him by mistake; perhaps he hadn't been meant to have it. (He was right in both these suppositions: Jreel had meant the egg for Krink, as a little gift.) Perhaps he ought to get rid of the egg. An unauthorized egg might be dangerous.

Hesitantly he raised the incubator lid. It would be a shame, but—yes, he'd throw the egg out. Anything, anything at all might be inside an egg. There was no sense in taking chances. He approached his hand. The imago, dimly aware that it was at a crucial point in its affairs, exerted itself.

George's hand halted a few inches from the egg. He had broken into a copious sweat, and his forearm was one large cramp. Why, he must have been crazy. He didn't want—he couldn't possibly want to—get rid of the egg. What had been the matter with him? He perceived very clearly now what he thought he must have sensed dimly all along; that there was a wonderful promise in the egg.

A promise of what? Of—he couldn't be sure—but of warmth, of sleep, of rest. A promise of something he'd been wanting all his life. He couldn't be any more specific than that. But if what he thought might be in the egg was actually there, it wouldn't matter any more that Mother was dead and that he was forty-six and lonely. He'd—he gulped and sighed deeply—he'd be happy. Satisfied.

The egg kept on enlarging, though more slowly, until late that evening. Then it stopped.

George was in a froth of nervous excitement. In the course of watching the egg's slow growth, he had chewed his fingernails until three of them were down to the quick and ready to bleed. Still keeping his eyes fixed on the egg, he went to the dresser, got a nail file, and began to file his nails. The operation soothed him. By midnight, when it became clear that nothing more was going to happen immediately, he was calm enough to go to bed. He had no dreams.

The fourth and fifth days passed without incident. On the sixth day George perceived that though the egg was the same size, its shell had hardened and become once more opaque. And on the eighth day—to this extent the molded mnxx bird egg was true to the schedule laid down in the booklet for the chu lizard—the egg began to crack.

George felt a rapturous excitement. He hovered over the incubator breathlessly, his hands clutching the air and water conduits for support. As the tiny fissure enlarged, he kept gasping and licking his lips. He was too agitated to be capable of coherent thought, but it occurred to him that what he really expected to come out of the egg was a bird of some sort, some wonderful, wonderful bird.

The faint pecking from within the egg grew louder. The dark fissure on the pale blue-green background widened and spread. The halves of the shell fell back suddenly, like the halves of a door. The egg was open. There was nothing inside.

Nothing. Nothing. For a moment George felt that he had gone mad. He rubbed his eyes and trembled. Disappointment and incredulity were sickening him. He picked up the empty shell.

It was light and chalky and faintly warm to the touch. He felt inside it unbelievingly. There was nothing there.

His frustration was stifling. For a moment he thought of crumpling up newspapers and setting the cabin on fire. Then he put the halves of the shell down on the dresser and went wobblingly toward the door. He'd—go for a walk.

The mnxx bird imago, left alone within the cabin, flitted about busily.

The moon had risen when George got back. In the course of his miserable wanderings, he had stopped on a slight rise and shed a few salty tears. Now he was feeling, if not better, somewhat more resigned. His earlier hopes, his later disappointment, had been succeeded by a settled hopelessness.

The mnxx bird was waiting behind the door of the cabin for him.

In its flittings in the cabin during his absence, it had managed to assemble for itself a passable body. It had used newspapers, grapes, and black wool from the afghan as materials. What it had made was short and squat and excessively female, not at all alluring, but it thought George would like it. It held the nail file from the dresser in its one completed hand.

George shut the cabin door behind him. His arm moved toward the light switch. He halted, transfixed by the greatest of the surprises of the day. He saw before him, glimmering wanly in the moonlight from the window, the woman of his—let's be charitable—dreams.

She was great-breasted, thighed like an idol. Her face was only a blur; there the mnxx bird had not felt it necessary to be specific.

But she moved toward George with a heavy sensual swaying; she was what George had always wanted and been ashamed of wanting. She was here. He had no questions. She was his. Desire was making him drunk. He put out his hands.

The newspaper surface, so different from what he had been expecting, startled him. He uttered a surprised cry. The mnxx bird saw no reason for waiting any longer. George was caressing one grape-tipped breast uncertainly. The mnxx raised its right arm, the one that was complete, and drove the nail file into his throat.

The mnxx bird was amazed at the amount of blood in its victim. Jreel, when he had been molding the imago with his death wishes for Krink, had said nothing about this. The inhabitants of the planet Morx do not have much blood.

After a momentary disconcertment, the mnxx went on with its business. It had, after all, done what it had been molded to do. Now there awaited it a more personal task.

It let the woman's body it had shaped collapse behind it carelessly. The newspapers made a wuffling sound. In a kind of rapture it threw itself on George. His eyes would be admirable for mnxx bird eyes, it could use his skin, his hair, his teeth. Admirable material! Trembling invisibly with the joy of creation, the mnxx bird set to work.

When it had finished, George lay on the sodden carpet flaccidly. His eyes were gone, and a lot of his vital organs. Things were over for him. He had had, if not all he wanted, all he was ever going to get. He was quiet. He was dead. He was satisfied.

The mnxx bird, on the fine strong wings it had plaited for itself out of George's head hair, floated out into the night.

WORDS TO KNOW

NOTE: When you write the definitions of the following words, make it a point to use at least three of them in conversation over the next day and three of them in your next writing assignment. Many times you'll find it difficult or impossible to use them in everyday speech or writing. What then is the point of defining them? Of learning them? At the very least, in all the following cases where you have unusual vocabulary terms to define, attempt to use them. How does attempting to use vocabulary that feels awkward or different change your view of your common speech and writing patterns? Learning how to use new vocabulary means just that—using the words. Write specifically how, where, when, and why you used the words and discuss with your class.

mnxx—
chu—
Jreel—
Krink—
grist—
incubator—
substation—
cleaving—
gesell—
Morx—
Amorgos—
soi-disant—
cuboid—
ovoid—
Café de la crème—
hygroscopic—
gelatinous—
copious—
afghan—
disconcertment—
wuffling—

QUESTIONS

Part of the power of technology lies in its reminder that morality is not inherent in the makeup of life; it's something we create—and, therefore, it is extremely fragile. Create a group of Text/You/Other and Three-Layered Questions from this reading. Have you dealt with any of the issues you raise in your questions previously in this text? Any of the questions? Do you keep coming back to them because you can't think of anything else to ask? Or because you're interested? Are you pushing yourself hard enough to really explore intricacies and complexities in your questions? Why or why not? What do you come up with for potential writing projects?

WRITING ACTIVITIES

1. Choose one of your questions on which to write.
2. Write a one to two page short essay on your question.
3. Now, set aside your words and create a visual essay using only images, photographs, artwork, or other pictorial information.
4. You could also choose to create an aural essay using only sounds and music (but use music without lyrics or words).
5. Present these nonverbal essays to your classmates. How do they respond? Do they "get it"? What are they supposed to get?
6. Follow up presenting your visual and/or aural essay with presenting your written essay. Now how does your audience respond? Why? Use their responses and feedback to revise your written essay.

GRAMMAR AND STYLE QUESTIONS

1. Using a standard grammar reference (e.g., Strunk and White's *Elements of Style*), find three exceptions (from any of the readings in this reader, including "An Egg a Month from All Over") to the rules such a standard reference has created, and discuss why the authors broke those rules.
2. Look at "exotic" punctuation (e.g., dashes, parentheses, exclamation points) and any exotic vocabulary and/or spelling within any of this reading, and discuss what effect the author's use of these forms of punctuation and/or spelling has on the reader. What does the use this author makes of style and vocabulary tell you about the written word as opposed to the spoken word?

Germs

Lewis Thomas

Born in 1913, research physician Lewis Thomas has studied hyper-sensitivity, the pathogenicity of mycoplasmas, and infectious diseases. Though he originally published in The New England Journal of Medicine, *many of his essays were published in mainstream books. Thomas is one of those doctors who loves his work but never forgets where it comes from: his audience, many of whom, like yourselves, are wondering what a mycoplasma is.*

Introduction Lewis Thomas's essay uses some of the conventional essay organization and presentation, specific examples that support his main idea and a fairly traditional opening with a misconception followed by the actual situation. But what really stands out in the essay is the way he skillfully mixes heavy duty science terminology with a conversation with you the reader. The effect of his humor and gentle ribbing is to get you past the difficulty with the terminology to see what the real problem is using the actual language of that field.

Watching television, you'd think we lived at bay, in total jeopardy, surrounded on all sides by human-seeking germs, shielded against infection and death only by a chemical technology that enables us to keep killing them off. We are instructed to spray disinfectants everywhere, into the air of our bedrooms and kitchens and with special energy into bathrooms, since it is our very own germs that seem the worst kind. We explode clouds of aerosol, mixed for good luck with deodorants, into our noses, mouths, underarms, privileged crannies—even into the intimate insides of our telephones. We apply potent antibiotics to minor scratches and seal them with plastic. Plastic is the new protector; we wrap the already plastic tumblers of hotels in more plastic, and seal the toilet seats like state secrets after irradiating them with ultraviolet light. We live in a world where the microbes are always trying to get at us, to tear us cell from cell, and we only stay alive and whole through diligence and fear.

We still think of human disease as the work of an organized, modernized kind of demonology, in which the bacteria are the most visible and centrally placed of our adversaries. We assume that they must somehow relish what they do. They come after us for profit, and there are so many of them that disease seems inevitable, a natural part of the human condition; if we succeed in eliminating one kind of disease there will always be a new one at hand, waiting to take its place.

These are paranoid delusions on a societal scale, explainable in part by our need for enemies, and in part by our memory of what things used to be like. Until a few decades ago, bacteria were a genuine household threat, and although most of us survived them, we were always aware of the nearness of death. We moved, with our families, in and out of death. We had lobar pneumonia, meningococcal meningitis, streptococcal infections, diphtheria, endocarditis, enteric fevers, various septicemias, syphilis, and, always, everywhere, tuberculosis. Most of these have now left most of us, thanks to antibiotics, plumbing, civilization, and money, but we remember.

In real life, however, even in our worst circumstances we have always been a relatively minor interest of the vast microbial world. Pathogenicity is not the rule. Indeed, it occurs so infrequently and involves such a relatively small number of species, considering the huge population of bacteria on the earth, that it has a freakish aspect. Disease usually results from inconclusive negotiations for symbiosis, an overstepping of the line by one side or the other, a biologic misinterpretation of borders.

Some bacteria are only harmful to us when they make exotoxins, and they only do this when they are, in a sense, diseased themselves. The toxins of diphtheria bacilli and streptococci are produced when the organisms have been infected by bacteriophage; it is the virus that provides the code for toxin. Uninfected bacteria are uninformed. When we catch diphtheria it is a virus infection, but not of us. Our involvement is not that of an adversary in a straightforward game, but more like blundering into someone else's accident.

I can think of a few microorganisms, possibly the tubercle bacillus, the syphilis spirochete, the malarial parasite, and a few others, that have a selective advantage in their ability to infect human beings, but there is nothing to be gained, in an evolutionary sense, by the capacity to cause illness or death. Pathogenicity may be something of a disadvantage for most microbes, carrying lethal risks more frightening to them than to us. The man who catches a meningococcus is in considerably less danger for his life, even without chemotherapy, than meningococci with the bad luck to catch a man. Most meningococci have the sense to stay out on the surface, in the rhinopharynx. During epidemics this is where they are to be found in the majority of the host population, and it generally goes well. It is only in the unaccountable minority, the "cases," that the line is crossed, and then there is the devil to pay on both sides, but most of all for the meningococci.

Staphylococci live all over us, and seem to have adapted to conditions in our skin that are uncongenial to most other bacteria. When you count them up, and us, it is remarkable how little trouble we have with the relation. Only a few of us are plagued by boils, and we can blame a large part of the destruction of tissues on the zeal of our own leukocytes. Hemolytic streptococci are among our closest intimates, even to the extent of sharing antigens with the membranes of our muscle cells; it is our reaction to their presence, in the form of rheumatic fever, that gets us into trouble. We can carry brucella for long periods in the cells of our reticuloendothelial system without any awareness of their existence; then cyclically, for reasons not understood but probably related to immunologic reactions on our part, we sense them, and the reaction of sensing is the clinical disease.

Most bacteria are totally preoccupied with browsing, altering the configurations of organic molecules so that they become usable for the energy needs of other forms of life. They are, by and large, indispensable to each other, living in interdependent communities in the soil or sea. Some have become symbionts in more specialized, local relations, living as working parts in the tissues of higher organisms. The root nodules of legumes would have neither form nor function without the masses of rhizobial bacteria swarming into root hairs, incorporating themselves with such intimacy that only an electron microscope can detect which membranes are bacterial and which plant. Insects have colonies of bacteria, the mycetocytes, living in them like little glands, doing heaven knows what but being essential. The microfloras of animal intestinal tracts are part of the nutritional system. And then, of course, there are the mitochondria and chloroplasts, permanent residents in everything.

The microorganisms that seem to have it in for us in the worst way—the ones that really appear to wish us ill—turn out on close examination to be rather more like bystanders, strays, strangers in from the cold. They will invade and replicate if given the chance, and some of them will get into our deepest tissues and set forth in the blood, but it is our response to their presence that makes the disease. Our arsenals for fighting off bacteria are so powerful, and involve so many different defense mechanisms, that we are in more danger from them than from the invaders. We live in the midst of explosive devices; we are mined.

It is the information carried by the bacteria that we cannot abide.

The gram-negative bacteria are the best examples of this. They display lipopolysaccharide endotoxin in their walls, and these macromolecules are read by our tissues as the very worst of bad news. When we sense lipopolysaccharide, we are likely to turn on every defense at our disposal; we will bomb, defoliate, blockade, seal off, and destroy all the tissues in the area. Leukocytes become more actively phagocytic, release lysosomal enzymes, turn sticky, and aggregate together in dense masses, occluding capillaries and shutting off the blood supply. Complement is switched on at the right point in its sequence to release chemotactic signals, calling in leukocytes from everywhere. Vessels become hyperreactive to epinephrine so that physiologic concentrations suddenly possess necrotizing properties. Pyrogen is released from leukocytes, adding fever to hemorrhage, necrosis, and shock. It is a shambles.

All of this seems unnecessary, panic-driven. There is nothing intrinsically poisonous about endotoxin, but it must look awful, or feel awful when sensed by cells. Cells believe that it signifies the presence of gram-negative bacteria, and they will stop at nothing to avoid this threat.

I used to think that only the most highly developed, civilized animals could be fooled in this way, but it is not so. The horseshoe crab is a primitive fossil of a beast, ancient and uncitified, but he is just as vulnerable to disorganization by endotoxin as a rabbit or a man. Bang has shown that an injection of a very small dose into the body cavity will cause the aggregation of hemocytes in ponderous, immovable masses that block the vascular channels, and a gelatinous clot brings the circulation to a standstill. It is now known that a limulus clotting system, perhaps ancestral to ours, is centrally involved in the reaction. Extracts of the hemocytes can be made to jell by adding extremely small amounts of endotoxin. The self-disintegration of the whole animal that follows a systemic injection can be interpreted as a well-intentioned but lethal error. The mechanism is itself quite a good one, when used with precision and restraint, admirably designed for coping with intrusion by a single bacterium: the hemocyte would be attracted to the site, extrude the coagulable protein, the microorganism would be entrapped and immobilized, and the thing would be finished. It is when confronted by the overwhelming signal of free molecules of endotoxin, evoking memories of vibrios in great numbers, that the limbulus flies into panic, launches all his defenses at once, and destroys himself.

It is, basically, a response to propaganda, something like the panic-producing pheremones that slave-taking ants release to disorganize the colonies of their prey.

I think it likely that many of our diseases work in this way. Sometimes, the mechanisms used for overkill are immunologic, but often, as in the limulus model, they are more primitive kinds of memory. We tear ourselves to pieces because of symbols, and we are more vulnerable to this than to any host of predators. We are, in effect, at the mercy of our own Pentagons, most of the time.

WORDS TO KNOW

NOTE: When you write the definitions of the following words, make it a point to use at least three of them in conversation over the next day and three of them in your next writing assignment. Many times you'll find it difficult or impossible to use them in everyday speech or writing. What then is the point of defining them? Of learning them? At the very least, in all the following cases where you have unusual vocabulary terms to define, attempt to use them. How does attempting to use vocabulary that feels awkward or different change your view of your common speech and writing patterns? Learning how to use new vocabulary means just that—using the words. Write specifically how, where, when, and why you used the words and discuss with your class.

irradiating—
demonology—
lobar pneumonia—
meningococcal meningitis—
streptococcal—
diphtheria—
endocarditis—
enteric fevers—
septicemias—

syphilis—
tuberculosis—
pathogenicity—
symbiosis—
bacilli—
streptococci—
bacteriophage—
tubercle bacillus—
syphilis spirochete—
meningococci—
staphylococci—
hemolytic—
antigens—
brucella—
retinculoendothelial—
symbionts—
legumes—
rhizobial—
mycetocytes—
microfloras—
mitochondria—
chloroplasts—
lipopolysaccharide endotoxin—
macromolecules—
leukocytes—
defoliate—
phagocytic—
lysosomal—
occluding—
chemotactic—
epinephrine—
necrotizing—
pyrogen—
hymocytes—
limulus—
coaguable—
vibrios—
limbulus—

QUESTIONS

It is important that you open yourself up to learning a vast amount of new scientific vocabulary in a short piece and a short period of time— not because you have to be a scientist, but because you need to practice remaining open to new words and new ways of expressing yourself in writing. Furthermore, if you don't let the vocabulary frighten you, you will find yourself enjoying Thomas's wit and insight. Create a group of Text/You/Other and Three-Layered Questions from this reading. Find another reading, either in this text or elsewhere, that matches Lewis Thomas's in wit, length, and style. Incorporate this reading into your question.

WRITING ACTIVITIES

1. Choose one of your questions on which to write.
2. Write a one to two page short essay on your question using the level of language and diction *you* would normally use.
3. Now, rewrite the piece using a jargon, technical, or other high-level, dense language and diction.
4. Write a third version in which you use as simplistic a level of language and diction as you can.
5. Read each version to your audience. Which do they like best and why? How much of their choice has to do with not wanting to work hard to understand what's being said? Why is that?

GRAMMAR AND STYLE QUESTIONS

1. Examine the use of punctuation in three different readings, including Thomas's reading. How is punctuation used to emphasize the authors' tone? Discuss specific examples from the readings in your answers.
2. Select a reading originally published on the Internet to compare and contrast to this reading of Thomas's, which is a text reading (written to be read on the page of a book or in a printed periodical). Analyze these examples. What is the difference in grammatical style, and why? Use specific examples from the readings as well as specific rules of grammar and details in your answer.

Male Birth Control Pill

Brad Wieners and David Pescovitz

Editor, critic, and reporter Brad Wieners has written for Wired, TimeOut, Details, *and the* San Francisco Review. *He lives in San Francisco, California. David Pescovitz has written for the* Los Angeles Times, bOING bOING, Cincinnati CityBeat, *and* The Net. *He is a contributing editor for* Wired, *for which he writes the monthly column, "Reality Check." He lives in Oakland, California.*

Introduction We all like to speculate about the future, but how many of us actually follow through with real guesses as opposed to just giving in to emotion and broad generalization? Brad Wieners and David Pescovitz have asked writers to speculate about the matter of male birth control. Examples vary from the general to the specific and the humor of the piece encourages you both to listen to the argument as well as to think more carefully about your own "quick" answers to big problems.

Fair is fair: if a woman can swallow a pill and alter her body's chemistry such that she can't get pregnant, why shouldn't there be a chemical or hormone men can take to neutralize their seed?

Even though it has been cited (perhaps not incorrectly) as a sexist excuse, it *is* true that engineering a method to deactivate sperm is biologically more difficult than disrupting a woman's monthly egg output. And it isn't as though attempts at a pill for men haven't been made; several male birth control regimens have entered trials, only to prove toxic or to have intolerable side effects such as impotence. Isadora Alman says that some of the trials have confirmed persistent suspicions that men are content to leave birth control to their partners. For instance, the only side effect of one pill that did well in trials, Alman says, is that it turned the eyes of its taker pink. For Alman, this hardly rates when compared to the bloating, risk of cancer, and other myriad side effects associated with the female birth control pill. In fact, she says, this neo-pink eye would actually be an advantage: a woman could tell on sight if her partner or liaison was actually on the pill.

As of this writing, a couple of promising new developments have been made public: Research Triangle Institute in North Carolina has announced a new male contraceptive compound, now in trials, and an Australian group at the Royal Women's Hospital and Melbourne's Prince Henry's Institute of Medical Research has announced male contraceptive injections. The injections, reminiscent of those developed for women, have proven as effective in weekly doses as a woman's daily pill. To make the injections more market-friendly, researchers are trying to make them monthly or quarterly.

In general, our experts are optimistic. They acknowledge gender bias in contraceptive R & D. For example, they pointed to a double standard: to merit financial support, new contraceptive techniques for men must also protect against HIV infection, whereas new contraceptive techniques for women that don't block HIV, such as Norplant, routinely receive funding. But, they insist, men *do* care about birth control—vasectomies, for example, have never been performed more frequently—and they have confidence that a chemical or hormone supplement will soon make it that much easier for men to wear the pants in family planning.

WORDS TO KNOW

NOTE: When you write the definitions of the following words, make it a point to use at least three of them in conversation over the next day and three of them in your next writing assignment. Many times you'll find it difficult or impossible to use them in everyday speech or writing. What then is the point of defining them? Of learning them? At the very least, in all the following cases where you have unusual vocabulary terms to define, attempt to use them. How does attempting to use vocabulary that feels awkward or different change your view of your common speech and writing patterns? Learning how to use new vocabulary means just that—using the words. Write specifically how, where, when, and why you used the words and discuss with your class.

neo-pink eye—
Research Triangle Institute—
vasectomies—

QUESTIONS

This short reading mixes science with humor in a different way than Thomas's piece. How and why? What do you see to be the differences in the audiences of these two readings? In the objectives of the writers of them? Create a group of Text/You/Other and Three-Layered Questions from this reading. Is this article about sex? Or politics? Explain. What do you come up with for potential writing projects?

WRITING ACTIVITIES

1. Choose one of your questions on which to write.
2. Select three forms of sources to verify points and information you will make in your essay. For instance, you could choose an expert in the field whom you could interview and/or bring into class, a Web Site, and a newspaper article.
3. Write your essay using those sources to help support your main idea. Which did you find most useful and why?
4. Now bring in a false "expert" and use both in the presentation of your paper. Obviously, you will need to alert your two presentors ahead of time so neither one lets on who is the real expert.
5. Watch the class carefully as you present your essay and speakers. Ask the speakers questions and see how your classmates respond.
6. To what extent do they follow your lead in deciding who is the real expert? Did they guess correctly?

GRAMMAR AND STYLE QUESTIONS

1. Select a reading originally published on the Internet to compare and contrast with this text reading, which almost appears to be an Internet reading. Analyze these examples. What is the difference in grammatical style and why? Use specific examples from the readings as well as specific rules of grammar and details in your answer.
2. Using a standard grammar reference (e.g., Strunk and White's *Elements of Style*), find three specific exceptions (from any of the readings in this reader, including this one) to the rules such a standard reference has created, and discuss why the authors broke those rules.

Man A Machine*

David Paul

Apocalypse Culture *begins with a quote by Werner Herzog which reads, "There is nothing more terrifying than stupidity." It contains a disturbing juxtaposition of images. The real question is why is this text so disturbing? Do we allow authority figures to lie to us a little too often? Why? Does it make us feel better? The question then becomes, about what?*

Introduction David Paul's essay utilizes an implied extended metaphor to connect you, the reader, to the subject of his essay: how the human body works. His piece contains a number of references to outside texts in the form of quotes and paraphrases as well as startling statements about the meaning of the human body—all of which will surprise-attack your conventional thoughts about what really makes us tick.

When driving a car, one's nervous system becomes linked with the vehicle in a very basic way. If the driver decides to brake, the body performs a complex sequence of maneuvers with the brake, accelerator and steering wheel, all acting as sense-extensions. The vehicle becomes body-like and responds in body-like fashion to the driver's thoughts. If the driver decides to accelerate, the brain signals the foot which responds by signaling the accelerator, which responds by increasing fuel flow, which enacts a series of events that causes the vehicle to increase speed. In a sense, the car is the driver's body and is directly controlled by the driver's brain and central nervous system.

*The title *Man a Machine* is taken from Julien Offray De La Mettrie's book of the same title, first published in 1748. La Mettrie was a physician who had seen military service, and put forth the view that the human body can be seen as simply a complex machine. This view was partly inspired by a "vision" La Mettrie experienced during a feverish attack of cholera on the battlefield in 1742.

The driver "feels" other objects external to the vehicle and judges distances from the car in a manner crudely analogous to the operations involved in judging one's environment from the physical body. The difference is that the signal flow from the brain to the auto is indirect and is impeded by the physical separation of the operator's appendages from the appropriate control mechanisms. A little over a decade ago, there was talk of an experimental automobile braking system which was to be engaged by simply lifting an eyebrow, cutting in half the reaction time of a conventional braking system and reducing physical effort and mechanical work. As we design increasingly subtle mechanisms responsive to heat, pressure, and biological signals, we appear to be approaching a time when "willing" a machine into action will be relatively common. The separate steps between thought and realization of a desired goal begin to blur and finally disappear. Signal flow between organic and mechanical units linked in a system gradually becomes continuous and unbroken.

This trend toward continuous communications has resulted in the transfer of the machine operator's work from ". . . the level of muscular activity to the level of perception, memory and thought—to internal mental processes."[1] MIT mathematician Norbert Wiener (1894–1964) noted that the Industrial Revolution concerned the machine primarily as an alternative to human muscle. According to Lewis Mumford in *The Pentagon of Power,* "Man's biological emergence during the last two million years has, indeed, accelerated; and it has done so mainly in one direction, in the enlargement of the nervous system, under an increasingly unified cerebral direction." Machines make the body expandable. If machines have accomplished nothing else, they've reduced the human self to the brain and central nervous system.

The history of simple tools is a chronology of extension and articulation of human functions. Tools, originally conceived about two million years ago as crude adjuncts of the body to increase its power and efficacy, are passive participants in accomplishing work.

"A machine is merely a supplemental limb; this is the be-all and end-all of machinery." (Butler, *Erewhon.*) Tools connected in series produce machines. Machinery has gone a step beyond the tool in that it is capable of varying degrees of automatism (self-regulated activity without human participation), contingent behavior (decision making) and reaction to sensory stimulus through artificial organs. Mechanical history involves not only extension but replacement of human activity. Mumford has actually called the machine ". . . a sort of minor organism, designed to perform a single set of functions."

You might say that extension of the limb evolved into extensions of the brain.

Technology improves itself in a Darwinian way, as seen in the electronic marketplace, where "unfit" contraptions become extinct every year. As technology absorbs more and more human work, the line separating biology and mechanics gradually becomes less distinct. Though we are still toolmakers and our "logic engines" are still tools in the general sense of the word, the context has changed. No one living at the time of Hero of Alexandria[2] had any idea that the five machines he defined would have produced offspring capable of instantaneous logarithmic calculation or incorporated into the body as working parts. By World War II, machines were exhibiting behavior originally thought to be characteristic of primitive life. Early guided missiles were designed with the ideas of goal-seeking and scanning in mind, which "had combined as the essential mechanical conception of a working model that would behave very much like simple animal" (Grey Walter, *The Living Brain*).

Occupying the gray area between biology and technology is cybernetic theory. The word's root is Greek for "steersman" and André Ampère used the word in 1834 to mean "science of control" or "the branch of politics which is concerned with the means of government." Norbert Wiener used the term to refer to "the study of control and communication in the animal and the machine" concerned especially with mathematical analysis of information flow between biological, electronic and mechanical systems, and maintenance of order in those systems.

The complexity of predicting trajectories of quickly moving targets during World War II sparked Wiener and Julian Bigelow's development of cybernetics. Constantly changing information about the target's direction and speed necessitated feedback devices which would allow a gun to regulate its own movements. Interestingly enough, human operators in Wiener's automatic gun (which was never built) were given equal status with electro-mechanical components in the feedback loop.

Information gleaned from the project concerning feedback and servo-mechanisms led Wiener and associates to devise a model of the central nervous system that "explained some of its most characteristic activities as circular processes, emerging from the nervous system into the muscles, and re-entering the nervous system through the sense organs" (McCorduck, *Machines Who Think*).

"The connecting link was electronics, and the almost mystical fit between mathematic logic and the behavior of electronic circuits.

The thrust of the new information sciences was to precisely define and measure information in mathematic terms; to add information to the list of fundamental definitions basic to science—matter, energy, electric charge and the like" (Hanson, *The New Alchemists*).

"It has long been clear to me," says Wiener in *Cybernetics*, "that the modern ultra-rapid computing machine was in principle an ideal central nervous system to an apparatus for automatic control; and that its input and output need not be in the form of numbers or diagrams but might very well be, respectively, the readings of artificial sense organs, such as photoelectric cells or thermometers, and the performances of motors or solenoids."

Information transfer is fundamental to discussing the current state of technology. Automata need only instructions to accomplish given tasks. The link with the machine is mental. Machine language carries out our work. Language, according to Wiener, "is not exclusively an attribute of living beings but one which they may share to a certain degree with the machines man has constructed."

"Cybernetics recorded the switch from one dominant model, or set of explanations for phenomena, to another. Energy—the notion central to Newtonian mechanics—was now replaced by information. The ideas of information theory, such as coding, storage, noise, and so on, provided a better explanation for a whole host of events, from the behavior of electronic circuits to the behavior of a replicating cell" (McCorduck, *Machines Who Think*).

Electrical powering of machinery allowed a dialogue between organic and mechanized systems. Galvani's discovery of electrical nervous stimulation in animal muscles around 1790 was the starting point of electrophysiology (apparently an inspiration to Mary Shelley). In 1875, electric brain currents were discovered and in 1924, Hans Berger devised a method of recording electrical activity from the surface of the scalp, later to become known as electroencephalography, central to biofeedback.

All living tissue is sensitive to electric current and generates small voltages. Our nervous system's activity is accompanied by electrical potentials and can be controlled externally by electricity, providing a means of direct communication between human and machine systems, the common thread of biofeedback and prosthetic research.

Technical history, then, involves extension and replacement of human functions in more than just a metaphorical sense. Wiener, again, was the first to suggest using myoelectric currents (produced by contracting muscle fiber) to control the motions of prosthetic limbs. He believed that signals from the brain to the muscle fiber in the stump of the limb could be tapped by electrodes. Small motors in the prosthesis could amplify the current to control the limb's movements. The "Boston Elbow" and "Utah Arm" are motor-driven prostheses that follow this procedure almost exactly, using electrodes that attach to the shoulder muscle or lay implanted in the arm socket. Through biofeedback the amputee learns to control the device somewhat like a normal limb.

The following is extracted from a paper explaining the design and construction of a microcomputer-controlled manipulator: "For an amputee to obtain motions when they are desired, he or she must give the microcomputer needed information. This information can come in the form of myoelectric signals picked up on the surface of the amputee's skin. These signals occur when the brain sends a signal to the muscle and the muscle tissues expand or contract to produce the requested motion. When a part of the body is amputated, many times the amputee continues to have a mental image of the missing part, a phenomenon known as the phantom limb syndrome. Mentally, the amputee can continue to move this phantom limb. Therefore, the brain continues to send signals to the remaining muscles and these muscles continue to try to produce the desired motion."[3]

Grey Walter experimented with the E-wave, or expectancy wave, which is a voltage that "arises in the brain about one second before a voluntary action, which can be either a motor act (such as pushing a button) or simply an action with respect to making a firm decision about something" (Rorvick, *As Man Becomes Machine*). The E-wave, like any electric signal from any source, can also be used to operate electrically controlled devices. Slow progress has finally resulted in a recent announcement that a researcher at Johns Hopkins University has learned to predict the arm movements of a monkey by analysis of its brain waves. These techniques, developed twenty years ago, are rather basic, but they're a first step in allowing machinery to be mentally or neurally controlled like alternate body parts. The opposite of thought-activated machinery is electrical brain stimulation which sinks electrodes into the brain and applies minor voltages. Just as thoughts and mental impulses produce electrical activity, most motor functions and emotions can be triggered or influenced by electrically stimulating the brain. "When a patient is conscious during a brain operation, the surgeon can give electrical stimulation in the motor strip and produce definite movements; here a twisting of the foot, there an arm movement, at a third point a clamping of the jaw" (Calder, *The Mind of Man*).

Electrical brain stimulation provides researchers with a means of mapping and controlling brain functions, including stimulating dormant sections (as in stroke victims) to produce useful body operation. Sequential computer control of serial stimulus has apparently been successful in producing "lifelike" movement in laboratory animals suffering paralysis. Stimulating the cortex directly to replace missing sensory input is another application. "Brindley and Lewin have described the case of a fifty-two-year-old woman, totally blind after suffering bilateral glaucoma, in whom an array of eighty small receiving coils were implanted subcutaneously above the skull, terminating in eighty platinum electrodes encased in a sheet of silicone rubber placed in direct contact with the visual cortex of the right occipital lobe. . . . With this type of transdermal stimulation, a visual sensation was perceived by the patient in the left half of her visual field . . . and simultaneous excitation of several electrodes evoked the perception of predictable simple visual patterns" (Delgado, *Physical Control of the Mind*). Electrical stimulation of the auditory nerve has produced auditory sensations. Appropriately placed electrodes can alter blood pressure, sleep, motor functions, the sensation of pain and even hostile behavior.

The following account illustrates one of the many possibilities opened up by the advent of these techniques: ". . . the ability to detect radiation has been bestowed on a group of experimental cats, each of which is wired into a portable, miniature geiger counter that telemeters electrical impulses directly to the feline brain via implanted electrodes. The square-wave electrical impulses are similar to normal nervous impulses. They are transmitted to a portion of the brain that is associated with fear reactions, causing the cats to shy away from radioactive sources" (Rorvik, *As Man Becomes Machine*). According to José Delgado, "It is reasonable to speculate that in the near future the stimoreceiver [instruments for radio transmission and reception of electrical messages to and from the brain] may provide the essential link from man to computer to man, with a reciprocal feedback between neurons and instruments which represents a new orientation for the medical control of neurophysiological functions. For example, it is conceivable that the localized abnormal activity which announces the imminence of an epileptic attack could be picked up by implanted electrodes, telemetered to a distant instrument room, tape-recorded, and analyzed by a computer capable of recognizing abnormal electrical patterns. Identification of the specific electrical disturbance could trigger the emission of radio signals to activate the patient's stimoreceiver and apply an electrical stimulation to a determined inhibitory area of the brain, thus blocking the onset of the convulsive episode" (Delgado, *Physical Control of the Mind*).

"By the turn of the century, every major organ except the brain and central nervous system will have artificial replacements," says Dr. William Dobelle, whose Institute for Artificial Organs in New York is working on replacements for the pancreas, heart, ear and eye ("Building the Bionic Man," *Newsweek,* July 12, 1982). The concept of total prosthesis seems plausible, if this is true. Creating an artificial human brain, however, is a little more difficult. Some say it will never happen. Since the first Artificial Intelligence experiments, attempts to mimic complex human neural activity with the crudities of current electronic hardware have been plagued with challenging problems.

Breakthroughs in this line of research might take place through electrobiological engineering or hybridization of computer architecture with molecular engineering. Naval Research Laboratories, the Japanese Ministry of International Trade and Industry, the U.S. Defense Advanced Research Projects Agency and other investors like Sharp and Sanyo-Denki are funding research into what is known as the Molecular Electronic Device (MED) or "biochip." There are several designs for these organic microprocessors, but the essential idea is to use protein molecules or synthetic organic molecules as computing elements to store information or act as switches with the application of voltage. Signal flow in this case would be by sodium or calcium ions. Others feel that artificial proteins can be constructed to carry signals by electron flow. Still another idea is to "metalize" dead neuronal tissue to produce processing devices. "The ultimate scenario," says geneticist Kevin Ulmer, of Genex Corporation, "is to develop a complete genetic code for the computer that would function as a virus does, but instead of producing more virus, it would assemble a fully operational computer inside a cell" ("Biochip Revolution," *Omni,* December, 1981).

The very notion that computer chips could be "grown" or that living and inert matter could be fused together on a molecular level promises surprises ahead for those with orthodox notions of mind and body. As machines become more and more responsive to human internal experiences (from the desire to move a limb or even rage or sexual pleasure), we'll probably reach a stage at which every subtle nuance of imagination and consciousness can be realized, stored and displayed through machinery. And at some point in the future it will be possible to "will" events to occur.

New twists in the evolution of the brain might be brought about through our own manipulation of the elements of biological science. If we seriously consider Spengler's suggestion that the hand and tool must have come into existence together, then it follows that the tool's transformation into an "organism" capable of monitoring and responding to our biological functions transforms us as well.

NOTES

1. Cole, M. & S., "Three Giants of Soviet Psychology." Interview with Alexei Nikolae-vitch Leontiev in *Psychology Today*, March, 1971.
2. Greek engineer whose credits include building a holy water slot machine and auto-mated religious shows featuring moving statues of gods.
3. Beeson, W., "A Microcomputer Controlled Manipulator for Biomedical Applica-tions," *Bioengineering: Proceedings of the Eight Northeast Conference*, Pergamon Press, 1980.

WORDS TO KNOW

NOTE: When you write the definitions of the following words, make it a point to use at least three of them in conversation over the next day and three of them in your next writing assignment. Many times you'll find it difficult or impossible to use them in everyday speech or writing. What then is the point of defining them? Of learning them? At the very least, in all the following cases where you have unusual vocabulary terms to define, attempt to use them. How does attempting to use vo-cabulary that feels awkward or different change your view of your common speech and writing patterns? Learning how to use new vo-cabulary means just that—using the words. Write specifically how, where, when, and why you used the words and discuss with your class.

appendages—
adjuncts—
automatism—
logarithmic—
cybernetic—
trajectories—
photoelectric—
electro-encephalography—
myoelectric—
E-wave—

bilateral glaucoma —
subcutaneously —
occipital —
transdermal —
telemeters —
stimoreceiver —
biochip —
metalize —
neuronal —

QUESTIONS

How does this reading affect your view of the human body and "what it is"? "What its purpose is"? Create a group of Text/You/Other and Three-Layered Questions from this reading. In what way is this reading covering new ground in its subject area? In terms of other readings in this text? Ask yourself again, have you dealt with any of the issues you raise in your questions previously in this text? Any of the questions? Do you keep coming back to them because you can't think of anything else to ask? Or because you're interested? Are you pushing yourself hard enough to really explore intricacies and complexities in your questions? Why or why not? What do you come up with for potential writing projects?

WRITING ACTIVITIES

1. This time, pool your questions as a class. Each student should draw a question to answer.
2. Write a one or two page short essay on your question which takes an unresearched approach to your subject and/or answers the question as though you didn't care what you were saying.
3. Now write a well-researched, original (this means don't just copy down what you find either in texts or on the Internet, but really think about and do something with the information that you find that turns it into a real idea) short essay that has a style and a voice. Create a pictorial source and incorporate it into what you've written.
4. To which version do your classmates respond, and why?
5. Do the same activity and writing for one of your own questions and present it to your classmates. Do you feel a difference in your writing and presentation when you are in control of the question — when

you've made the question? Which is the better of your two essays and presentations? Why?

GRAMMAR AND STYLE QUESTIONS

1. An important aspect of good usage is the concise and active expression of thoughts and ideas. Looking through "Man a Machine," find concise, active, grammatical expressions, put them into your own words, and see how you can make them still more concise.
2. Now take wordy, general expressions from your own writing that you've done based on this reading, and revise to make them concise, active expressions that are correct grammatically.

First Cryonic Reanimation

Brad Wieners and David Pescovitz

Editor, critic, and reporter Brad Wieners has written for Wired, TimeOut, Details, *and the* San Francisco Review. *He lives in San Francisco, California. David Pescovitz has written for the* Los Angeles Times, bOING bOING, Cincinnati CityBeat, *and* The Net. *He is a contributing editor for* Wired, *for which he writes the monthly column, "Reality Check." He lives in Oakland, California.*

Introduction We all like to speculate about the future, but how many of us actually follow through with real guesses as opposed to just giving in to emotion and broad generalization? Brad Wieners and David Pescovitz have cleverly asked writers to speculate about the matter of cryogenics. They consulted with some experts in the field and related fields including Steve Bridge of the Alcor Life Extension Foundation and Charles Pratt of the Cryo-Care Foundation among others. Examples vary from the general to the specific and straightforward definitions and hypothetical situations encourage you both to listen to the argument as well as think more carefully about your own "quick" answers to big problems.

It's a desire as old as life, and among some cryonicists it's a rallying cry: "Abolish Mortality!"

Here's what they envision: One day you die (or deanimate, as the advocates say), and over the next few days, technicians slowly but surely freeze either your head or entire body, eventually submerging what's left of you in liquid nitrogen (-196 degrees Celsius). Then, years from now, you are brought back to life. Disorientated at first, memories soon remind you of who you are. By that time, advanced surgical techniques have reversed the effects of freezer burn on your gray matter and have jump-started stalled metabolic processes (see "Cell Repair Technology," page 119). You undergo extensive physical therapy in an effort to adjust to your new body—one that has been cloned for you from your own DNA. Welcome to a brave new world where the Big Chill no longer means death and where true death occurs only when the DNA needed to construct new tissue has been destroyed.

Cryonics, the latest and arguably most promising technology yet for achieving longevity, is the science of deep-freezing tissue before it has begun to decay with an eye toward reanimating it later. The term dates to 1965 and Robert C. W. Ettinger's book, *The Prospect of Immortality.* Interestingly, as early as 1773 Benjamin Franklin considered the possibility of "a method of embalming drowned persons, in such a manner that they may be recalled to life at any period, however distant."

At least four companies make good on Ettinger's idea, insofar as we have the front-end (deep-freezing) technology today and can theoretically keep someone frozen until we have the back-end (reviving) technology. In fact, as this book went to press, these four organizations were maintaining 67 heads and/or bodies in cryosuspension. Alcor Foundation, perhaps the best known of the four, sustains 13 whole body and 19 neuro (head) suspensions. (Walt Disney's body and head, by the way, are not among them. His cryosuspension is an urban myth.)

Far-fetched as cryonics strikes some, it is, according to Ralph C. Merkle, "feasible in principle, if not yet in practice." Already, he and others note, kidneys and other internal organs have been frozen and later restored to their functions. The trick, he says, will be to revive a brain—with the memory intact. "Within ten years," says Steve Bridge optimistically, "we'll know how memory functions well enough to see if particular structures that are vital to it have survived."

To reach that point, says Art Quaife, will require investment in R & D. Quaife points to recent interest from Wall Street in "spin-off" cryonic technologies like BioTime's blood substitute (which, in context of cryonics, could serve as a biological antifreeze); to advances in cloning (lizards are already cloned in labs); and to the ability to repair tissue damaged by ice crystals.

Significantly, our experts suggest that the reanimation of people currently in cryonic suspension may not be the best measure of this technology. Instead, they point to cryogenic medicine as a better indicator of progress in cryonics. Imagine, says Merkle, "being able to operate on a person as a mechanic does a car—to turn off the motor completely, fix what is wrong, and then turn it back on again."

WORDS TO KNOW

NOTE: When you write the definitions of the following words, make it a point to use at least three of them in conversation over the next day and three of them in your next writing assignment. Many times you'll find it difficult or impossible to use them in everyday speech or writing. What then is the point of defining them? Of learning them? At the very least, in all the following cases where you have unusual vocabulary terms to define, attempt to use them. How does attempting to use vocabulary that feels awkward or different change your view of your common speech and writing patterns? Learning how to use new vocabulary means just that—using the words. Write specifically how, where, when, and why you used the words and discuss with your class.

cryonicists—

deanimate—

cryosuspension—

Alcor Foundation—

QUESTIONS

Clearly you can see some relationship between this reading and the last. How do both make you feel? Make you think? Create a group of Text/You/Other and Three-Layered Questions from this reading. Are these readings offensive? Intelligent? Insightful? What potential writing projects can you think of?

WRITING ACTIVITIES

1. Choose one of your questions on which to write.
2. List all the possible responses you can think of to your question from most clichéd to most original.
3. Where do you rate your own response on that scale and why?
4. On what materials, sources do you base your response?
5. Mix those sources with brand-new sources as you write your essay. Make the fact that a source is new to you or quite familiar a part of the

essay, in terms of its style and organization as well as in terms of its content.

6. Present your essay to your classmates. How do they respond?
7. How do you respond to their essays?
8. Use their responses and feedback to revise your written essay.

GRAMMAR AND STYLE QUESTIONS

1. An important aspect of good usage is the concise and active expression of thoughts and ideas. Reread the article by Wieners and Pescovitz and find concise, active, expressions that are correct grammatically, put them into your own words, and see how you can make them still more concise.

2. Now take wordy, general expressions from your own writing that you've done based on this reading, and revise them to make them more concise, active expressions that are correct grammatically.

Spanish Cats
and The Body Electric

Arthur Kroker and Michael A. Weinstein

Arthur Kroker is the author of Spasm, The Possessed Individual, *and* The Postmodern Scene, *among others. A contributing editor of* Mondo 2000 *and co-editor of the electrical journal,* CTHEORY, *he is Professor of Political Science at Concordia University, Montreal. Michael Weinstein is Professor of Political Philosophy at Purdue University, photography critic for* NEW CITY *in Chicago, and a rap poet. He's published 19 books, ranging from culture theory to metaphysics.*

Introduction Look closely at the layers of implication Arthur Kroker suggests just through his one opening example about stray pets in Spain. Notice in particular how Kroker transitions from the pets and their identification chips to an analogy (parallel correlation) with the concentration camp tattoos. What effect does this transition produce, and why?

The fate of animals in Spain prefigures the fate of the virtual body. In the name of greater animal safety, Spanish cats and dogs must be either tattooed at birth or have a micro-chip surgically implanted in their skin. When found as strays on the city streets, their electronic history can be pulled up (from a distance) by roving scanners, and their owners traced. Spanish officials are now considering adding new data files to the encrypted micro-chips of these telematic cats and dogs: their medical history of vaccinations, records of sexual sterilization, and a history of (cat) offenses against the public order.

What happens now to the virtualized animals in Spain anticipates the future of the electronic (sub-human) body. With this difference: the surgical implanting of a micro-chip in the virtual body will not be resisted, but welcomed, actually demanded, in the name of safety. What mother would not want her baby to be electronically identifiable from birth? Here, the tattoo of the concentration camps comes inside, and is electronically inscribed in the skin of the virtual body. Not only will micro-chips be used for electronic scanning, but molecular micro-computers straight from Silicon Valley will be inserted directly into the blood stream. Who does not want to be healthy? Who does not want to be warned in advance of the undetectable breakdowns of vital bodily organs? This is health fascism: the archiving of the medicalized body in the name of the preservation of good health. A virtual body, therefore, that emits a steady stream of electronic data about its identity, the health of its vital organs, its white blood cell count, the speed and circulability of its credit financing: like a spacecraft at the outer edge of the galaxy that beams digital radio messages about its electronic journey across the Milky Way.

The 1990s as the closing days of the slaughterhouse century. And Nietzsche's body vivisectionists? They are those gloating scientists from MIT and Harvard who performed radiation experiments on the "mentally retarded," and called it progress. Philosopher George Grant was correct when he predicted that the ethics of technological liberalism would be the ethics of the "petty conveniences" on the other hand, and radical injustice against the weak, the powerless, and the poor on the other. Such is the doubled language of cynical power at the fin-de-millenium. The virtual surveillance system has warped out of the bodies of those Spanish cats and dogs, and phase-shifted into the bloodstream of the virtual population of America.

WORDS TO KNOW

NOTE: When you write the definitions of the following words, make it a point to use at least three of them in conversation over the next day and three of them in your next writing assignment. Many times you'll find it difficult or impossible to use them in everyday speech or writing. What then is the point of defining them? Of learning them? At the very least, in all the following cases where you have unusual vocabulary terms to define, attempt to use them. How does attempting to use vocabulary that feels awkward or different change your view of your common speech and writing patterns? Learning how to use new vo-

cabulary means just that—using the words. Write specifically how, where, when, and why you used the words and discuss with your class

encrypted—
health fascism—
circulability—
vivisectionists—
prefigures—
undetectable—
surveillance—
medicalized—

QUESTIONS

Create a group of Text/You/Other and Three-Layered Questions from this reading. What visual images appear in your mind as you read this short excerpt? What potential writing projects can you think of?

WRITING ACTIVITIES

1. Gather from your classmates what images they saw as they read this piece.
2. Use these images in writing your essay on your question.
3. What becomes more important in the end upon finishing your essay? The point you want to make? Or what you want people to see as they read what you wrote?
4. How do you read writing? Visually? Do you see words? Pictures? Describe how you take in the language. Share this discussion with your class.
5. Revise your essay to incorporate a style and diction that will respond to how your classmates read, what appeals to them.
6. What does this experiment do to your writing? Do you like it or not? Why?

GRAMMAR AND STYLE QUESTIONS

1. Examine the use of punctuation in three different readings in this book, including this one by Kroker. How does each author use punctuation to emphasize his or her tone? To further his or her purpose? Does the

choice of punctuation make a difference with regard to these two elements, tone and purpose? Why or why not? Use specific examples in your answer.

2. Select an additional text reading and a reading originally published on the Internet to compare and contrast to this text reading by Kroker. Analyze these three readings. What are the differences stylistically? Use specific examples from the readings as well as specific rules of grammar and details in your answer.

One Student, One Computer

Stewart Brand

In his introduction to The Media Lab, *written in March 1988, Stewart Brand writes, "The time to understand a subject whole is when it's changing. Understanding is easier then because everything— even the deep premise structure—is up for grabs. And, with whole understanding, there's a better chance that the changes will be directed toward improvement." Brand founded, edited, and published the* Whole Earth Catalog *and the* Whole Earth Review.

Introduction Stewart Brand has written this piece (whose original purpose is as an essay within a chapter in his nonfiction book on media labs and how they change learning and communication) as a narrative essay where he tells a story about going to observe students learning with computers in the classroom. Through his narration about his interaction with the students and the principal, you learn what his point is. Of course, a number of strong statements throughout also serve as thesis points. Which are they and why have you chosen them?

I visited Hennigan School in early 1986, only five months after the project had begun. It's the kind of place that's easy to find parking near, a random-feeling, freeway-bruised, non-neighborhood. The concrete-slab walls of the school, built in 1972, are covered with faded graffiti. The spacious common areas inside have signs in Spanish as well as English. One of the reasons the school was selected was because of its racial makeup: 40 percent black, 40 percent Hispanic, 18 percent white, 2 percent Asian. Many of the kids are from single-parent, illiterate homes. Of the 600 children in the school, 220 are involved in the computer project.

Hennigan had the usual loud, busy feel of any school, but it had almost none of the usual "SIT DOWN AND SHUT UP" tenseness from the teachers. The kids seemed to be too interested in learning to hassle the system. I found the place so gleeful to be around that I went back a couple of more times later just for the pleasure of it.

I strolled through two computer common areas, each with two large circles of IBM PCjr personal computers facing outward, thirteen in each circle, classrooms fanning out all around. Scattered around the circles were kids at the keyboards messing around. Apparently a new spelling game had just turned up, so many were exploring what it had to offer.

On the walls were signs with the main Logo commands—PD (pen down), PU (pen up), HT (hide turtle), FD (forward), etc.—and pinned-up word-processed stories ("MI CARRO ES ROJO. MI PAPA TIENE UN CARRO ROJO . . ."). The kids evidently treated visiting grownups with aplomb, so I sat down next to one Rachel, fifth-grader, who was using Logo to animate a story. She typed "SETBG1." The screen responded, "I DON'T KNOW HOW TO SETBG1." Rachel shrugged and corrected, "SET BG1." The screen background obligingly turned blue, and she ran the end of the story. A flashing-color snowflake tumbled down a slope as words appeared:

> ALL OF A SUDDEN
>
> OCCY TRIPED. HE
>
> ROLLED AND
>
> ROLLED
>
> AND ROLLED.

At the next console Mike Travers from the Vivarium group was watching a boy of light-brown complexion and intent demeanor making a stick figure walk on his screen. Travers' eyebrows were up: "He's discovered transformational geometry." A bell, classes changed, and the number of kids in the circle went from three to ten, picking up projects on the computers where they'd left off. They were on their own time.

Before visiting Hennigan I had talked with Papert in his office at the Media Lab about why the density of computers might matter. He's a soulful man—warm brown eyes always seeming about to smile, eyebrows canted up at the outside, gentle cottony voice with a British colonial accent from his South African origins overlaid with a French flavor from his five years working with Jean Piaget on child development in Geneva. His beard blurring grayly down and his hair grayly up, he seems devoid of hard edges.

"There are a million computers in American schools," he told me, "and 50 million students. What do you do with one-fiftieth of a computer? Boston has the highest ratio of large American cities, a computer for every eighteen students. Each one gets about an hour a week. It's like having one pencil for every eighteen students. At Hennigan there's about 100 computers for 220 students—enough for the kids always to be able to get at one. They can get an hour of two of computer time a day.

"It's too soon to know what the real difference that will make, but you can see some things. At Hennigan the girls play with computers *just* as much as the boys, unlike most schools, where computers are competed for, and the girls drop out of that game."

"Kids like computers?" I asked. Papert: "It's a total love affair between kids and computers." "Why?" I wondered.

Papert: "I think it corresponds to children wanting to be able to control an important part of the world. They're always reaching out to grab what is perceived as important in the adult world. They grab a pencil and scribble with it. They can feel the flexibility of the computer and its power. They can find a rich intellectual activity with which to fall in love. It's through these intellectual love affairs that people acquire a taste for rigor and creativity." Me: "And they see games right away that are fun to play." Papert: "And they see games right away that are fun to play."

Part of the attraction of Logo is that it has lived up to its original design principle: "low threshold and no ceiling." Anybody can get into it and quickly start being amused by doing things, and in time they can use it for anything a computer can do—drawing, writing, doing math, making music. From the very start they are programming the computer rather than being programmed by it. Since the child is alone with the utterly nonjudgmental machine, activities like guessing, playing, imitating, inventing, all come easily—exactly the real-world learning behavior that is cramped or suppressed in most classroom settings.

They're not quite alone with the computer, actually. Kids naturally help each other and show each other things they've made and peek at each other's work, and the teachers soon catch on it's better to let that happen. It's not cheating. It's the kind of joint exploration that is group learning at its best. Teachers who are committed to being the imparters and arbiters of all knowledge in the classroom can have a tough time making the switch.

Hennigan is a classic Media Lab situation. With sufficiently personalized technology, power shifts toward the no-longer-passive individual.

Music amid the computers at Hennigan is an interesting case. Papert: "Almost all the fourth- and fifth-grade children know music notation—that's considered impossible in most music teaching—and they're all writing music. Some are writing some extremely beautiful things that you'd admire. In our society music creativity is poorly represented. At school you don't learn to compose, you learn to sing in tune and play the piano. Composition is only for specialists, and there's no reason it should be. Everybody draws, everybody writes, everybody talks, everybody does theater. I think one reason is that you need too much performance skill with music to be able to listen to your piece. With the computer as a musical instrument it becomes possible to create a piece of music and hear it independently of your performance skill."

And the kids do, but the computer angle is so blended in you hardly notice it. A Hennigan music class that I watched consisted mostly of singing and "body movement"—fiercely inventive dancing led by the black students—along with enthusiastic improvisation on traditional instruments and homemade ones. I saw an upright piano, slide whistle, bottle-cap rattlers, and a toy xylophone in use as well as an Apple computer and a Yamaha keyboard and attached computer. Discussion with the teacher between pieces was of chords and harmonies, tempo and composition.

Before at Hennigan, Papert recalled, "music was the most hated subject. It was hated worse than math, even worse than punishment. The change has affected the teachers as much as anyone. "The other day one of the teachers was sitting on the floor with the children making bird sounds. Six months ago that would have been unthinkable. If we told them at the beginning that would be expected, they would have said, 'Do your experiments somewhere else.'"

WORDS TO KNOW

NOTE: When you write the definitions of the following words, make it a point to use at least three of them in conversation over the next day and three of them in your next writing assignment. Many times you'll find it difficult or impossible to use them in everyday speech or writing. What then is the point of defining them? Of learning them? At the very least, in all the following cases where you have unusual vocabulary terms to define, attempt to use them. How does attempting to use vocabulary that feels awkward or different change your view of your common speech and writing patterns? Learning how to use new vo-

cabulary means just that—using the words. Write specifically how, where, when, and why you used the words and discuss with your class.

Logo—
PD—
PU—
HT—
FD—
Mi—
Carro—
Es—
Rojo—
Tiene—
aplomb
Vivarium—
Jean Piaget—
arbiters—

QUESTIONS

Remember this reading was written in 1987, over ten years ago. What's changed? What's your own experience and relationship with computers? With computers in school? Computers in learning? Create a group of Text/You/Other and Three-Layered Questions from this reading. What do you come up with for potential writing projects?

WRITING ACTIVITIES

1. Choose one of your questions on which to write.
2. Give yourself a pseudonym and start an essay from your selected question on the computer and save it on a disk.
3. Trade disks with your classmates two other times, each time making sure you get a different disk and that no one knows whose disk is whose.
4. Continue the essay from where you get it, which the first time will mean you write the middle of the essay, and the second time will mean you write the conclusion to the essay.
5. Return disks to the rightful owners.

6. Present the essays. Don't reveal who wrote what until after you've read the essays as a group. How do you like the body and conclusion that were written for your essay and its introduction?

GRAMMAR AND STYLE QUESTIONS

1. Compare and contrast the previous reading of Brand's with this reading of his. How does he use grammar to get his points across? How does his use of grammar to get his points across in each reading differ? What do both readings have in common in terms of how they use grammar? Use specific rules of grammar and details in your answer.

2. One of the most difficult tasks for any new writer is to express time and timelines consistently and to match actions to those times and timelines. Take a paragraph from this Brand reading (or the previous one) that has a strong sense of either past, present, or future tense, rewrite it using a different verb tense (i.e., if it was written in the present tense, rewrite it in the past tense, and so forth). What is the effect of such a change? Were you consistent with your new selection of verb tense in your revision? And, if you had difficulty with consistency, without referring back to the text, restore the original tense and see how closely the paragraph matches how Brand originally wrote it.

Oil Spills: Dispersing Pollution

Edward Tenner

Edward Tenner, former executive editor for physical science and history at Princeton University Press, holds a visiting research appointment in the Department of Geological and Geophysical Sciences at Princeton University. He received an A.B. from Princeton and a Ph.D. in history from the University of Chicago and has held visiting research positions at Rutgers University and the Institute for Advanced Study. In 1991–92 he was a John Simon Guggenheim Memorial Fellow and in 1995–96 a Fellow of the Woodrow Wilson International Center for Scholars.

Introduction Edward Tenner's essay is also a subchapter within a chapter in his book, and he takes a fairly conventional essayist approach in terms of his writing and style. What he does that makes his essay stand out is challenge your notions of what the "right" solution is. He dares you to fall back on the now famous "Can't we all just get along?" line without knowing what your facts are. How many of you know what he reveals about the real solution to cleaning up an oil spill? Where does his essay start busting clichés?

When the *Exxon Valdez* hit Bligh Reef off the Alaska Coast in 1988, the murky discharge of 35,000 tons of crude oil was an ethical Rorschach test. To some it was simply another example of human failure—resulting from flaws of character and responsibility, and of course from drinking on the job. To others it expressed the heedlessness of corporate capitalism at its worst, the inevitable outcome of putting profits above safe operation. And to still others, the real fault was neither the captain's nor the corporation's but the consumer's: an inexorable price of the industrial world's insatiable hunger for energy. In fact, as the next chapter will argue, great oil spills threaten species diversity far less than some other consequences of shipping do. They may not even be the ugliest fruits of marine traffic. One report in 1986 estimated that ships and drilling rigs were dumping hundreds of thousands of tons of plastic debris into the world's oceans each year, the U.S. Navy alone accounting for sixty tons a day. Plastics strangle birds and seals, poison turtles, and fatally ensnarl whales. But litter, excepting medical waste, isn't newsworthy. Television spreads the more spectacular ugliness of spills electronically around the world, and it would take a very stony-hearted policy analyst to argue that shippers and governments are already spending too much money to prevent them.

Decades of megaspills from the world's growing supertanker fleet before the *Valdez* affair suggest that the problem is indeed structural. The even larger wrecks of the *Torrey Canyon* (120,000 tons) in 1967 and *Amoco Cadiz* (220,000 tons) in 1978 had already shown it was worldwide. Europe's coasts have suffered much more than America's. And the U.S. National Research Council and others have pointed to a potential technological revenge effect. Computerized design lets naval architects model the result of stresses on larger and larger ships; the *Seawise Giant* of 1980 has a deadweight of 565,000 tons, though today's very large crude carriers (VLCCs) have typical deadweights of about half of that. Far from making shipping safer, new design technology like Humphrey Davy's mining lamp, which initially resulted in deeper shafts and more accidents encouraged owners to push the limits of risk. They specified lighter, high-tensile steel which saved fuel but could rupture when repeated stresses began to produce small but potentially deadly cracks. Stronger steel is less ductile and more likely to break under some circumstances (in the early 1980s, wings fell off airplanes, storage tanks exploded, and hip implants cracked). It is harder to weld properly, and shipbuilders don't always provide suitable internal framework.

The search for safer designs shows that the conversion of catastrophic problems to chronic ones can sometimes be reversed. When treaties in the 1970s forbade ballast water in empty petroleum tanks, they slashed the steady pollution of seas and harbors from the flushed water. Unfortunately, oil in the higher-riding ships with separate ballast tanks has ever since been under greater pressure relative to the sea. If a hull is ruptured, more oil pours out. The most popular recommendation for tanker safety, adding a second hull about a meter or more from the ship's exterior, might let petroleum vapors seep into the space between hulls and explode. Safety inspections, already covering twelve hundred kilometers of welded seam on the vast hulls, could be so daunting that more sources of leaks could be missed. Keeping tanks partly empty to reduce pressure relative to the sea might retain most oil within tanks in small accidents, but it could increase dangerous stresses in high waves. Pumps to maintain negative pressure after accidents could also promote explosions, And owners argue that larger numbers of smaller, safer ships might actually result in more accidents and more oil spillage than conventional supertankers do now. (They also warn of a social revenge effect: if liability under the U.S. Oil Pollution Act is too risky, serving the U.S. market will be left to doubtful operators.) Fortunately there are technological solutions that in time will reduce the risks of marine accidents. Intermediate decks can limit spills from the largest tankers. Automatic ocean sounding and Global Positioning System satellites can cut the time and expense of producing more accurate and comprehensive nautical charts. And offshore petroleum receiving stations like the Louisiana Offshore Oil Port, linked to the mainland with underwater pipelines, appear to reduce the risk of collision.

Once a spill does happen, it is ugly. There is a grandeur in natural hazards, even where they devastate natural habitats, as the eruption of Mount St. Helens did in Washington State and Hurricane Andrew did in the Southeast. The horrific images of an oil slick, the struggles of oil-coated seabirds and mammals, the contaminated shorelines—all assault cameras and consciences. They call for technologies to repair what technology has wrought. Unfortunately the record of cleanup technology has so far been filled with revenge effects of its own. England experienced some of these problems as early as 1967, when napalm failed to burn off the oil from *Torrey Canyon* and shores and harbors were treated to ten thousand tons of chemical dispersants. These turned out to kill many of the remaining crustaceans and other animals and plants that the oil itself had spared. Even in the 1990s, dispersants have potential revenge effects. By breaking down petroleum into minute globules that will mix with water and sink below the surface, they relieve some of the unsightly signs of a leak. They also keep blobs of oil from washing up onto the shoreline and from contaminating sediments. But as the petroleum is free to sink below the water's surface, it is also more likely to harm the reproduction of organisms on the seafloor, from fish eggs to lobsters.

Tidying up an oil spill mechanically can have even more serious revenge effects. The $2 billion cleanup of the *Exxon Valdez* disaster relied heavily on hot water applied to the shoreline through high-velocity pumps—Exxon's response to outrage. A later independent report for the Hazardous Materials Response unit of the National

Oceanic and Atmospheric Administration (NOAA) showed just how unexpected the consequences of purification could be. David Kennedy of NOAA's Seattle office explained: "The treatment scalded the beach, killing many organisms that had survived the oil, including some that were little affected by it. It also blasted off barnacles and limpets. And it drove a mixture of sediment and oil down the beach face, depositing them in a subtidal area richer in many forms of marine life—one where there hadn't been much oil." A report commissioned by NOAA suggested that the high-pressure cleanup had disrupted rock-surface ecology by destroying mussel and rockweed populations, "relatively tolerant" to petroleum, making surfaces more vulnerable to waves and predators. Fewer mollusks also encouraged opportunistic algae to preempt surfaces from rockweed and red algae. The oil flushed from the surface killed hard-shelled clams and crustaceans in intertidal and subtidal zones. It apparently also reduced the productivity of the eelgrass that shelters young fish and shrimp. The water pressure itself was even more damaging. At up to one hundred pounds per square inch it disrupted the natural sediments of beaches, both gravel and sand, smothering clams and worms.

Rescuing animals from spills may also result in revenge effects. Of the 357 sea otters saved from the spill and treated by veterinarians and volunteers, 200 could be returned to the sea. A number of biologist now believe, though, that these spread a herpes virus to otters in eastern Prince William Sound that had avoided the spill itself. The transplanted otters also died in unusual numbers. While some form of the virus appears to be endemic in the waters off Alaska, the treated otters had lesions that could have transmitted the disease, or a more virulent strain of it. Stressed animals are potentially dangerous, and some biologists and veterinarians now favor keeping them in captivity. They also point out that efforts to save the most seriously injured otters may only have made them suffer longer.

The *Torrey Canyon* and especially the *Exxon Valdez* disasters show the perils of purification. Contamination anywhere in the world can become so unbearably visible that it seems to cry out for equally televisable remedies. Exxon officials still defend cleanup methods even though most scientists now believe a less costly strategy—for Exxon, too—would have been more effective. This does not mean that cleanup never works. It should not discourage us from reducing and correcting our degradation of nature—whether chronic or acute. But the big marine spills underscore how complex natural systems are, and how creative and flexible human management of them has to be. It is fortunate for us that crude petroleum seeps into the ocean on its own, since natural selection has already engineered bacteria that thrive on it. In fact, the existence of natural pollution of Prince William Sound sped its recovery; local spruce trees produce hydrocarbons related to those in the Prudhoe Bay crude spilled by the *Exxon Valdez*. (Refined products are less likely to find preadapted bacteria.) Recovery rates have varied from one site to another, but a study by the Congressional Research Service specialist James E. Mielke underscored the ability of marine ecosystems to recover from even severe impacts. Fishing and hunting have a far greater impact than oil spills do on those species that are harvested; most species recolonize polluted areas quickly.

The closer we look at marine oil pollution, the less catastrophic and more chronic it turns out to be. During the 1980s, global oil pollution from sea and land disasters like spills, shipwrecks, and fires declined from 328 million gallons to between 8 and 16 percent of that figure annually. In 1985, tanker accidents accounted for only 12.5 percent of oil pollution—not much more than natural marine seeps and sediment erosion. In spite of the ban on ballast water in tanks, routine bilge and fuel oil pollution from tankers was almost as bad a problem as tanker accidents, and other "normal" tanker operations caused as much pollution as the last two combined. Municipal and industrial sources put nearly three times as much oil pollution in the sea as all tanker accidents combined.

On land, too, it is smaller leaks, seepage, and waste-oil storage—not catastrophic—that pose the most dangerous threats to both wildlife and human health. The U.S. Fish and Wildlife Service has estimated that more than twice as many migratory birds died after landing in open ponds and containers of waste oil in five Southwestern states alone in one year as were lost in the *Exxon Valdez* spill. Tank farms and pipelines on a Brooklyn site have been slowly leaking over one and a half times the spill of the *Exxon Valdez*. Another tank farm in Indiana is being forced to remedy leaks that could have been three times as large. Rusting pipes, bad welding, leaking valves, and sloppy maintenance account for most of the loss. Leak detectors are so unreliable that in January 1990, 567,000 gallons of heating oil were discharged from an Exxon facility in New Jersey where warnings had been ignored after twelve years of false alarms. And the problem extends to the retail level. Richard Golob, publisher of an oil pollution newsletter, has calculated that at any time, 100,000 of America's 1.5 million underground fuel storage tanks are leaking or starting to leak; the safer tanks that local service stations are required to put in their place may leak anyway after careless, cut-rate installation. In fact, the chronic leakage problem

can turn into a catastrophic risk of explosion if the electrical conduits needed by the new systems are not sealed expertly.

WORDS TO KNOW

NOTE: When you write the definitions of the following words, make it a
point to use at least three of them in conversation over the next day
and three of them in your next writing assignment. Many times you'll
find it difficult or impossible to use them in everyday speech or writing.
What then is the point of defining them? Of learning them? At the very
least, in all the following cases where you have unusual vocabulary
terms to define, attempt to use them. How does attempting to use vocabulary that feels awkward or different change your view of your
common speech and writing patterns? Learning how to use new vocabulary means just that—using the words. Write specifically how,
where, when, and why you used the words and discuss with your class.

VLCCs—
high-tensile—
ballast—
dispersants—
crustaceans—
limpets—
preadapted—

QUESTIONS

We are always taught that whenever you make a mess, clean it up and
leave the place cleaner than when you found it. Have you ever questioned this rule? Why or why not? Have you ever considered that to follow it would have negative consequences? Why or why not? To what
extent have you ever followed up on the aftereffects of any kind of pollution cleanup? On the after effects of a disaster? Create a group of
Text/You/Other and Three-Layered Questions from this reading. What
potential writing projects can you think of?

WRITING ACTIVITIES

1. Choose one of your questions on which to write.
2. Write a one to two page essay on that question, and be sure to include a conclusion.
3. Trade papers with a classmate.
4. Upon receiving your classmate's paper, write a paper that picks up where his or hers concluded and that really follows through on what happens or has happened after or since "the paper ends or ended."
5. Present your essay to your classmates. How do they respond?
6. How do you respond to their essays?
7. Use their responses and feedback to revise your written essay and write a more challenging, more in-depth conclusion.

GRAMMAR AND STYLE QUESTIONS

1. One of the most difficult tasks for any new writer is to express time and timelines consistently and to match actions to those times and time-lines. Take a paragraph from this reading that has a strong sense of either past, present, or future tense, and rewrite it using a different verb tense (i.e., if it was written in the present tense, rewrite it in the past tense, and so forth). What is the effect of such a change? Were you consistent with your new selection of verb tense in your revision? And, if you had difficulty with consistency, without referring back to the text, restore the original tense and see how closely the paragraph matches how the author originally wrote it.
2. One of the best ways to learn grammar, in addition to learning the names and rules of grammatical elements, is to read other people's writing and determine how and why they write well. Take a grammatically imperfect piece of your own work, read two or three readings from this reader (including this one by Tenner), and rewrite your piece afterwards. Is it grammatically better? Why or why not? What was the impact of seeing how other people put together words? Whose did you like best and why?

Tiny Indian Tribe Stalls Columbia's Rush for Oil

Michael McCaughan

Oil takes on a very different role and meaning in the following article that follows about a group of 5,000 people willing to die to save it. This story challenges you also to view the "importance of the needs of the many outweighing the need of the few."

Introduction Michael McCaughan's piece is a newspaper article that contains exposition about a particular situation in Colombia. But in addition to the facts and players in the case, he uses single sentence turning points at various places in the article which have the effect of showing you each time you think "that's the end of it," it's not. There are also several different environmental issues at stake, and McCaughan has skillfully blended them. Can you determine what they are and how they defy what you might consider to be typical environmental issues?

The small air force plane dropped off its dozen passengers in the middle of an army camp near this humid jungle town in northeastern Colombia.

Just beyond the airport, a row of oil drums and sandbags provided makeshift cover for dozens of soldiers crouched in combat position, awaiting guerrillas who strike from the hills beyond. Signs labeled "Minefield—Don't Walk" dissuade visitors from straying off the main road.

Saravena is at the heart of Colombia's spectacular oil boom, which has transformed this country from an importer to a self-sufficient exporter, with annual revenues worth $3 billion. Projected figures for 1998 show a 50 percent increase in the revenues, but reserves are low and pressure is on to exploit new deposits.

The latest deposits to be discovered are located within the territory of the U'wa. an indigenous people who attracted international attention last year by threatening to commit collective suicide by jumping off a 1,400-foot cliff if drilling proceeds.

The border of the U'wa reservation is two hours by foot from Saravena across unpaved roads and rising rivers. The tribe has trekked through the cloud forests of the Colombian Andes for centuries, shifting their home base three times a year, rotating subsistence crops between snow-capped peaks, lush jungle forest and scorched, arid lands. The U'was' stewardship of the land has been so exemplary that satellite photos are unable to distinguish land under cultivation from virgin terrain.

They are standing on top of a billion-dollar fortune that would bring them health clinics, VCRs and washing machines, catapulting the 5,000-member tribe into the modern age.

But the U'wa are not interested.

Each year their spiritual leaders, known as "Werjayas," sing the world into existence—fasting for weeks on end as they seek guidance from gods above and below the land. According to U'wa tradition, oil is the vital element that holds the Earth together, and its extraction would bring an end to their world.

"The oil is working right where it is now. It is alive and cannot be extracted," said Roberto Cobaria, president of the U'wa Council of tribal authorities. "There is no possible compensation for this."

The U'wa conflict has been played out in other guises countless times in Latin America, as Indian tribes from Oaxaca in Mexico to the Amazon cave in to foreign investors and local politicians who promise prosperity and development.

The results have mostly been catastrophic—entire communities disappearing, swallowed up by the influx of non-Indian laborers, alcoholism, prostitution, and the end of traditional hunting and fishing lifestyles.

In Colombia, the situation is aggravated by the presence of two guerrilla armies who have found in the oil conflict an ideal battleground for their war on gringo capital.

In the past decade, pipeline sabotage by the rebels has spilled 1.5 million barrels of crude oil into nearby forests and rivers. In comparison, 240,000 barrels were spilled by the Exxon Valdez. The oil companies pay a "war tax" to the state to offset the costs involved in maintaining thousands of soldiers to guard isolated oil installations.

An estimated 1.5 billion barrels of crude are waiting to be extracted in the U'wa territory, about the amount the United States uses in three months, according to the Rainforest Action Network. The deposit is known to oil companies as the "Samore block" and Los Angeles-based giant Occidental Petroleum wants to begin exploration work.

But the U'was' suicide threat has paralyzed the project.

"We do not want to engage in a project that means conflict," said Robert Stewart, Occidental's spokesman in Colombia, during an interview in the company's bunker-like Bogota office.

Colombia's revised 1991 constitution contains some of Latin America's most progressive legislation concerning Indian rights, upholding the principle of Indian land as "non-negotiable, nontransferable and ineligible for seizure under any conditions."

The matter would seem to end there.

But in February 1997, the Supreme Court upheld the validity of Occidental's environmental license, which was granted after a single consultation with the U'wa authorities.

Colombian politicians make no bones about the outcome they expect in the U'wa case.

"You can't compare the interests of 38 million Colombians with the worries of an indigenous community," said Rodrigo Villamizar, who recently stepped down as energy minister. "The resources belong to all Colombians, and the government has the final say on the issue."

The U'was' suicide threat can be traced back to the arrival of the Spanish in the 16th century. Rather than become slaves for the invaders, and entire U'wa community threw themselves off the same "cliff of glory" they are threatening to jump off today.

Their determination is symbolized by Cobaria's bravery in the face of intimidation.

Last July five hooded men dragged him from his bed and pressed a piece of paper into his hands, ordering him to sign.

"Kill me now, I cannot sign anything away for my tribe," shouted Cobaria, who cannot read or write.

The unidentified assailants then beat him with the butts of their rifles, threatened him with hanging, flung him off an embankment into a river and ran off.

The attack occurred during a period in the summer when outsiders are forbidden to enter U'wa territory because of ceremonial fasting by the tribe.

The Werjayas have allegedly agreed on the suicide ritual to be followed should oil exploration begin, but the details remain a well-kept secret.

Occidental takes the threat seriously enough that it has halted all work in the region until further negotiations are held.

Last year, in an effort to break the impasse, Colombian authorities commissioned a joint report by Harvard University and Organization of American States experts to analyze the conflict and suggest a way forward.

In August, the Harvard-OAS team recommended a formal definition of U'wa territory (the dimensions of which are disputed by the government), allowing Occidental to begin work now within clearly demarcated limits and to discuss future exploration inside U'wa land "in the distant future."

The situation has grown more volatile of late.

In early March, the U'wa issued a statement that is in essence their response to the recommendations.

They demand that the government and Occidental recognize their right to refuse or accept oil activity on their land as a precondition to any dialogue about oil development. The tribe also demands an immediate withdrawal of the military presence in U'wa territory, which has increased dramatically since the beginning of the year.

The statement also accused Occidental of attempting to "create conflicts" within the tribe and of falsely implying that the U'wa are linked to the guerrillas.

Colombia's National Indigenous Organization, (ONIC), a lobbying group set up in 1982 to offer legal advice to Indian peoples and act as a representative before national authorities, has readied a nationwide emergency protest plan should the U'wa conflict reach a crisis point.

The ONIC linked up with the U'wa just as Occidental began work in the region, bringing 4,000 Indians from all over the country to visit the area and facilitating Cobaria's contact with U.S. environmental groups.

Occidental, meanwhile is waiting things out, confident that the drilling will go ahead.

"We're under contract with the government; we couldn't leave if we wanted," said Stewart, who seems keen to distance Occidental from any direct role in the process.

But Abadio Green, ONIC's president, asks: "The U'wa oil would keep the U.S. in gas for three months. Is that worth the extinction of the U'wa people?"

❖   ❖   ❖

WORDS TO KNOW

NOTE: When you write the definitions of the following words, make it a point to use at least three of them in conversation over the next day and three of them in your next writing assignment. Many times you'll find it difficult or impossible to use them in everyday speech or writing. What then is the point of defining them? Of learning them? At the very least, in all the following cases where you have unusual vocabulary terms to define, attempt to use them. How does attempting to use vocabulary that feels awkward or different change your view of your common speech and writing patterns? Learning how to use new vocabulary means just that—using the words. Write specifically how, where, when, and why you used the words and discuss with your class.

U'wa—
guerrillas—
Werjayas—
guises—

QUESTIONS

Technology versus morality plays itself out here in a manner which calls into question much of the United States' modern way of life. Search the Internet for follow-up news on what action was taken as well as letters to the world from the U'wa. Create a group of Text/You/Other and Three-Layered Questions from this reading. What potential writing projects can you think of?

WRITING ACTIVITIES

1. Choose one of your questions on which to write.
2. Write a one to two page essay on that question addressing it in the way in which you want to address it, regardless of having to use sources, or what those sources say. Make the paper reflect your own feelings, beliefs, whims, and desires.
3. Now write a version that takes into account source material and other information that would insist you rein in your own agenda.
4. Present your two essays to your classmates. How do they respond?
5. How do you respond to their essays? Why?
6. Where do you draw the line at what's right for the work?

GRAMMAR AND STYLE QUESTIONS

1. Compare and contrast McCaughan's reading with another author's reading in this book. How do they use grammar to get their points across? How does their use of grammar to get their points across differ? What are the common features of both? Use specific rules of grammar and details in your answer.

2. Look at the uses of punctuation from a journalistic reading and a storytelling reading (use McCaughan's reading as your journalistic selection). How is punctuation used stylistically? Use specific examples from the readings as well as specific rules of grammar and details in your answer.

Twenty Evocations

Bruce Sterling

Of Schismatrix Plus *Bruce Sterling writes:* Schismatrix Plus *is a creeping sea-urchin of a book—spiky and odd. It isn't very elegant, and it lacks bi-lateral symmetry, but pieces of it break off inside people and stick with them for years.*

Of "Twenty Evocations" he writes that he was taking "his crammed prose technique as far as it would go."

Introduction One of the meanings of evoke is to conjure up a particular image. Rather than present you with a traditionally formatted and organized short story, Sterling has chosen to evoke twenty images from the life of this "machine" boy Nikolai (remember our earlier reading "Man a Machine"?) What impact do these word "photographs" have on you as reader? How does such a presentation affect the way you learn what happens in the story versus if you had received the information in the way that you do in the Margaret St. Clair story "An Egg a Month from All Over"?

1. Expert Systems

When Nikolai Leng was a child, his teacher was a cybernetic system with a holographic interface. The holo took the form of a young Shaper woman. Its "personality" was an interactive composite expert system manufactured by Shaper psychotechs. Nikolai loved it.

2. Never Born

"You mean we all came from Earth?" said Nikolai, unbelieving.

"Yes," the holo said kindly. "The first true settlers in space were born on Earth—produced by sexual means. Of course, hundred of years have passed since then. You are a Shaper. Shapers are never born."

"Who lives on Earth now?"

"Human beings."

"Ohhhh," said Nikolai, his falling tones betraying a rapid loss of interest.

3. A Malfunctioning Leg

There came a day when Nikolai saw his first Mechanist. The man was a diplomat and commercial agent, stationed by his faction in Nikolai's habitat. Nikolai and some children from his crèche were playing in the corridor when the diplomat stalked by. One of the Mechanist's legs was malfunctioning, and it went click-whirr, click-whirr. Nikolai's friend Alex mimicked the man's limp. Suddenly the man turned on them, his plastic eyes dilating. "Gene-lines," the Mechanist snarled. "I can buy you, grow you, sell you, cut you into bits. Your screams: my music."

4. Fuzz Patina

Sweat was running into the braided collar of Nikolai's military tunic. The air in the abandoned station was still breathable, but insufferably hot. Nikolai helped his sergeant strip the valuables off a dead miner. The murdered Shaper's antiseptic body was desiccated, but perfect. They walked into another section. The body of a Mechanist pirate sprawled in the feeble gravity. Killed during the attack, his body had rotted for weeks inside his suit. An inch-think patina of grayish fuzz had devoured his face.

5. Not Meritorious

Nikolai was on leave in the Ring Council with two men from his unit. They were drinking in a free-fall bar called the ECLECTIC EPILEP-TIC. The first man was Simon Afriel, a charming, ambitious young Shaper of the old school. The other man had a Mechanist eye implant. His loyalty was suspect. The three of them were discussing semantics. "The map is not the territory," Afriel said. Suddenly the second man picked an almost invisible listening device from the edge of the table. "And the tap is not meritorious," he quipped. They never saw him again.

. . . A Mechanist pirate, malfunctioning, betraying gene-lines. Invisible listening devices buy, grow, and sell you. The abandoned station's ambitious young Shaper, killed during the attack. Falling psychotechs produced by sexual means the desiccated body of a commercial agent. The holographic interface's loyalty was suspect. The cybernetic system helped him strip the valuables off his plastic eyes. . . .

6. Speculative Pity

The Mechanist woman looked him over with an air of speculative pity. "I have an established commercial position here," she told Nikolai, "but my cash flow is temporarily constricted. You, on the other hand, have just defected from the Council with a small fortune. I need money; you need stability. I propose marriage."

Nikolai considered this. He was new to Mech society. "Does this imply a sexual relationship?" he said. The woman looked at him blankly. "You mean between the two of us?"

7. Flow Patterns

"You're worried about something," his wife told him. Nikolai shook his head. "Yes, you are," she persisted. "You're upset because of that deal I made in pirate contraband. You're unhappy because our corporation is profiting from attacks made on your own people."

Nikolai smiled ruefully. "I suppose you're right. I never knew anyone who understood my innermost feeling the way you do." He looked at her affectionately. "How do you do it?'"

"I have infrared scanners," she said. "I read the patterns of blood flow in your face."

8. Optic Television

It was astonishing how much room there was in an eye socket, when you stopped to think about it. The actual visual mechanisms had been thoroughly miniaturized by Mechanist prostheticians. Nikolai had some other devices installed: a clock, a biofeedback monitor, a television screen, all wired directly to his optic nerve. They were convenient, but difficult to control at first. His wife had to help him out of the hospital and back to his apartment, because the subtle visual triggers kept flashing broadcast market reports. Nikolai smiled at his wife from behind his plastic eyes. "Spend the night with me tonight," he said. His wife shrugged. "All right," she said. She put her hand to the door of Nikolai's apartment and died almost instantly. An assassin had smeared the door handle with contact venom.

9. Shaper Targets

"Look," the assassin said, his slack face etched with weariness, "don't bother me with any ideologies. . . . Just transfer the funds and tell me who it is you want dead."

"It's a job in the Ring Council," Nikolai said. He was strung out on a regimen of emotional drugs he had been taking to combat grief, and he had to fight down recurrent waves of weirdly tainted cheerfulness. "Captain-Doctor Martin Leng of Ring Council Security. He's one of my own gene-line. My defection made his own loyalty look bad. He killed my wife."

"Shapers make good targets," the assassin said. His legless, armless body floated in a transparent nutrient tank, where tinted plasmas soothed the purplish ends of socketed nerve clumps. A body-servo waded into the tank and began to attach the assassin's arms.

10. Child Investment

"We recognize your investment in this child, shareholder Leng," the psychotech said. "You may have created her—or hired the technicians who had her created—but she is not your property. By our regulations she must be treated like any other child. She is the property of our people's corporate republic."

Nikolai looked at the woman, exasperated. "I didn't create her. She's my dead wife's posthumous clone. And she's the property of my wife's corporations, or, rather, her trust fund, which I manage as executor. . . . No, what I mean to say is that she owns, or at least has a lienhold on, my dead wife's semiautonomous corporate property, which becomes hers at the age of majority. . . . Do you follow me?"

"No, I'm an educator, not a financier. What exactly is the point of this, shareholder? Are you trying to re-create your dead wife?"

Nikolai looked at her, at face carefully neutral. "I did it for the tax break."

. . . Leave the posthumous clone profiting from attacks. Semi-autonomous property has an established commercial position. Recurrent waves of pirate contraband. His slack face bothers you with ideologies. Innermost feelings died almost instantly. Smear the door with contact venom. . . .

11. Allegiances Resented

"I like it out here on the fringes," Nikolai told the assassin. "Have you ever considered a breakaway?"

The assassin laughed. "I used to be a pirate. It took me forty years to attach myself to this cartel. When you're alone, you're meat, Leng. You ought to know that."

"But you must resent those allegiances. They're inconvenient. Wouldn't you rather have your own Kluster and make your own rules?"

"You're talking like an ideologue," the assassin said. Biofeed-back displays blinked softly on his prosthetic forearms. "My allegiance is to Kyotid Zaibatsu. They own this whole suburb. They even own my arms and legs."

"I own Kyotid Zaibatsu," Nikolai said.

"Oh," the assassin said, "Well, that puts a different face on matters."

12. Mass Defection

"We want to join your Kluster," the Superbright said. "We must join your Kluster. No one else will have us."

Nikolai doodled absently with his light pen on a convenient videoscreen. "How many of you are there?"

"There were fifty in our gene-line. We were working on quantum physics before our mass defection. We made a few minor breakthroughs. I think they might be of some commercial use."

"Splendid," said Nikolai. He assumed an air of speculative pity. "I take it the Ring Council persecuted you in the usual manner—claimed you were mentally unstable, ideologically unsound, and the like."

"Yes. Their agents have killed thirty-eight of us." The Superbright dabbed uneasily at the sweat beading on his swollen forehead. "We are not mentally unsound, Kluster-Chairman. We will not cause you any trouble. We only want a quiet place to finish working while God eats our brains."

13. Data Hostage

A high-level call came in from the Ring Council. Nikolai, surprised and intrigued, took the call himself. A young man's face appeared on the screen. "I have your teacher hostage," he said.

Nikolai frowned. "What?"

"The person who taught you when you were a child in the crèche. You love her. You told her so. I have it on tape."

"You must be joking," Nikolai said. "My teacher was just a cybernetic interface. You can't hold a data system hostage."

"Yes, I can," the young man said truculently. "The old expert system's been scrapped in favor of a new one with a sounder ideology. Look." A second face appeared on the screen; it was the superhumanly smooth and faintly glowing image of his cybernetic teacher. "Please save me, Nikolai," the image said woodenly. "He's ruthless."

The young man's face reappeared. Nikolai laughed incredulously. "So you've saved the old tapes?" Nikolai said. "I don't know what your game is, but I suppose the data has a certain value. I'm prepared to be generous." He named a price. The young man shook his head. Nikolai grew impatient. "Look," he said "What makes you think a mere expert system has any objective worth?"

"I know it does," the young man said. "I'm one myself."

14. Central Question

Nikolai was aboard the alien ship. He felt uncomfortable in his brocaded ambassador's coat. He adjusted the heavy sunglasses over his plastic eyes. "We appreciate your visit to our Kluster," he told the reptilian ensign. "It's a very great honor."

The Investor ensign lifted the multicolored frill behind his massive head. "We are prepared to do business," he said.

"I'm interested in alien philosophies," Nikolai said. "The answers of other species to the great questions of existence."

"But there is only one central question," the alien said. "We have pursued its answer from star to star. We were hoping that you would help us answer it."

Nikolai was cautious. "What is the question?"

"'What is it you have that we want?'"

15. Inherited Gifts

Nikolai looked at the girl with the old-fashioned eyes. "My chief of security had provided me with a record of your criminal actions," he said. "Copyright infringement, organized extortion, conspiracy in restraint of trade. How old are you?"

"Forty-four," the girl said. "How old are you?"

"A hundred and ten or so. I'd have to check my files." Something about the girl's appearance bothered him. "Where did you get those antique eyes?"

"They were my mother's. I inherited them. But you're a Shaper, of course. You wouldn't know what a mother was."

"On the contrary," Nikolai said. "I believe I knew yours. We were married. After her death, I had you cloned. I suppose that makes me your—I forget the term."

"Father."

"That sounds about right. Clearly you've inherited her gifts for finance." He reexamined her personal file. "Would you be interested in adding bigamy to your list of crimes?"

. . . The mentally unstable have a certain value. Restraint of trade puts a different face on the convenient videoscreen. A few minor breakthroughs in the questions of existence. Your personnel file persecuted him. His swollen forehead can't hold a data system. . . .

16. Pleasure Roar

"You need to avoid getting set in your ways," his wife said. "It's the only way to stay young." She pulled a gilded inhaler from her garter holster. "Try some of this."

"I don't need drugs," Nikolai said, smiling. "I have my power fantasies." He began pulling off his clothes.

His wife watched him impatiently. "Don't be stodgy, Nikolai." She touched the inhaler to her nostril and sniffed. Sweat began to break out on her face, and a slow sexual flush spread over her ears and neck.

Nikolai watched, then shrugged and sniffed lightly at the gilded tube. Immediately a rocketing sense of ecstasy paralyzed his nervous system. His body arched backward, throbbing uncontrollably.

Clumsily, his wife began to caress him. The roar of chemical pleasure made sex irrelevant. "Why . . . why bother?" he gasped.

His wife looked surprised. "It's traditional."

17. Flickering Wall

Nikolai addressed the flickering wall of monitor screens. "I'm getting old," he said. "My health is good—I was very lucky in my choice of longevity programs—but I just don't have the daring I once did. I've lost my flexibility, my edge. And the Kluster has outgrown my ability to handle it. I have no choice. I must retire."

Carefully, he watched the faces on the screens for every flicker of reaction. Two hundred years had taught him the art of reading faces. His skills were still with him—it was only the will behind them that had decayed. The faces of the Governing Board, their reserve broken by shock, seemed to blaze with ambition and greed.

18. Legal Targets

The Mechanists had unleashed their drones in the suburb. Armed with subpoenas, the faceless drones blurred through the hallway crowds, looking for legal targets.

Suddenly Nikolai's former Chief of Security broke from the crowd and began a run for cover. In free-fall, he brachiated from handhold to handhold like an armored gibbon. Suddenly one of his prosthetics gave way and the drones pounced on him, almost at Nikolai's door. Plastic snapped as electromagnetic pincers paralyzed his limbs.

"Kangaroo courts," he gasped. The deeply creased lines in his ancient face shone with rivulets of sweat. "They'll strip me! Help me, Leng!"

Sadly, Nikolai shook his head. The old man shrieked: "You got me into this! You were the ideologue! I'm only a poor assassin!"

Nikolai said nothing. The machines seized and repossessed the old man's arms and legs.

19. Antique Splits

"You've really got it through you, right? All that old gigo stuff!" The young people spoke a slang-crammed jargon that Nikolai could barely comprehend. When they watched him their faces showed a mixture of aggression, pity, and awe. To Nikolai, they always seemed to be shouting. "I feel outnumbered," he murmured.

"You *are* outnumbered, old Nikolai! This bar is your museum, right? Your mausoleum! Give our ears your old frontiers, we're listening! Those idiot video ideologies, those antique spirit splits. Mechs and Shapers, right? The wars of the coin's two halves!"

"I feel tired," Nikolai said. "I've drunk too much. Take me home, one of you."

They exchanged worried glances. "This *is* your home! Isn't it?"

20. Eyes Closed

"You've been very kind," Nikolai told the two youngsters. They were Kosmosity archaeologists, dressed in their academic finery, their gowns studded with awards and medals from the Terraform-Klusters. Nikolai realized suddenly that he could not remember their names.

"That's all right, sir," they told him soothingly. "It's now our duty to remember you, not vice versa." Nikolai felt embarrassed. He hadn't realized that he had spoken aloud.

"I've taken poison," he explained apologetically.

"We know," they nodded. "You're not in any pain, we hope?"

"No, not at all. I've done the right thing, I know. I'm very old. Older than I can bear." Suddenly he felt an alarming collapse within himself. Pieces of his consciousness began to break off as he slid toward the void. Suddenly he realized that he had forgotten his last words. With an enormous effort, he remembered them and shouted them aloud.

"Futility is freedom!" Filled with triumph, he died, and they closed his eyes.

✛　✛　✛

WORDS TO KNOW

NOTE: When you write the definitions of the following words, make it a point to use at least three of them in conversation over the next day and three of them in your next writing assignment. Many times you'll find it difficult or impossible to use them in everyday speech or writing. What then is the point of defining them? Of learning them? At the very least, in all the following cases where you have unusual vocabulary terms to define, attempt to use them. How does attempting to use vocabulary that feels awkward or different change your view of your common speech and writing patterns? Learning how to use new vocabulary means just that—using the words. Write specifically how, where, when, and why you used the words and discuss with your class.

holographic—
Shaper—
psychotech—
Mechanist—
crèche—
patina—
desiccated—
meritorious—
free-fall—
eclectic—
quipped—
gene-line—
body-servo—
posthumous—
semiautonomous—
Kluster—
ideologue—
kangaroo court—

QUESTIONS

Have you ever read a short story like this one? What comes closest to describing what it's like to read this? Create a group of Text/You/Other and Three-Layered Questions from this reading. What potential writing projects can you think of?

WRITING ACTIVITIES

1. Choose one of your questions on which to write.
2. This time, keep the writing to less than a page, but still make sure you have a complete essay. "Cram your prose," as Sterling does.
3. Make each line of your essay or story as full as the different colors, lines, areas of a picture. Don't tell anything. Instead, show everything.
4. If it makes it easier, start with a phrase or sentence long theme or subject to give you a focus. For inspiration, reread Sterling's piece and come up with a one phrase or one sentence theme or subject for it. Then go back and revise your piece of writing.
5. Present your essay/story to your classmates. How do they respond?
6. How do you respond to their essays?
7. What was it like trying to write in this way and why?

GRAMMAR AND STYLE QUESTIONS

1. Select a reading originally published on the Internet to compare and contrast to this reading by Sterling. Analyze these examples. What are the differences stylistically, and why? Use specific examples from the readings as well as specific rules of grammar and details in your answer.
2. Using a standard grammar reference (e.g., Strunk and White's *Elements of Style*), find three exceptions (from any of the readings in this reader, including this reading by Sterling) to the rules such a standard reference has created, and discuss why the authors broke those rules. Use specific examples from each reading in your answer.

The Ideology of Machines: Medical Technology

Neil Postman

Neil Postman's insights and sardonic wit have made and kept him a strong media psychiatrist and psychologist. Postman's insights into technology and its manipulative effects on us as audience, consumers, and creators keep him at the forefront of millennium forecasters.

Introduction Neil Postman uses a traditional essay writing style combining research, analysis, and specific examples to support his point, but he also makes strong use of sarcasm and humor—tones of voice which are integral to getting his words across to his audience. What effect does this use of humor have on you? Where do you find specific signs of his humor? Where do his questions and/or insights make you uncomfortable and why? Is this his intended effect? Why or why not?

A few years ago, an enterprising company made available a machine called Hagoth, of which it might be said, this was Technopoly's most ambitious hour. The machine cost $1,500, the bargain of the century, for it was able to reveal to its owner whether someone talking on the telephone was telling the truth. It did this by measuring the "stress content" of a human voice as indicated by its oscillations. You connected Hagoth to your telephone and, in the course of conversation, asked your caller some key question, such as "Where did you go last Saturday night?" Hagoth had sixteen lights—eight green and eight red—and when the caller replied, Hagoth went to work. Red lights went on when there was much stress in the voice, green lights when there was little. As an advertisement for Hagoth said, "Green indicates no stress, hence truthfulness." In other words, according to Hagoth, it is not possible to speak the truth in a quivering voice or to lie in a steady one—an idea that would doubtless amuse Richard Nixon. At the very least, we must say that HAGOTH's definition of truthfulness was peculiar, but so precise and exquisitely technical as to command any bureaucrat's admiration. The same may be said of the definition of intelligence as expressed in a standard-brand intelligence test. In fact, an intelligence test works exactly like HAGOTH. You connect a pencil to the fingers of a young person and address some key questions to him or her; from the replies a computer can calculate exactly how much intelligence exists in the young person's brain.[1]*

HAGOTH has mercifully disappeared from the market, for what reason I do not know. Perhaps it was sexist or culturally biased or, worse, could not measure oscillations accurately enough. When it comes to machinery, what Technopoly insists upon most is accuracy. The idea embedded in the machine is largely ignored, no matter how peculiar.

Though HAGOTH has disappeared, its idea survives—for example, in the machines called "lie detectors." In America, these are taken very seriously by police officers, lawyers, and corporate executives who ever more frequently insist that their employees be subjected to lie-detector tests. As for intelligence tests, they not only survive but flourish, and have been supplemented by vocational aptitude tests, creativity tests, mental-health tests, sexual-attraction tests, and even marital-compatibility tests. One would think that two people who have lived together for a number of years would have noticed for themselves whether they get along or not. But in Technopoly, these subjective forms of knowledge have no official status, and must be confirmed by tests administered by experts. Individual judgments, after all, are notoriously unreliable, filled with ambiguity and plagued by doubt, as Frederick W. Taylor warned. Tests and machines are not. Philosophers may agonize over the questions "What is truth?" "What is intelligence?" "What is the good life?" But in Technopoly there is no need for such intellectual struggle. Machines eliminate complexity, doubt, and ambiguity. They work swiftly, they are standardized, and they provide us with numbers that you can see and calculate with. They tell us that when eight green lights go on someone is speaking the truth. That is all there is to it. They tell us that a score of 136 means more brains than a score of 104. This is Technopoly's version of magic.

What is significant about magic is that it directs our attention to the wrong place. And by doing so, evokes in us a sense of wonder

*The footnotes can be found in the original text listed on the Credits page of this book.

rather than understanding. In Technopoly, we are surrounded by the wondrous effects of machines and are encouraged to ignore the ideas embedded in them. Which means we become blind to the ideological meaning of our technologies. In this chapter and the next, I should like to provide examples of how technology directs us to construe the world.

In considering here the ideological biases of medical technology, let us begin with a few relevant facts. Although the U.S. and England have equivalent life-expectancy rates, American doctors perform six times as many cardiac bypass operations per capita as English doctors do. American doctors perform more diagnostic tests than doctors do in France, Germany, or England. An American woman has two to three times the chance of having a hysterectomy as her counterpart in Europe; 60 percent of the hysterectomies performed in America are done on women under the age of forty-four. American doctors do more prostate surgery per capita than do doctors anywhere in Europe, and the United States leads the industrialized world in the rate of cesarean-section operations—50 to 200 percent higher than in most other countries. When American doctors decide to forgo surgery in favor of treatment by drugs, they give higher dosages than doctors elsewhere. They prescribe about twice as many antibiotics as do doctors in the United Kingdom and commonly prescribe antibiotics when bacteria are likely to be present, whereas European doctors tend to prescribe antibiotics only if they know that the infection is caused by bacteria *and* is also serious.[2] American doctors use far more X-rays per patient than do doctors in other countries. In one review of the extent of X-ray use, a radiologist discovered cases in which fifty to one hundred X-rays had been taken of a single patient when five would have been sufficient. Other surveys have shown that, for almost one-third of the patients, the X-ray could have been omitted or deferred on the basis of available clinical data.[3]

The rest of this chapter could easily be filled with similar statistics and findings. Perhaps American medical practice is best summarized by the following warning, given by Dr. David E. Rogers in a presidential address to the Association of American Physicians:

> As our interventions have become more searching, they have also become more costly and more hazardous. Thus, today it is not unusual to find a fragile elder who walked into the hospital, [and became] slightly confused, dehydrated, and somewhat the worse for wear on the third hospital day because his first 48 hours in the hospital were spent undergoing a staggering series of exhausting diagnostic studies in various laboratories or in the radiology suite.[4]

None of this is surprising to anyone familiar with American medicine, which is notorious for its characteristic "aggressiveness." The question is, why? There are three interrelated reasons, all relevant to the imposition of machinery. The first has to do with the American character, which I have previously discussed as being so congenial to the sovereignty of technology. In *Medicine and Culture,* Lynn Payer describes it in the following way:

> The once seemingly limitless lands gave rise to a spirit that anything was possible if only the natural environment . . . could be conquered. Disease could also be conquered, but only by aggressively ferreting it out diagnostically and just as aggressively treating it, preferably by taking something out rather than adding something to increase the resistance.[5]

To add substance to this claim, Ms. Payer quotes Oliver Wendell Holmes as saying, with his customary sarcasm:

> How could a people which has a revolution once in four years, which has contrived the Bowie Knife and the revolver . . . which insists in sending out yachts and horses and boys to outsail, outrun, outfight and checkmate all the rest of creation; how could such a people be content with any but "heroic" practice? What wonder that the stars and stripes wave over doses of ninety grams of sulphate of quinine and that the American eagle screams with delight to see three drachms [180 grains] of calomel given at a single mouthful?[6]

The spirit of attack mocked here by Holmes was given impetus even before the American Revolution by Dr. Benjamin Rush, perhaps the most influential medical man of his age. Rush believed that medicine had been hindered by doctors placing "undue reliance upon the powers of nature in curing disease," and specifically blamed Hippocrates and his tradition for this lapse. Rush had considerable success in curing patients of yellow fever by prescribing large quantities of mercury and performing purges and bloodletting. (His success was probably due to the fact that the patients either had mild cases of yellow fever or didn't have it at all.) In any event, Rush was particularly enthusiastic about bleeding patients, perhaps because he believed that the body contained about twenty-five pints of blood, which is more than twice the average actual amount. He advised other doctors to continue bleeding a patient until four-fifths of the body's blood was removed. Although Rush was not in attendance during George Washington's final days, Washington was bled seven times on the night he died, which, no doubt, had something to do with why he died. All of this occurred, mind you, 153 years after Harvey discovered that blood circulates throughout the body.

Putting aside the question of the available medical knowledge of the day, Rush was a powerful advocate of action—indeed, gave additional evidence of his aggressive nature by being one of the signers of the Declaration of Independence. He persuaded both doctors and patients that American diseases were tougher than European diseases and required tougher treatment. "Desperate diseases require desperate remedies" was a phrase repeated many times in American medical journals in the nineteenth century. The Americans, who considered European methods to be mild and passive—one might even say effeminate—met the challenge by eagerly succumbing to the influence of Rush: they accepted the imperatives to intervene, to mistrust nature, to use the most aggressive therapies available. The idea, as Ms. Payer suggests, was to conquer both a continent and the diseases its weather and poisonous flora and fauna inflicted.

So, from the outset, American medicine was attracted to new technologies. Far from being "neutral," technology was to be the weapon with which disease and illness would be vanquished. The weapons were not long in coming. The most significant of the early medical technologies was the stethoscope, invented (one might almost say discovered) by the French physician René-Théophile-Hyacinthe Laënnec in 1816. The circumstances surrounding the invention are worth mentioning.

Working at the Necker Hospital in Paris, Laënnec was examining a young woman with a puzzling heart disorder. He tried to use percussion and palpation (pressing the hand upon the body in hope of detecting internal abnormalities), but the patient's obesity made this ineffective. He next considered auscultation (placing his ear on the patient's chest to hear the heart beat), but the patient's youth and sex discouraged him. Laënnec then remembered that sound traveling through solid bodies is amplified. He rolled some sheets of paper into a cylinder, placed one end on the patient's chest and the other to his ear. *Voilà!* The sounds he heard were clear and distinct. "From this moment," he later wrote, "I imagined that the circumstance might furnish means for enabling us to ascertain the character, not only of the action of the heart, but of every species of sound produced by the motion of all the thoracic viscera." Laënnec worked to improve the instrument, eventually using a rounded piece of wood, and called it a "stethoscope," from the Greek words for "chest" and "I view."[7]

For all its simplicity, Laënnec's invention proved extraordinarily useful, particularly in the accuracy with which it helped to diagnose lung diseases like tuberculosis. Chest diseases of many kinds were no longer concealed: the physician with a stethoscope could, as it were, conduct an autopsy on the patient while the patient was still alive.

But it should not be supposed that all doctors or patients were enthusiastic about the instrument. Patients were often frightened at the sight of a stethoscope, assuming that its presence implied imminent surgery, since, at the time, only surgeons used instruments, not physicians. Doctors had several objections, ranging from the trivial to the significant. Among the trivial was the inconvenience of carrying the stethoscope, a problem some doctors solved by carrying it, crosswise, inside their top hats. This was not without its occasional embarrassments—an Edinburgh medical student was accused of possessing a dangerous weapon when his stethoscope fell out of his hat during a snowball fight. A somewhat less trivial objection raised by doctors was that if they used an instrument they would be mistaken for surgeons, who were then considered mere craftsmen. The distinction between physicians and surgeons was unmistakable then, and entirely favorable to physicians, whose intellect, knowledge, and insight were profoundly admired. It is perhaps to be expected that Oliver Wendell Holmes, professor of anatomy at Harvard and always a skeptic about aggressiveness in medicine, raised objections about the overzealous use of the stethoscope; he did so, in characteristic fashion, by writing a comic ballad, "The Stethoscope Song," in which a physician makes several false diagnoses because insects have nested in his stethoscope.

But a serious objection raised by physicians, and one which has resonated throughout the centuries of technological development in medicine, is that interposing an instrument between patient and doctor would transform the practice of medicine; the traditional methods of questioning patients, taking their reports seriously, and making careful observations of exterior symptoms would become increasingly irrelevant. Doctors would lose their ability to conduct skillful examinations and rely more on machinery than on their own experience and insight. In his detailed book *Medicine and the Reign of Technology,* Stanley Joel Reiser compares the effects of the stethoscope to the effects of the printing press on Western culture. The printed book, he argues, helped to create the detached and objective thinker. Similarly, the stethoscope

> helped to create the objective physician, who could move away from involvement with the patient's experiences and sensations, to

a more detached relation, less with the patient but more with the sounds from within the body. Undistracted by the motives and beliefs of the patient, the auscultator [another term for the stethoscope] could make a diagnosis from sounds that he alone heard emanating from body organs, sounds that he believed to be objective, bias-free representations of the disease process.[8]

Here we have expressed two of the key *ideas* promoted by the stethoscope: Medicine is about disease, not the patient. And, what the patient knows is untrustworthy; what the machine knows is reliable.

The stethoscope could not by itself have made such ideas stick, especially because of the resistance to them, even in America, by doctors whose training and relationship to their patients led them to oppose mechanical interpositions. But the ideas were amplified with each new instrument added to the doctor's arsenal: the ophthalmoscope (invented by Hermann von Helmholtz in 1850), which allowed doctors to see into the eye; the laryngoscope (designed by Johann Czermak, a Polish professor of physiology, in 1857), which allowed doctors to inspect the larynx and other parts of the throat, as well as the nose; and, of course, the X-ray (developed by Wilhelm Roentgen in 1895), which could penetrate most substances but not bones. "If the hand be held before the fluorescent screen," Roentgen wrote, "the shadow shows the bones darkly with only faint outlines of the surrounding tissues." Roentgen was able to reproduce this effect on photographic plates and make the first X-ray of a human being, his wife's hand.

By the turn of the century, medicine was well on its way to almost total reliance on technology, especially after the development of diagnostic laboratories and the discovery and use of antibiotics in the 1940s. Medical practice had entered a new stage. The first had been characterized by direct communication with the patient's experiences based on the patient's reports, and the doctor's questions and observations. The second was characterized by direct communication with patients' bodies through physical examination, including the use of carefully selected technologies. The stage we are now in is characterized by indirect communication with the patient's experience and body through technical machinery. In this stage, we see the emergence of specialists—for example, pathologists and radiologists—who interpret the meaning of technical information and have no connection whatsoever with the patient, only with tissue and photographs. It is to be expected that, as medical practice moved from one stage to another, doctors tended to lose the skills and insights that predominated in the previous stage. Reiser sums up what this means:

> So, without realizing what has happened, the physician in the last two centuries has gradually relinquished his unsatisfactory attachment to subjective evidence—what the patient says—only to substitute a devotion to technological evidence—what the machine says. He has thus exchanged one partial view of disease for another. As the physician makes greater use of the technology of diagnosis, he perceives his patient more and more indirectly through a screen of machines and specialists; he also relinquishes control over more and more of the diagnostic process. These circumstances tend to estrange him from his patient and from his own judgment.[9]

There is still another reason why the modern physician is estranged from his own judgment. To put it in the words of a doctor who remains skilled in examining his patients and in evaluating their histories: "Everyone who has a headache wants and expects a CAT scan." He went on to say that roughly six out of every ten CAT scans he orders are unnecessary, with no basis in the clinical evidence and the patient's reported experience and sensations. Why are they done? As a protection against malpractice suits. Which is to say, as medical practice has moved into the stage of total reliance on machine-generated information, so have the patients. Put simply, if a patient does not obtain relief from a doctor who has failed to use all the available technological resources, including drugs, the doctor is deemed vulnerable to the charge of incompetence. The situation is compounded by the fact that the personal relationship between doctor and patient now, in contrast to a century ago, has become so arid that the patient is not restrained by intimacy or empathy from appealing to the courts. Moreover, doctors are reimbursed by medical-insurance agencies on the basis of what they *do,* not on the amount of time they spend with patients. Nontechnological medicine is time-consuming. It is more profitable to do a CAT scan on a patient with a headache than to spend time getting information about his or her experiences and sensations.

What all this means is that even restrained and selective technological medicine becomes very difficult to do, economically undesirable, and possibly professionally catastrophic. The culture itself—its courts, its bureaucracies, its insurance system, the training of doctors, patients' expectations—is organized to support technological treatments. There are no longer methods of treating illness; there is only one method—the technological one. Medical competence is now defined by the quantity and variety of machinery brought to bear on disease.

As I remarked, three interrelated reasons converged to create this situation. The American character was biased toward an aggressive approach and was well prepared to accommodate medical technology; the nineteenth-century technocracies, obsessed with invention and imbued with the idea of progress, initiated a series of remarkable and wondrous inventions; and the culture reoriented itself to ensure that technological aggressiveness became the basis of medical practice. The ideas promoted by this domination of technology can be summed up as follows: Nature is an implacable enemy that can be subdued only by technical means; the problems created by technological solutions (doctors call these "side effects") can be solved only by the further application of technology (we all know the joke about an amazing new drug that cures nothing but has interesting side effects); medical practice must focus on disease, not on the patient (which is why it is possible to say that the operation or therapy was successful but the patient died); and information coming from the patient cannot be taken as seriously as information coming from a machine, from which it follows that a doctor's judgment, based on insight and experience, is less worthwhile than the calculations of his machinery.

Do these ideas lead to better medicine? In some respects, yes; in some respects, no. The answer tends to be "yes" when one considers how doctors now use lasers to remove cataracts quickly, painlessly, and safely; or how they can remove a gallbladder by using a small television camera (a laparoscope) inserted through an equally small puncture in the abdomen to guide the surgeon's instruments to the diseased organ through still another small puncture, thus making it unnecessary to cut open the abdomen. Of course, those who are inclined to answer "no" to the question will ask how many laparoscopic cholecystectomies are performed *because* of the existence of the technology. This is a crucial point.

Consider the case of cesarean sections. Close to one out of every four Americans is now born by C-section. Through modern technology, American doctors can deliver babies who would have died otherwise. As Dr. Laurence Horowitz notes in *Taking Charge of Your Medical Fate*, ". . . the proper goal of C-sections is to improve the chances of babies at risk, and that goal has been achieved."[10] But C-sections are a surgical procedure, and when they are done routinely as an elective option, there is considerable and unnecessary danger; the chances of a woman's dying during a C-section delivery are two to four times greater than during a normal vaginal delivery. In other words, C-sections can and do save the lives of babies at risk, but when they are done for other reasons—for example, for the convenience of doctor or mother—they pose an unnecessary threat to health, and even life.

To take another example: a surgical procedure known as carotid endarterectomy is used to clean out clogged arteries, thus reducing the likelihood of stroke. In 1987, more than one hundred thousand Americans had this operation. It is now established that the risks involved in such surgery outweigh the risks of suffering a stroke. Horowitz again: "In other words, for certain categories of patients, the operation may actually kill more people than it saves."[11] To take still another example: about seventy-eight thousand people every year get cancer from medical and dental X-rays. In a single generation, it is estimated, radiation will induce 2.34 million cancers.[12]

Examples of this kind can be given with appalling ease. But in the interests of fairness the question about the value of technology in medicine is better phrased in the following way: Would American medicine be better were it not so totally reliant on the technological imperative? Here the answer is clearly, yes. We know, for example, from a Harvard Medical School study which focused on the year 1984 (no Orwellian reference intended), that in New York State alone there were thirty-six thousand cases of medical negligence, including seven thousand deaths related in some way to negligence. Although the study does not give figures on what kinds of negligence were found, the example is provided of doctors prescribing penicillin without asking the patients whether they were hypersensitive to the drug. We can assume that many of the deaths resulted not only from careless prescriptions and the doctors' ignorance of their patients' histories but also from unnecessary surgery. In other words, iatrogenics (treatment-induced illness) is now a major concern for the profession, and an even greater concern for the patient. Doctors themselves feel restricted and dominated by the requirement to use all available technology. And patients may be justifiably worried by reports that quite possibly close to 40 percent of the operations performed in America are not necessary. In *Health Shock,* Martin Weitz cites the calculations of Professor John McKinlay that more deaths are caused by surgery each year in the United States than the annual number of deaths during the wars in Korea and Vietnam. As early as 1974, a Senate investigation into unnecessary surgery reported that American doctors had performed 2.4 million unnecessary operations, causing 11,900 deaths and costing about $3.9 billion.[13] We also know that, in spite of advanced technology (quite possibly because of it), the infant-survival rate in the United States ranks only fourteenth in the world, and it is no exaggeration to say that American hospitals are commonly regarded as among the most dangerous places in the nation. It is also well documented that, wherever doctor strikes have occurred, the mortality rate declines.

There are, one may be sure, very few doctors who are satisfied with technology's stranglehold on medical practice. And there are far too many patients who have been its serious victims. What conclusions may we draw? First, technology is not a neutral element in the practice of medicine: doctors do not merely use technologies but are used by them. Second, technology creates its own imperatives and, at the same time, creates a wide-ranging social system to reinforce its imperatives. And third, technology changes the practice of medicine by redefining what doctors are, redirecting where they focus their attention, and reconceptualizing how they view their patients and illness.

Like some well-known diseases, the problems that have arisen as a result of the reign of technology came slowly and were barely perceptible at the start. As technology grew, so did the influence of drug companies and the manufacturers of medical instruments. As the training of doctors changed, so did the expectations of patients. As the increase in surgical procedures multiplied, so did the diagnoses which made them seem necessary. Through it all, the question of what was being *undone* had a low priority if it was asked at all. The Zeitgeist of the age placed such a question in a range somewhere between peevishness and irrelevance. In a growing Technopoly, there is no time or inclination to speak of technological debits.

WORDS TO KNOW

NOTE: When you write the definitions of the following words, make it a point to use at least three of them in conversation over the next day and three of them in your next writing assignment. Many times you'll find it difficult or impossible to use them in everyday speech or writing. What then is the point of defining them? Of learning them? At the very least, in all the following cases where you have unusual vocabulary terms to define, attempt to use them. How does attempting to use vocabulary that feels awkward or different change your view of your common speech and writing patterns? Learning how to use new vo-

cabulary means just that—using the words. Write specifically how, where, when, and why you used the words and discuss with your class.

HAGOTH—
Technopoly—
oscillations—
ferreting—
drachms—
calomel—
Hippocrates—
thoracic viscera—
ophthalmoscope—
laryngoscope—
laparoscope—
cholecystectomies—
carotid endarterectomy—
iatrogenics—
zeitgeist—

QUESTIONS

Ending with a look to the past, into the present, and turning towards the future, Postman brings us news which we should heed, news that is directly and indirectly connected to virtually all the issues and conflicts discussed in these readings and more than likely, in your writings. How? Think about it. Create a group of Text/You/Other and Three-Layered Questions from this reading. What do you come up with for potential writing projects?

WRITING ACTIVITIES

1. For your last piece, combine two or more questions (which should relate to each other in some way) and plan to lengthen your essay by two pages, bringing the total to four pages.
2. Remember to include a range of sources, but consider those which will leave a real impression on the reader throughout the piece, making your introduction as memorable as your conclusion—think of it as asking your reader to look up from the paper and see the image you show

him/her in the beginning, make him or her directly experience it before going on with facts, figures, and more abstract sorts of details.

3. Take the three parts of your paper—the introduction, the body, and the conclusion—and present each piece separately to the class as a draft run, complete with accompanying presentation aides (music, pictures, readings, and so forth) and get feedback from your classmates before putting it into its final form.

4. Try trading parts of the papers with your classmates and presenting on their different sections; this will give everyone new ideas and take pressure off you to produce everything all at once.

5. After you get some ideas from what they're doing, both with their own work as well as with yours, revise your essay and presentation again.

6. Present your essay to your classmates. How do they respond?

7. How do you respond to their essays? Why is it important to always be responding? To always be listening? To always be learning? To always be creating?

GRAMMAR AND STYLE QUESTIONS

1. One of the most difficult tasks for any new writer is to express time and timelines consistently and to match actions to those times and timelines. Take a paragraph from this reading that has a strong sense of either past, present, or future tense, and rewrite it using a different verb tense (i.e., if it was written in the present tense, rewrite it in the past tense, and so forth). What is the effect of such a change? Were you consistent in your new selection of verb tense in your revision? And, if you had difficulty with consistency, without referring back to the text, restore the original tense and see how closely the paragraph matches how Postman originally wrote it.

2. Compare and contrast this latest reading of Postman's with his earlier reading. How does he use grammar to get his points across? How does his use of grammar to get his points across differ from one piece to the next? What are the common features of both? Use specific rules of grammar and details in your answer.

Credits

"The African Fang Legends: Eboka" from John Miller and Randall Koral (eds.), *White Rabbit: A Psychedelic Reader* (San Francisco: Chronicle Books, 1995). Reprinted with permission.

Art on the Edge of Fashion, "A Conversation Between Curators on Art on the Edge of Fashion," "Performance—Angela Ellsworth" and "Performance—April Flanders, Annette Foster and Angela Bettridge." Reprinted with the permission of the Arizona State University Art Museum, Tempe, Arizona.

Associated Press, "Pet shop fish touched by deity?" from *The San Francisco Examiner* (June 29, 1997). Reprinted with the permission of the Associated Press.

Carol Bowman, excerpt from *Children's Past Lives: How Past Life Memories Affect Your Child*. Copyright © 1997 by Carol Bowman and Steve Bowman. Reprinted with the permission of Bantam Books, a division of Random House, Inc.

Doug Boyd, "The Story of False Face" from Mad Bear: Spirit, Healing and the Sacred in the Life of a Native American Medicine Man. Copyright © 1994 by Doug Boyd. Reprinted with the permission of Simon & Schuster.

Serge Bramly, "The Descent of the Gods," translated by Meg Bogin, from *Macumba: The Teachings of Maria-José, A Mother of the Gods*. Copyright © 1975 by Editions Seghers, Paris. English translation copyright © 1977 by St. Martin's Press. Reprinted with the permission of St. Martin's Press Incorporated.

Stewart Brand, excerpt from the Introduction,"Fading Nations" and "One Student, One Computer" from *The Media Lab*. Copyright © 1987, 1988 by Stewart Brand. Reprinted with the permission of Viking Penguin, a division of Penguin Books Inc.

Andrei Codrescu, excerpt from the Introduction and "Until I Got Here—America Boring" from *The Dog with the Chip in His Neck*. Copyright © 1996 by Andrei Codrescu. Reprinted with the permission of St. Martin's Press Incorporated.

Edward Colimore, "Collecting kids' stories of past lives: The author's own past-life regressions motivate her to reach out to these children" from *The Philadelphia Inquirer*. Reprinted with the permission of *The Philadelphia Inquirer*.

Kaz Cooke, "Weight for Me: Food" from *Real Gorgeous: The Truth About Body and Beauty*. Copyright © 1996 by W. W. Norton & Company. Copyright © 1994 by Kaz Cooke. Reprinted with the permission of W. W. Norton & Company, Inc.

Esther Grassian, "Thinking Critically about World Wide Web Resources" from online *UCLA College Library Instruction Guide*. Reprinted with permission.

Lisa Jones, excerpt from the Introduction and "color therapy by deandra" from *bulletproof diva: Tales of Race, Sex and Hair*. Originally published in *The Village Voice*. Copyright © 1994 by Lisa Jones. Doubleday, a division of Random House, Inc.

Nancy Kress, "Out of All Them Bright Stars" from *Trinity and Other Stories*. Originally published in *The Magazine of Fantasy and Science Fiction* (March 1985). Copyright © 1985 by Mercury Press, Inc. Copyright © 1985 by Nancy Kress. Reprinted with the permission of the author.

Arthur Kroker and Michael Weinstein, "Spanish Cats and the Body Electric" from *Data Trash: The Theory of the Virtual Class*. Copyright © New World Perspectives ald

Index